The Extraordinary Adirondack Journey of

C L A R E N C E   P E T T Y

The Extraordinary Adirondack Journey of

C L A R E N C E P E T T Y

Wilderness Guide, Pilot, and Conservationist

C H R I S T O P H E R A N G U S

With a Foreword by Anne LaBastille

Syracuse University Press

First Edition 2002
02 03 04 05 06 07   6 5 4 3 2 1

The paper used in this publication meets the minimum requirements
of American National Standard for Information Sciences—Permanence of Paper
for Printed Library Materials, ANSI Z39.48–1984.∞™

Library of Congress Cataloging-in-Publication Data

Angus, Christopher.
  The extraordinary Adirondack journey of Clarence Petty : wilderness
  guide, pilot, and conservationist / Christopher Angus ; with a foreword
  by Anne LaBastille.— 1st ed.
       p. cm.
  Includes bibliographical references and index.
  ISBN 0-8156-0741-5 (cloth : alk. paper)
  1. Petty, Clarence, 1905– 2. Adirondack Mountains (N.Y.)—Biography.
  3. Environmentalists—New York (State)—Biography. 4.
  Conservationists—New York (State)—Biography. 5. Adirondack Park
  (N.Y.)—History. I. Title.
  F127.A2 A2755 2002
  333.7'2'092—dc21   2002002149

Manufactured in the United States of America

FOR KATHY AND EMMA

❧

I cannot but regard it as a kindness
[that] I have been nailed down to this
my native region so long and steadily,
and made to study and love this spot
of earth more and more.

—Henry David Thoreau

CHRISTOPHER ANGUS is book review editor for *Adirondac* magazine and, for many years, wrote a weekly column for the *St. Lawrence Plaindealer* and the *Advance News.* He has been involved in lobbying for the passage of the Environmental Protection Act and in efforts to reopen Adirondack rivers to the public. He is the author of *Reflections from Canoe Country: Paddling the Waters of the Adirondacks and Canada,* 1997, also published by Syracuse University Press.

Contents

Illustrations

Foreword

Anne LaBastille

Three words always personify for me the Adirondack Mountains. Granite. Waves. Trunks.

These three words also personify for me Clarence Petty. Granite. Waves. Trunks.

The Adirondacks are made up of enduring granite rock. It is stable, rugged, ancient, dependable.

Adirondack waters form waves. On ponds, lakes, rivers. On windy open snow fields and on icefalls down steep cold cliffs. Yet these waves always have an orderliness, a fluid form, and a calmness. They may be of various colors, sizes, heights, and feel. Yet there is always a sameness.

Clarence's life has seen many changes, many places, many people, many events. Somehow he always moves forward with the same orderliness and purposefulness as do waves.

Adirondack trunks hold up millions of trees in the Forest Preserve and beyond. They support branches, leaves, fruits, nuts, and buds. Trunks channel life-giving sap and cradle life-giving nests.

Clarence is like a burly trunk. He helps many friends. He supports dozens of conservation organizations. He has taught many people to fly. He is a stalwart tree of the Adirondacks.

Two vignettes of outings with Clarence remain fixed in my mind. One autumn day he invited me out for the first time in his vintage, varnished, cedar guide boat. He wanted to show me the three Stony Creek Ponds strung out like aquamarine beads beneath the brooding bulk of Stony Creek Mountain. My two German shepherds leapt into the craft

Clarence and Anne LaBastille push off in Clarence's one-hundred-year-old guideboat, 2001. Courtesy of Anne LaBastille.

and settled down on a bed of life jackets and old shirts. Clarence began rowing, carefully crossing his oars so as not to hit each other or his hands. He headed for a passage between two ponds, precisely cutting around a rock. There was poetry in his skill and the responsiveness of this Cadillac of guide boats.

Chekika and Xandor fidgeted. The boat's ribs were poking into *their* ribs. Clarence began sliding this way and that on his seat, trying to balance the boat. Finally, he politely asked me to center the dogs. I crawled forward, pushing one, then the other. They would not stay put.

Nevertheless our day passed pleasantly. We soaked up the fall colors, watched wildlife, and chatted about the different camps along the shores. I was conscious, however, that this was Clarence's special craft, and that he—like the good pilot he is—was trying to "trim the plane."

When we returned to his place late in the day, Clarence said quietly, "Maybe next time we'd better leave the 'wolves' in your truck."

The next summer, I invited Clarence to visit my cabin for the first time. I had told him of the terrible twister (microburst) of July 15, 1995, and the damage done to my land. He immediately offered to come up next afternoon with his pack basket, scarred ax, large chain saw, own gas and oil, and two sackfuls of groceries. I showed him around the cabin, lean-tos, woodshed, and outhouse, plus my canoes. Then we sat on the dock to watch the sun set over my lake.

I eyed him speculatively and asked, "Would you like to see my little writing retreat, Thoreau II, rather than work here tomorrow?"

Clarence looked pleased and nodded.

"I haven't had time to hike up there and check for damages. I'm worried sick it may have been flattened," I explained.

Later, we ate ravenously from a roast with his homegrown potatoes and squash. Then we polished off a large can of peaches in heavy syrup. Clarence began rummaging in his pack basket, produced a sleeping bag from the 1940s, and disappeared into the guest room.

At breakfast he sat on the kitchen stool and produced his own instant oatmeal and dried milk. "You're absolutely no trouble at all as a guest," I murmured, pouring boiling water into his bowl. Clarence was showing me new ways to be the perfect houseguest.

"It's how I was brought up," he said matter-of-factly.

We started out for Thoreau II with two paddles, two packs, and two German shepherds. A small yellow canoe would take us halfway there. This time the dogs were good as gold. Then we walked without talking. As we neared the tiny log shack, my heart was in my throat. What would we find?

It was still standing! Pure luck!

The top of a huge, dead spruce had snapped off, flown thirty feet through the air, and fallen on the opposite side of the cabin. Its bushy top was totally blocking the door. All we had was Clarence's cruising ax and our lunch. While I looked for firewood and started a campfire, he set to work clearing a burrow to the door. I could just manage to reach the door and unlock it. The air inside felt cold and smelled musty, yet the room looked in order.

"Oh, Clarence," I beamed, "*thanks* for doing that."

He said, "You need this place to escape to, away from the outside world and its too many people."

I started the fire and put a package of hotdogs on the grill. Then I laid out bread, mustard, another can of peaches in heavy syrup, and a Coke. Clarence and I split the Coke and we each ate one "dog," while Chekika and Xandor polished off the other eight.

Lying back on the crimson and saffron leaves, I gazed out across the pond toward the vast wilderness tract and then up at the cerulean sky. A blue jay called. We two experienced guides were in the kind of place we loved to be. I felt safe with Clarence and felt a glow of deep pleasure.

Acknowledgments

It says something about one's subject when virtually everyone contacted is bursting to talk about him. Many old colleagues and friends of Clarence's sought me out just to be able to tell me how much they thought of him and how glad they were that someone was finally writing his story. This certainly made my job easier and more enjoyable.

I am grateful to Mary Peterson Moore of Syracuse University Press and Dick Beamish, publisher of the *Adirondack Explorer*, for jointly suggesting this project to me. Thanks also to Dick for offering many suggestions and stories about his friend Clarence, and for putting his vast Adirondack experience to work checking for errors. Any errors still in evidence must be strictly credited to the author.

All those interviewed were enormously helpful. They are mentioned in the references. I would like to especially thank the members of the Petty family, including Ed Petty, Donald Petty, Archibald Petty, and Richard Petty. It was a pleasure to get to know Ed, who was always a sure resource for fact checking, for rare photographs, and for plenty of stories, suggestions, and even the odd bit of gardening advice. My thanks to George Davis, Gary Randorf, Neil Stout, Jay Hutchinson, and Harold Jerry, who offered stories, factual information, and pictures from their private collections. Jerry, who passed away in June 2001, was named executive director of the Temporary Study Commission on the Adirondacks in 1967 and played a major role in saving the Adirondacks from overdevelopment. Ken Alger, Stanley C. Bingham, Stephanie Coyne

DeGhett, and Gus Thomaris were extremely open and helpful in relating their stories about flying with Clarence.

Clarence's Coreys neighbors—Janet and Fritz Decker, Claire Stratford, Jean Freeman, Paul, Nancy, and Rebecca Soderholm—offered their comments, stories, meals, and encouragement throughout this process, for which I am very grateful. Janet Decker also reviewed an early draft on Clarence's childhood, and her research on the history of Coreys was invaluable. My thanks also to Ken and Alice Hollenbeck, who parted with a very special place, allowing me to also become one of Clarence's neighbors.

I am indebted, as always, to Neal Burdick, editor of *Adirondac,* for his professional editing talents, which improved the book immeasurably, and for his encyclopedic knowledge of all things Adirondack. An equally large debt is owed to Peter Van de Water, who offered the use of his unpublished manuscript on the Adirondack Park Agency along with his recollections on Citizens to Save the Adirondack Park.

My profound gratitude to Anne LaBastille for her foreword to this work. She needed no encouragement to write about her longtime friend, Clarence, with whom she shares a deep and committed love for the Adirondacks.

Joan and Jim Barrick did yeoman and highly professional service in transcribing the many hours of interviews with Clarence and others. And, as always, O. J. Audet never seems to tire of guiding me, his most illiterate of computer friends, through the morass of my own incompetence.

My thanks to Michelle Tucker and the Adirondack Collection of the Saranac Lake Free Library, to Jim Meehan of the Adirondack Museum in Blue Mountain Lake, and to Jane Eaton Gage at St. Lawrence University's Launders Science Library.

Finally, this work could not have been done without the support of my family. My wife, Kathy, pushed me to take on a project that I at first found daunting, given the depth of Clarence's long life and many experiences. My sister, Jamie, and brother-in-law, Jim, gave me honest and tough criticism that sent me back to the drawing board and made the book much more readable. And my daughter, Emma, gave me encouragement every time she bounced into my study, shined her two bright eyes on me, and asked, "How's it going?"

Most of all, it was an indescribable experience to be able to spend so many hours with Clarence. Whoever first coined the term "one of a kind" must surely have had him in mind.

The Extraordinary Adirondack Journey of

C L A R E N C E   P E T T Y

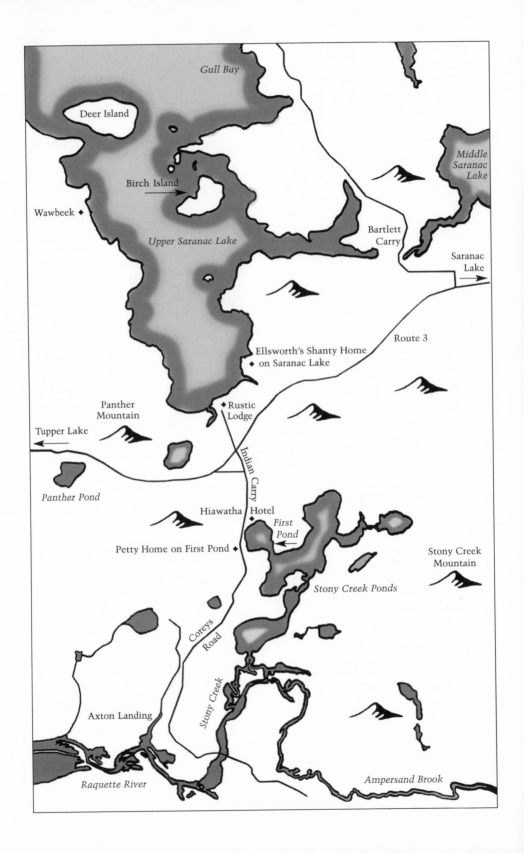

CHAPTER 1

A Death on Upper Saranac

Clarence got the call at eight o'clock at night. His ninety-three-year-old father was overdue, his mother, Catherine, said, and the weather was bad. It was May 9, 1956.

Ellsworth Petty first rowed the familiar six-mile round trip to and from Deer Island on Upper Saranac Lake in another century. His craft, a sixteen-foot blue guide boat with gunwales painted black, had handled high winds and waves many times. Just a few years earlier, at the age of eighty-eight, he had made the same crossing in gale-force winds in the wake of the devastating 1950 hurricane. Everyone on the lake knew Ellsworth's boat.

By the time Clarence drove from Parishville to the family home at Coreys between Tupper and Saranac Lakes, his older brother, Bill, a ranger stationed at Saranac Inn, had already begun the search with help from the Department of Environmental Conservation.

Ellsworth was an indomitable figure, the sort the Adirondack heartland seems to produce in abundance. He had come to Upper Saranac Lake in the 1880s to work as a guide with his cousin, Carlos Whitney. Ellsworth was then in his mid-twenties, and Carlos was some twenty-five years older. They earned two dollars a day, high wages for the Adirondacks.

Carlos first became familiar with the Indian Carry that connected Upper Saranac with the Stony Creek Ponds in the 1850s. There were still Indians around back then. They hunted along the banks of the Sounding River (the Raquette) and fished in the Wampum Waters

3

(Stony Creek Ponds). The women grew corn along the shores and the boys proved their manhood, or so the legend goes, by tying knots in young saplings. The taller the sapling, the stronger the youth. Years later, white men supposedly puzzled over the strange burls clustered in stands of mature trees.

Carlos invited Ellsworth to come over from Crown Point and join him as a guide at the Alfred L. White camp on Deer Island. Perhaps Carlos wanted his cousin to join him because Ellsworth could swim, while Carlos, who made his living paddling across vast, gray, windy lakes, had never learned that skill.

But more likely, Carlos simply needed help rowing "sports" to the best fishing and hunting spots, carrying guide boats along endless woodland trails, and hauling deer back to camp. City folks did not have the stamina for such chores, nor did they want it. Those were jobs for the hired help.

Carlos knew the sort of helper he was getting in Ellsworth, a man with the temperament and persistence of a bulldog. His forearms were huge, almost outsize, like Popeye on a three-can-of-spinach day. You might not have guessed it to look at him, but at five-foot-nine and 150 pounds, Ellsworth Petty was built for endurance, for the long haul. After decades of rowing, hauling wood, sawing lake ice, and packing innumerable deer down steep mountain trails, those muscles would grow into taut knots of sinew.

Ellsworth holding the day's catch. Clarence Petty collection.

When he arrived at Coreys, Clarence was uncertain as to the seriousness of the emergency reported by Catherine. He and his brothers had come to understand that Ellsworth, even at ninety-three, was a man who never needed help. Indeed, he was the helper, the one who carried the boats, chopped the firewood, built the shelters, and told his clients where to cast their lines. Ellsworth was not a man anyone would ever expect to turn out a search party for.

On the night of May 9, 1956, Ellsworth rowed hard for the Indian Carry and home as he tried one last time to forge his way across the vast, steel-gray waters of Upper Saranac Lake. The ice had only been out for a few days, and the water was still winter cold. A southwest wind pushed and pounded waves into whitecaps. The labor of straining on the oars and keeping his guide boat balanced against the wind required intense concentration. Yet one has to believe that he never doubted his ability to come through. He had done it before, countless times. Indeed, if Ellsworth were to choose among his favorite times in the North Woods, he would likely have selected a blustery day out on the water, with tall pines snapping in the wind and clouds boiling across the sky.

Concentrating, rowing rhythmically, he probably thought of his wife, Catherine, who had been the linchpin of the Petty family for more than half a century. There would be a meal waiting for him and the comfort of the home they had shared since 1911. Catherine had urged him to come home early that day, but early had come and gone. Now, fierce winds shook the Petty home.

By ten P.M. that night, Bill told searchers that there was little more to be done until morning. But Clarence said to his brother, "Let's take our flashlights and we'll go up to the camp. We'll start right there. The wind's blowing from the southwest. We'll cut around the lake shore, and we can at least try to find the boat."

They rowed out into the dark, overcast night. Studying the wind, they determined that it would have blown their father's guide boat to the east shore. They began their search in Gull Bay, with Clarence rowing their guide boat from the bow while Bill shined a flashlight from the stern. The light flickered eerily, bobbing up and down, picking out strange shapes of twisted cedars and protruding logs. The wind and waves pounded the shoreline, adding to the confusion.

Finally, well past midnight, Bill's flashlight halted its ceaseless wandering. "Look, there!" he said. Clarence turned and followed the beam of yellow. Up against the shore behind Birch Island, a blue guide boat rocked on the waves. It was upright and banging against the rocks, and inside Ellsworth Petty lay on his back in six inches of water, his hands close by the oars.

"His heart just gave out," says Clarence. The wind and waves had not really defeated the old guide. His boat never turned over, and the trusty craft carried him safely to shore, back to his family one last time.

Finding their father dead in his boat was a blow that the brothers would feel all the remaining days of their lives. That moment, seeing Ellsworth unmoving in the storm, was the first time they had ever witnessed their father in defeat.

Today, nearly half a century later, Clarence sometimes stares out across Upper Saranac Lake and imagines his father rowing for home. It was once the favorite sight of a little three-year-old boy who lived in a shanty on a knoll overlooking the woods and waters that his father called home.

CHAPTER 2

The Shanty Years

When Ellsworth arrived on the Saranacs in the 1880s, he listened avidly to the stories Carlos told him. His cousin was a huge man who was used to being listened to. "He could pick up a 200 pound deer and walk off with it," said Clarence years later in Charles Brumley's *Guides of the Adirondacks*. "He was one of those guys you think of carrying a bull moose under each hand. Great big husky guy!"

Carlos told of seeing corn stubble where the Rustic Lodge would later be built and of the Indian artifacts that Jesse Corey, proprietor of the lodge, had collected along the carry. He told of coming upon Indian women fishing through holes in the lake ice on Upper Saranac, proof that the Indians had not always avoided the frigid Adirondack highlands.

Ellsworth took in the stories and took to the mountains like a fish to water. His first home was a camp in the woods atop a knoll with a good spring. It was built out of spruce logs and rough-sawn boards and had a canvas fly for a roof. Over time he would add to the twelve-by-twenty-foot structure, turning it into an open camp with a bark roof, then enclosing it into a primitive shack in which to raise a family.

Ellsworth met his future wife at Bartlett's Carry, one of the preeminent Adirondack camps for wealthy visitors at the turn of the century. Catherine had been raised in New York City but left home when she was about ten, becoming almost a waif living in the streets. Eventually, she was taken in by a Mrs. Cobb, from whom she got her religious upbringing. At the age of about twenty, Catherine traveled to

The shanty on Upper Saranac Lake, 1910. Clarence Petty collection.

Bartlett's,[1] where she got a job preparing food. She was always very "particular" in her preparation of food, Clarence recalls, which made her an attractive employee to deal with the fussiness of rich tourists.

The backwoods lodge, located on the carry between Upper Saranac and Round Lake (known today as Middle Saranac Lake), had been purchased by Virgil Bartlett in 1854. The low, rambling, two-story structure soon became renowned for its speckled trout fishing and for the hearty cuisine provided by Mrs. Bartlett.

Virgil ruled his little kingdom with an iron hand and was known for his quick temper. One sportsman of the period who engaged in wrestling matches with the hotel owner related that "for pure meanness Bartlett took the prize." Though he never held office, Virgil was a towering figure in local politics. Each election day he delivered a solid

---

1. Many place names have variations in the literature. Bartlett's Carry is also Bartlett's Landing, Bartlett Carry or simply Bartlett's. Coreys Road is sometimes Corey's Road. The Hiawatha Lodge is also Hiawatha House or Hotel. The Wawbeek is also Wawbeek Hotel, Lodge, or Club. I have tried to be consistent throughout, though Clarence often uses the old names.

*Bartlett's, Saranac Lake, 1870s. S. R. Stoddard photo,
courtesy of Adirondack Museum.*

block of his thirty or so workers to election headquarters, where they were expected to vote as Virgil told them. In the sparsely populated district, Virgil's voters generally carried the day.

Bartlett ran his hotel until his death in 1884. His wife then took it over and continued running it for another fifteen years. In 1899 Mrs. Bartlett sold the establishment to a group of former guests who turned it into a private club, albeit one willing to accept the dollars of the touring public. In *Little Rivers* Henry Van Dyke described Bartlett's in the 1880s:

> It was the homeliest, quaintest, coziest place in the Adirondack . . . the only dwelling within a circle of many miles. The deer and bear were in the majority. At night one could sometimes hear the scream of the panther or the howling of wolves. But soon the wilderness began to wear the traces of a conventional smile. The desert bloomed a little— if not as the rose, at least as the gillyflower. Fields were cleared, gardens planted; half a dozen log cabins were scattered along the river; and the old house, having grown slowly and somewhat irregularly for twenty years came out, just before the time of which I write, in a modest coat of paint and a broad-brimmed piazza.

Ellsworth's father, Harry Petty, at Crown Point, 1908. Clarence Petty collection.

Bartlett's had thus enjoyed a long and esteemed history as a hostelry and superb backcountry eatery when Catherine arrived to work at the turn of the century. It is not hard to imagine the pretty young cook taking a shine to the hard-working, if taciturn, Ellsworth. He exhibited his wiry strength as he carried his boat from Upper Saranac to Round Lake, where he often took groups to sample the fabulous northern pike fishing.

They were married in 1901, and the New York City girl found herself living in a tent on a platform on state land, in the middle of the greatest wilderness east of the Mississippi. It was a humble beginning, but the young couple could watch twenty-pound trout leap in the lake from their porch and feel the strong west wind in their faces.

A few days before Clarence was born, Ellsworth took Catherine to Crown Point, where he owned a small house that he rented out and where there was a doctor. Clarence's brother, Bill, one and one-half years older, had been born in one of the cabins at Rustic Lodge. On August 8, 1905, the second of the three Petty sons was born.

The family ancestry is not well documented. Catherine's parents were first or second generation Dutch immigrants who lived in New York City. The family name was probably Wandruska or possibly Van Druska. Ellsworth Petty was of Welsh extraction and was born in Crown Point. His father may have been born in Vermont and later crossed over to New York, where he became a farmer on the shores of

Lake Champlain. But most of this history has been lost. There were rumors of Petty connections in Ohio and, Clarence declares, "There were a bunch of Pettys in Texas, probably horse thieves or something."

Catherine's stay at the Crown Point house was brief. Two days after Clarence's arrival, they were back on the shores of Upper Saranac in the one-room shack with the big wood stove in the middle. It was primitive living for a city-bred girl with two babies to care for. Water was hauled from the spring for drinking, cooking, and filling the big washtub for baths. There was a small garden where they grew potatoes and tomatoes. In the spring black flies made life miserable. In the winter it was cold beyond imagining. But this was how many people lived, unless they were some of the wealthy New Yorkers who showed up after the black flies and left after the fall hunting.

It was always a scramble to make the best of the short Adirondack summer and fall, since this was the only time of year when real money could be made. It was a long, tough winter. Trapping was practically the only way to make any money. Almost everyone followed the same pattern, living off the land in winter and off the tourists the rest of the time.

The struggle to earn hard currency led to some creative business ventures. Clarence remembers Ellsworth boiling skinned skunk to make lard: "It was just a white grease and it still had some skunk smell to it. Mother didn't like that very much. My father had a big iron kettle, the kind they used to scald hogs in, and that's how he boiled it up. He sold it in jars to May's Drugstore in Tupper Lake. It was considered the finest kind of grease for a cold, and people'd rub it on their chests like Vicks VapoRub."

Remarkably, there are pictures from these early years because Catherine owned a camera. It was unusual for

Clarence, about age two, 1907.
Courtesy of Ed Petty.

anyone in such a remote area, much less a woman of working-class origins, to have photographic equipment at the turn of the century. The camera had been given to her by a friend in New York City. It was mounted on a tripod, and Catherine would disappear under a black hood to take big glass slides.

That camera was the first of many indications of Catherine's active and determined mind. Though she and Ellsworth had only fifth-grade educations, Catherine had many interests and a wide view of the world. Partly this must have been the result of her early days living in New York City. She maintained contact with family and friends in the city and occasionally returned for visits. Ellsworth was of an entirely different nature. A natural introvert, his method of raising children was basically to leave them to do as they wished. This was undoubtedly how he had been raised, and it had successfully produced a hard-working, if somewhat narrowly focused, adult.

But Catherine would have none of Ellsworth's laissez-faire approach. Education was the key in her mind to a better life. Her boys would have that education no matter what, even if they had to walk sixteen miles to attend school and board during the week with friends in Saranac Lake.[2] "You boys are not going to grow up in these woods living like Indians," she would say, and this was one reason that the family eventually moved to Coreys, where there was a small, one-room elementary school. Years later Catherine's youngest son, Archie, wrote, "Mother's pride in our academic accomplishments was overwhelming."

Life in the little shanty on Upper Saranac was hard but good for the Petty family. But in 1908 the Forest, Fish and Game Commission decided that there were too many squatters on state land. They were having a serious impact as a result of their illegal timber cutting. Ellsworth's good friend, Game Warden Jason Vosburgh, stopped by one day to break the news. "Sorry to tell you," he said, "but all squatters have gotta get off state land."

---

2. The old road that the boys walked measured sixteen miles before the curves were straightened by later improvements to the highway. Today, the distance is closer to thirteen miles.

Catherine with Bill and Clarence (right) in front of their shanty on Upper Saranac Lake after a June snowstorm, 1907. Clarence Petty collection.

The Pettys moved into a house built by a man named Putnam, located about three-quarters of a mile from Bartlett's Carry. Putnam was a retailer of groceries in Saranac Lake who had the idea that by building a storage place for meat near Upper Saranac, he could peddle meat and groceries on the lake. This was the time when more and more large camps were being built. Putnam constructed an icehouse and next to it built the house the Pettys would live in. The would-be grocer's door-to-door, or rather, guide boat-to-door delivery scheme never caught on. By 1908, when the Pettys were looking for a place to live, Putnam's had been sold to a Dr. Woods, whose main claim to fame seems to have been that he was a vegetarian. This must have been a rare proclivity in the mountains. That Dr. Woods became the owner of a former meat shop was an irony not lost on Clarence in later years. Before the family members could move into their newly rented home, they had to haul large amounts of spoiled meat out of the basement.

The Pettys lived at Putnam's for three years, until Clarence was six

Catherine at Rustic Lodge with Bill, Clarence, and Archie, 1910. Clarence Petty collection.

years old. In an effort to make life marginally easier, Ellsworth dug a trench and ran a galvanized pipe back to a spring to bring water to the house. In 1986, when Clarence returned to walk over the property with writer Ed Hale, Adirondack correspondent for the *Watertown Daily Times*, he uncovered portions of the old galvanized pipe. Decades after the family left Putnam's, Clarence would still see water coming out of that pipe down by the road.

One of Clarence's most vivid memories from this period was going to the dentist in Saranac Lake. Ellsworth insisted that the boys visit the dentist at least once a year. This was a considerable commitment, since the expedition took an entire day. The family traveled by guide boat a distance of perhaps eighteen miles by the winding lake route, including the carry at Bartlett's.

The trip by guide boat took longer than walking, but the family needed the boat to bring back various supplies from town. It is not hard to imagine little Clarence's day of fear and trepidation as they slowly rowed to town. The dentist operated a foot-pumped treadle drill that was excruciatingly painful. "That was the most painful thing I've ever experienced," remembers Clarence. "And on the trip home, by the time we reached Bartlett's Carry, I would be so dog-tired I could barely walk. I remember stumbling over the roots in the trail."

In 1911 the Pettys moved one more time, the last time. It would be the best move, and Catherine, with her fierce intent to educate her boys, would be behind it. That home, which still belongs to Clarence ninety years later, would become the focal point of his long Adirondack journey.

CHAPTER 3

To Catch a Fish for Fun

The Adirondacks Clarence was born into in 1905 was still very much a wilderness. But it was a wilderness increasingly under assault from a variety of forces, virtually all of them manmade.

Timber cutting had made a mess of the Adirondack forest. Ever since the very first log drive down the Schroon River tributary of the Upper Hudson in 1813, logging had been carried out with little concern for the well-being of the forest or its future production. By 1845 there were seven thousand sawmills in New York. The very heart of the industry was located around Tupper and Saranac Lakes, literally Clarence's future backyard.

The advent of pulp-wood processing in the 1860s and 1870s further increased the scale of destruction. The new technique meant that the biggest and oldest trees were no longer the central focus. Now virtually any species of any size could be utilized, including poplar, spruce, hemlock, pine, and balsam. By 1900 more than a hundred pulp mills were savaging the state's forests. "A hundred years ago," wrote Bill McKibben in a 1991 *Outside* article, "you'd have been lucky to find a tree to climb, and if you had you'd have looked out on desolation. Almost every acre in the Adirondacks was logged to the ground."

The depredations of the timber industry were the primary factor leading to the creation of the Forest Preserve in 1885, the park itself in 1892, and the "Forever Wild" Amendment to the New York State Constitution, which went into effect on January 1, 1895. The new amendment was also the outgrowth of a series of droughts that struck the

15

region in 1893 and 1894, resulting in numerous fires. Smoke hung over the Upper Hudson, and New York City residents were reminded of their long-standing worries about the depletion of their water supply should the northern watersheds be destroyed.[1] In addition, many of the wealthy owners of clubs and hunting camps in the Adirondacks were upset over the slashed and burned appearance of "their" wilderness.

Free-wheeling timber-cutters attacked the Forever Wild clause with a vengeance. Under the onslaught, enforcement of regulations was lax. Huge timber thefts occurred as the state all but surrendered title to its lands. In 1905 the Association for the Protection of the Adirondacks (with which Clarence would later have a long relationship) investigated the removal of timber from state lands. Its report found that millions of board feet of timber "had been removed unlawfully from State land during the preceding year with the knowledge of the authorities whose duty it was to prevent it."

Flourishing alongside the thousands of mid-nineteenth-century sawmills were the tanneries. Some fifteen hundred were already polluting streams and rivers before the Civil War. The industry relied on hemlock bark, which was ground and leached to provide tannin to turn cowhide into shoe leather. Historian Barbara McMartin estimates in *The Great Forest of the Adirondacks* that the tanning industry accounted for greater land clearing than logging between 1850 and 1880.

Iron mining was another draw on the forests. The production of iron required huge amounts of charcoal to fire the blast furnaces and forges. Charcoal could be made using virtually any species of hardwood. McMartin calculates that 250,000 acres were cleared to fuel the nineteenth century's iron manufactory.

As if these direct human assaults were not enough, the Adirondack heartland took yet another hit from forest fires. Large burns occurred in 1899, 1903, and 1908. During this time the forest was nearly always on fire somewhere. Again, it was human presence that was largely respon-

---

1. A concern that never seems to die. Watershed protection was used as partial justification for the expansion of the Sterling Forest State Park 40 miles northwest of New York City in the year 2000.

Pushing back the wilderness—pile driving for the bridge over Cranberry Pond stream near Rustic Lodge, 1900. Photograph by Catherine Petty, Clarence Petty collection.

sible. Many of the fires were started by sparks from coal-burning locomotives. Louis Marshall, the dedicated conservationist who helped secure passage of the Forever Wild clause, branded locomotives as "instruments of arson."

After the Civil War, the increasing numbers of people living in the Adirondacks began to bring about still another change. Private preserves, hunting clubs, and the grand hotels brought thousands of tourists to the region. Writers extolled the marvels of the wilderness, enticing ever-greater numbers of city dwellers to visit. William H. H. Murray's *Adventures in the Wilderness* (1869) was only the most successful in a series of works trumpeting the Adirondacks. Returning anglers and hunters wrote countless articles for publications such as *Forest and Stream* (later *Field and Stream*).

By the late nineteenth century the incredible abundance of wildlife was suffering the consequences. Gone were the moose, panther, lynx, and wolf. Beaver had been trapped to near extirpation. A Conservation Department report in 1905, the year of Clarence's birth, estimated that there were just forty beaver left in the entire Adirondacks. Longtime Adirondack guides such as Clarence's father, Ellsworth, found both the numbers of wildlife and their size decreasing.

Despite this assault upon the Adirondacks, the turn of the century also marked the awakening of a conservation movement that would shape much of the twentieth century. It would also shape Clarence Petty's life.

The fires of the early part of the century were, in large measure, responsible for the creation of a conservation lobby. The Association for the Protection of the Adirondacks, established in 1901, was dedicated to purchasing private lands to expand the Forest Preserve, to halting illegal logging on state land, to improving fire-fighting ability, and to opposing efforts to weaken the Forever Wild clause of the constitution. By the time of the state constitutional convention of 1915, the specter of devastating fires combined with the lobbying of the association spurred delegates to reaffirm Forever Wild.

But the mindset that led to the rise of a conservation lobby had begun to form much earlier. In 1864 George Perkins Marsh published *Man and Nature*, a work that Lewis Mumford called "the fountainhead of the conservation movement." *Man and Nature* set the stage for the widespread public fear at the end of the 1800s that deforestation would lead to desertification. Once that happened, the watershed that downstate depended upon would dry up. Though this was hardly a plausible outcome in the damp Adirondacks, Marsh's work contributed to the growing clamor in the 1870s and 1880s to save what remained of the Adirondack forest.

The first person to call for the creation of an Adirondack Park was the state land surveyor, Verplanck Colvin, in 1868. For the next thirty years, he was constantly surveying, compiling reports, and lobbying for the protection of the region. He was the first to argue for saving the watersheds for the future use of New York City. Preservation of the wilderness for its own sake, however, was not in Colvin's lexicon: "The idea of such an unproductive and useless park we utterly and entirely repudiate."

In 1901 Theodore Roosevelt, the nation's first great conservationist president, assumed command after the assassination of President McKinley. TR's famous midnight dash by carriage from the clubhouse at the foot of Mount Marcy to North Creek, after receiving word of McKinley's worsening condition, is one of America's most exciting tales of presidential succession. At the North Creek railroad station, Roosevelt learned that he was president of the United States, while much of the nation first learned about the Adirondack Mountains.

The remote setting was appropriate for the elevation of a new president who would preserve more of the American landscape, some 230 million acres, than any other leader until President Clinton.[2] Roosevelt's actions would be largely responsible for creating the constituency for conservation that made later environmental reforms politically feasible. His was a fitting presidency for Clarence to be born under.

Roosevelt's partnership with his friend Gifford Pinchot, the leader of the early Division of Forestry,[3] led to some of the most important conservation triumphs of the early twentieth century. But it also broke the conservation movement into two factions: the preservationists led by John Muir and the "wise use" advocates led by Pinchot. Roosevelt came down on the "wise use" side, advocating conservation of resources primarily for economic reasons.

Though the new president enjoyed the rugged outdoor life and was a committed bird-watcher, he nonetheless viewed nature in terms of its worth as a commodity. He spent little time worrying about the aesthetic values of wilderness, choosing to concentrate on pragmatic reasons to protect wildlife (in TR's lexicon, game animals) and forests. Today, this is not considered advanced environmental thinking and, combined with the president's incredible thirst for the hunt, has diminished his reputation as a conservationist.

2. Clinton was only able to surpass him as a result of TR's signing of the Antiquities Act of 1906, allowing presidents to protect wild lands as national monuments. President Carter, who presided over Congressional action setting aside a large part of Alaska as wilderness, joins TR and Clinton as America's greatest conservationist presidents.

3. Under Pinchot's leadership, it would become a bureau and then the Forest Service.

But Roosevelt's thinking evolved in this area over time. In 1903 he visited Yosemite with John Muir and Yellowstone with John Burroughs, and later wrote that such places should be protected "not merely for the sake of preserving the forests and the water, but for the sake of preserving all its beauties and wonders unspoiled by greedy and short-sighted vandalism." That same year TR established the nation's first federal wildlife refuge.

This progression of thought from use of the land for its products alone to valuing it in its own right mirrored the later development of Clarence Petty's thinking. Clarence's early days were spent earning a living as a guide. But he later expressed regret for all the killing he had done, even though his predation was born of economic necessity rather than a desire to kill for "sport," which is what Roosevelt engaged in.

"I never liked to kill anything, really, even a deer," says Clarence nearly a century after Roosevelt's presidency. "I killed it to eat, and I would never want to catch a fish for fun. I can't understand why anybody would want to catch a fish and throw it back just for the fun of catching it." Clarence's respect for the intrinsic value of wilderness would become the basis for his later commitment to the preservation of the Adirondacks.

This transition from one who lived off the land to one who lived to protect it is one of the signatory elements of Petty's life, for it represents a personal growth in philosophy that was highly unusual among those who lived in the Adirondacks and who had, traditionally, been closest to the land. It was an outlook that would repeatedly get Clarence into hot water in the years to come.

Backcountry Beginnings

Life on Coreys Road could hardly have been more perfect, at least in the eyes of young Clarence and his brothers, Bill and Archie. They lived in the heart of Adirondack wilderness, a natural paradise for adventurous boys. The cast of characters in their tiny community included colorful backwoods guides, lumberjacks, hermits, and, perhaps strangest of all, wealthy New Yorkers, whose lives could not have been more different from the Petty family's if they had been aliens from another planet.

The surrounding Shangri-la of mountains, lakes, and forests was a vast playground where the boys could hunt, fish, and run traplines to help support their family. The string of jewel-like Stony Creek ponds and outlet that connect the Raquette River with the Saranacs via the old Indian Carry was steeped in Indian lore. Many of the older guides who worked with Clarence's father had actually known Indians and told stories about the lives of the first real Americans.

One of these was Dan Emmett, an Abenaki Indian who made birch bark canoes and sold them to camp owners. "He was the only Indian I really had contact with," recalls Clarence.

> His face was just like the Indian on the nickel. He was a big guy, about 230 pounds, and he stood straight as a ram. His first camp was over by the Rustic Lodge golf course. He was a jolly fellow, and he'd stick his head out when my brother and I went by and say, "How much money did you make today?" He'd give us little sweet grass baskets that he made.

Dan would cut black ash that he found in the swamp and carry it back to camp. Then he'd take a wooden mallet to it, and he'd hammer on it to separate the spring wood from the summer wood, and that's what he peeled off and used for his pack baskets. I can still hear that sound, echoing over to our house, bang, bang, bang. He also used it for the ribs in his canoes. He'd take the hammered wood down to the pond in front of Hiawatha Lodge, put stones on it, and leave it underwater for two or three weeks, until it got well soaked. Then he'd bring it up and form it into the ribs for his canoes and pack baskets. He could bend it in any direction.

Indian Dan, as he was called, spent the winters in Canada at a little village on the St. Lawrence near Sorel, Quebec. His birch bark canoes, along with his services as a guide, were highly sought after by well-to-do camp owners such as the Rockefellers. Emmett is mentioned in Noah John Rondeau's diary and may have been instrumental in teaching the famous Adirondack hermit some of his woodcraft.

Overlooking First Pond, near the Petty home and on the spot where an Algonquin Indian village reputedly stood a one and one-half centuries before, the old Hiawatha Lodge still endured in 1911. The big hotel operated from spring to fall, housing the guides who worked there

Hiawatha Lodge on First Pond, Stony Creek Ponds, 1915.
Clarence Petty collection.

in its substantial boathouse. It then closed its doors, keeping only a caretaker for the winter months. One employee listed in Wallace's 1887 *Guide to the Adirondacks* was a man named John Dukett. He and Jesse Corey, who ran the Rustic Lodge at the other end of the Indian Carry, used teams of horses to haul boats and baggage across the portage for seventy-five cents a load.

There were three successive Hiawatha Lodges on the site, at least two of which burned, one in 1910, before the Pettys moved to Coreys, and one in 1918, after it had been rebuilt five years earlier. The building had acetylene lights, which used a highly flammable and explosive gas. This may have caused or contributed to the fires.

One of the many stories Clarence heard concerned the high mound near the Hiawatha that was reputedly the thronelike seat where the chief of the Saranacs kept watch for his enemies. Here too, it was pointed out, was the impress in solid rock of an Indian's foot.

Sometimes in the spring the boys would go out in the guide boat on Upper Saranac with their parents. Catherine and Ellsworth would leave them on an island while they went fishing. "We'd pick up stones and skip them," says Clarence. "One time, Bill picked up a stone and he said, 'Look at this.' He had a perfect arrowhead. So then I looked around and found another one. We found a lot of chippings made out of this real black rock which wasn't natural in that area at all. It must have come

The school at Coreys. Teacher on left, Bill and Clarence in front, Clarence wearing the fuzzy hat he hated. Clarence Petty collection.

from someplace else. Why the Indians used the island to make their arrowheads, I don't know."

Up the hill from the house stood the Coreys school. Harry Freeman's children, Ross, Alice, and Grace, and Bob Canning's daughter, Gertrude, were among Clarence's classmates. Freeman and Canning were both guides on the carry. There were about eight children in the one-room school when the Pettys arrived. Their teacher snowshoed to work from the home where she boarded. There is a picture of that first class taken by Catherine with her big camera.

The importance of school went hand in hand with the work ethic the elder Pettys instilled in their boys. Archie remembers leaving the house every morning by 7 A.M. to do chores. He mowed lawns, pumped water, filled ice boxes, and caddied at the golf course. If any free time was left over prior to supper, there were more chores.[1]

There was no indoor plumbing in the house. Everyone used the privy out back that Ellsworth called the "parliament building." It was advisable to take care of personal business of this nature before dark, especially in the winter, when the temperature regularly fell to thirty or forty below zero. One time Ellsworth got a porcupine quill in his derrière when the door to the parliament building was inadvertently left open. Porcupines could be an ongoing nuisance. They had a passion for salt and would even chew on the wooden toilet seats for the salt from urine. On one occasion, after ice cream had been churned on the wheelbarrow, the creatures chewed the handles off, much to Ellsworth's displeasure.

Bringing water into the house was no easy matter, as Archie recalls:

> After many years of carrying pails of water down off the hill, it was decided to get water piped in from the spring. It took seven years to lay the pipeline 750 feet from the spring to the house. Weekends became the time for ditch digging and even blasting. At the time, I was very small. My job was to hold the star-nosed drill with a gunnysack while dad or my brothers swung the sledge. No one had ever heard of eye pro-

---

1. Archibald Petty was eight years younger than his brothers, which is why he is mentioned less frequently in the descriptions of the boys' younger years.

Ellsworth cutting ice on First Pond with youngest son, Archie. Hiawatha Lodge in background. Photograph by Catherine Petty, Clarence Petty collection.

tection, but I was lucky and received no metal particles in the eyes. It took many days to drill into the granite. Keeping the smudge pot going was another job, for the biting insects were plentiful.

The construction of this pipeline became one of the perennial jobs of the boys' youth. After digging through the thin topsoil, they had to drill and blast to get down below the frost line, a distance of about five feet. It was a constant struggle to break through the bedrock.

This sort of hard work was the norm for the Petty sons from virtually the time they could toddle. It was subsistence living. Catherine grew vegetables and preserved them for the winter. The boys trapped animals on the weekends and sold the pelts at a store on Main Street in Saranac Lake when they went in for school. They fished and ate rabbit stew, even as Ellsworth made his real living working for the rich families along Upper Saranac Lake: the Guggenheims, the Seligmans, and the Goldmans.

It seems clear that Clarence accepted early on, perhaps even more resolutely than his brothers, the heavy responsibility that children car-

Upper Saranac Lake, from Rustic Lodge Golf Links. Clarence Petty collection.

ried in this economy. He took the importance of contributing to the family seriously, even at a very young age, and this sense of duty would stay with him, contributing to his lifelong commitment to hard work.

Clarence emulated his father's industry, also earning money from the wealthy families who lived close by during the warm months. He stacked wood, shoveled snow from rooftops, and caddied at the Rustic Lodge golf course. The lodge had been purchased from Jesse Corey in 1897 by the Swenson brothers, who constructed a nine-hole golf course for their patrons by pulling out the massive pine stumps with teams of horses and oxen. Incredibly, there was a second nine-hole course just down the road at Bartlett's Carry. Two such courses nearly side-by-side in the remote wilderness was proof of how established the Gilded Age was in this area by the turn of the century.

One reason for the appearance of wealthy Jewish families on Upper Saranac Lake was anti-Semitism. In 1877 Joseph Seligman had been turned away from the Grand Union Hotel in Saratoga. This was the first well-publicized case of anti-Semitism in America, and the trend spread to other Adirondack resorts, most famously, the Lake Placid Club run by Melvil Dewey, inventor of the Dewey Decimal System. Dewey did not discriminate in his discrimination. His club was off-limits to Jews, blacks, tuberculars, and anyone else he took a disliking to. As a result, families such as the Seligmans and Goldmans built their own retreats, and Upper Saranac became a favored locale.

Clarence was paid thirty-five cents an hour to caddy. If he was lucky enough to get two bags to carry, he made seventy cents. One of his chores was to make the golf tees. At each hole there was a little stand with two boxes on it. One box contained clay and the other water. Golfers fashioned their own tees on the spot by mixing water with a bit of clay. The clay came all the way from England, imported by the wealthy camp owners to line their walkways and surface their tennis courts.

Later, when Clarence was in high school and was working summers at the Santa Clara Lumber Company, he sometimes boarded at the Wawbeek Lodge. "Only they called it the Wawbeek Club," he remembers.

> That made it private, so then they didn't have to let Jewish people in. At that time, all these places, Saranac Inn, the Lake Placid Club, didn't want the Jews. It was kind of crazy because they were the ones supplying us with money. In fact, we didn't like to caddy for anybody that wasn't Jewish because they wouldn't tip you anything. Swensons were ranch people, and I caddied for them, but they'd never give you a tip. If you worked two hours, you got seventy cents. But if you worked for Bache or the Guggenheims or any of those people, boy, you'd get a nice tip.

The Wawbeek Hotel, 1900. Photograph by Catherine Petty, Clarence Petty collection.

By the time he was eight in 1913, Clarence was caddying for a variety of famous people. One was Jules S. Bache, the banker and art collector who made a fortune on Wall Street. In the 1940s Bache would give his magnificent art collection, including works by Rembrandt, Raphael, and Titian, to the Metropolitan Museum.

For two summers Bache paid Clarence a dollar a day to be on hand to meet his guests at the financier's "Wenonah Lodge." Bache himself sometimes went out alone with Clarence to golf. "He was a short fellow," Clarence remembers, "wore glasses and was real gruff talking. He'd golf alone in the morning and then come back with a bunch of guests in the afternoon. He had a daughter, Hazel, who was the most profane talking person I ever met. She couldn't golf worth a damn. She was a duffer and she'd hit the ground instead of the ball, and she'd swear like a trooper."

In addition to the wealthy Jewish financiers, Clarence met many other famous people who had camps or who came to visit those who did. Among them were the Rockefellers, who would later construct a camp on the point on Upper Saranac that would be called "Wonundra." When Clarence was seven or eight, he met five-year-old Nelson Rockefeller during a trip to Saranac Inn. Young Nelson tried to give him a toy birch bark canoe. Clarence did not want to take it, because his mother had always told him never to accept anything. But Nelson's governess assured him it would be all right. More than half a century later, Governor Nelson Rockefeller would create a commission to study the Adirondacks, and Clarence, who still had that little canoe in his home, would be asked to help.

Among others that Clarence met were Maxine Elliot, the grandam of the Broadway stage, and a tall, heavyset young man who would later become the well-known actor Monty Wooley. Wooley is best remembered as the crotchety but loveable invalid in *The Man Who Came to Dinner.*

This was a far cry from the world the young caddy was familiar with. It was not uncommon for a family residing on Upper Saranac Lake to bring twenty or thirty servants with them. They arrived for the season, loaded down with trunks, aboard the steamboat from Saranac Inn at the northern end of the lake. Dinners were formal affairs. Swenson himself, an amazed Clarence was once told, spent an hour getting his hands manicured before the evening meal. Sometimes Clarence played with the children of these people, and every midday and evening the kids would reluctantly depart, saying they had to go home and get cleaned up, bathed, and dressed for their meals.

Clarence, Bill, and young Archie with the day's catch, 1914. Clarence Petty collection.

Thus the entire Petty family earned livings from rich New Yorkers and their guests. As a result, the Petty family developed an early understanding of the importance of outsiders to the Adirondack economy. That seemingly rare insight by a native would become the foundation for Clarence's conservationist view: the preservation of the wilderness was all-important to the economy of the region. It was what kept the outsiders coming.

One colorful guide in the area was Mart Moody, who operated a succession of hotels for sportsmen on Tupper Lake. Moody guided presidents, philosophers, writers, historians, surveyors, and photographers. He became so renowned for his storytelling that sportsmen's clubs in New York City would pay to bring him down to entertain their members. Moody's technique was to begin with factual information and then, bit by bit, augment his story until no one knew where the facts left off and the fiction began.

Clarence relates one Moody tale in which the guide told of seeing a deer after he had run out of shot. He grabbed some pin cherries off a bush, sucked them dry, and thrust them down his barrel. He shot at the deer but missed. A year later he saw what appeared to be bushes moving along the top of a ridge. They were cherry trees growing right off a deer's back.

Guides such as Moody and Ellsworth, often dirt poor and uneducated, frequently found themselves in the exalted company of their rich, famous, and literary clientele. No doubt, some of this cultural exposure rubbed off on the more naturally loquacious and intelligent guides. But the influence was a two-way street. Men such as Ralph Waldo Emerson and James Russell Lowell were equally attracted to the "natural wits" who guided them through the dark woods.

The trip from the Saranacs across the Indian Carry, past Clarence's front door, and on down to the Raquette River was the most fabled in the Adirondacks. Writer Paul Jamieson called Indian Carry "The Times Square of the wilderness." The elite group of philosophers who encamped at Follensby Pond in 1858 steeped themselves in forests that would already be much changed by the time Clarence was born. In *Adirondack Pilgrimage* Jamieson described the setting that Emerson and company enjoyed: "From the third pond they wound down the 'charming stream' that flows into the Raquette, and hence past Axton for five miles to the marshy outlet of Follensby Pond coming in from the south. The Raquette then was bordered, not by the shaggy, meager deciduous forest of today, but by noble white pines that made a gorge up to 200 feet high for the dark, silent stream to slip through."

There can be little question as to the impact these surroundings had on the philosophers. But for all his poetic genius, by the time Emerson reached Axton, Jamieson tells us, he was already so lost that he misidentified the mountains surrounding them and even the direction that the Raquette flowed. Without men such as Moody and, later, Ellsworth and Clarence, few of the high and mighty, much less the literarily befogged, could have found their way through the leafy realms.

Farther along Coreys Road was the old Axton Hotel, run by Fred Wood and his wife. The building had formerly been part of the state forestry college run by Cornell University and Bernhard Fernow until the school folded in 1903. The hotel was used by lumberjacks when they went back into the Cold River country, since it was located about halfway on the two-day walk from Tupper Lake to number four camp at Raquette Falls. In about 1912 the structure was removed for use as a private camp. After the original site was abandoned, Clarence and Bill, exploring as usual, found jars of frogs and snakes in the meadow near where the hotel had stood. They were lab specimens, preserved in formaldehyde and left behind when the school was closed.

Fernow was at the center of one of the more interesting stories of this period. A professional forester who received his training at the Forest Academy of Prussia, he came to America in 1876. After managing a timber tract in Pennsylvania, he went on to work in Washington, D.C., as chief of the Forestry Division. In 1898 he was asked to head the new Cornell College of Forestry, established by the legislature to educate future foresters and to demonstrate good forestry techniques. The land selected for the college was a thirty-thousand-acre tract in Franklin County, the approximate center of which was at Axton, the site of an old lumber settlement originally called Axe-town.

Fernow wanted to illustrate that forestry could be successfully carried out on public lands. In order to find a market for his hardwoods, he enlisted the Brooklyn Cooperage Company to establish a plant at Tupper Lake to make hardwood barrel staves and wood alcohol. A six-mile rail line was constructed from the plant to the state tract to haul the hardwoods. In order to produce softwoods to reforest the area, Fernow established the first tree nursery in New York State at Axton. Some of the species he planted, such as Scotch Pine and Norway Spruce, were not native to the Adirondacks and did not fare well for many years.

Harvesting hardwoods while leaving behind the young spruce and reforesting with nonnative species proved to be impractical. But this was not the main reason that Fernow's plan failed. The first hardwoods to be cut were those closest to the railhead and also to the wealthy camp owners on Upper Saranac Lake. In short order, the foresters denuded the area, leaving behind a mess of slash and bleak landscapes.

Not only was Fernow a poor businessman and manager, but he was also a prickly character who alienated virtually everyone he came into contact with. In 1901, at the urging of the landowners and guides who furiously protested what Fernow was doing (Ellsworth Petty was among those who wrote to the governor), the state legislature assigned a special Committee of the Adirondacks to tour the site. It concluded that "the college has exceeded the original intention of the State when the tract was granted the university for conducting silvicultural experiments." In 1903 Governor Odell vetoed the annual appropriation for the College of Forestry.

Fernow was vilified for his actions and spent many years trying to defend himself. In 1911 the state reestablished the College of Forestry, awarding it to Syracuse University, where Clarence would later attend school. The entire episode soured relations between Cornell and Syracuse for many years. Clarence recalls that the ferocity of booing that went on at football games between the two colleges some twenty years later was a direct outgrowth of the forestry school conflict.

The cleared lands and nursery at Axe-town slowly reverted to wilderness. But Coreys Road remained one of the routes lumbermen took to get into the timberlands along the Cold River, at Raquette Falls, and around Ampersand Pond. Anyone familiar with Axton today would be astonished to see photographs of the completely open and cleared land that existed in 1900. Ironically, the beautiful forest that now blankets the area serves as partial vindication of Fernow's approach, since many of the trees he planted did in fact survive.

In 1911 Will Wardner, who operated the post office out of Rustic Lodge, asked Catherine Petty if she would be willing to take over the job. Thus almost as soon as the family moved in, the post office, which consisted of a bunch of cubbyholes to keep letters in, took up residence

Bill and Clarence shoveling in front of their home, the Coreys Post Office, 1911. Clarence Petty collection.

in the Pettys' front bedroom. It is still possible to see the marks made by the hobnail boots of the loggers in that front room as they came for their mail. The half-inch spikes tore splinters out of the floor, and Clarence remembers how his mother would grimace at the sound. Catherine's job was at first listed under Ellsworth's name, Archie recalls, for women were not allowed to hold the title of postmaster.

Letters required a two-cent stamp, and postcards were one cent. Catherine kept a list of the items she mailed and once a month sent the list to the U.S. Post Office. Sometimes she would earn as much as ten dollars a month. The mail arrived in big gray sacks with padlocks on them, and Catherine would dump them out and sort through the letters. She opened the post office at seven o'clock in the morning and closed at six, but customers paid little attention to the official hours. People hammered on the door early Sunday morning. Most of the tourists who came up to climb mountains or to paddle were only there for the weekend, and they wanted to get their letters out before they left. Clarence, Bill, and Archie each took turns waiting on postal customers.

In the winter the mail was delivered by stagecoach from Tupper Lake, but in the summer Saranac Inn had a post office. Here the mail would be sorted and then loaded aboard the mail boat for delivery all around the lake. Clarence still remembers the melodic, echoing sound of the mail boat's whistle. His family could hear it clearly as the boat arrived at Rustic Lodge at the foot of the lake.

The Pettys received a pouch of mail for the few people who lived at Coreys. But there was a bay on the lower part of Upper Saranac Lake that was too shallow for the mail boat, so the mail for the Houstons, who had a camp on the bay, was sent overland to Coreys. Every day, six days a week, Clarence would deliver the Houston's mail. For this he received a dollar a week. This was a great deal of money, and Clarence remembers, for a very good reason, the first dollar he earned in this manner. He lost it.

After he was paid, Clarence was walking back to Coreys with his head full of thoughts about his upcoming birthday. Catherine had told the boys that she was going to buy them a St. Lawrence skiff. He was thinking about this and fighting off clouds of deer flies when he reached the Hiawatha Lodge, only to discover that he had lost his money. He turned around and dashed back down the trail. He went around Cranberry Pond, and right there in the path he found his dollar. Just six years old, Clarence never forgot the first money he ever earned. His mother made him put it in the bank.

Catherine managed the post office until 1938. Eventually, she sold cameras, film, and candy to make a little extra money. The home overlooking Stony Creek Pond became a popular stop and meeting place for residents and for the lumbermen who sometimes walked back and forth to Tupper Lake from work at the camps. Catherine's house became known as a good place to stop for fresh baked goods. It was fourteen miles from number four camp to the Coreys Post Office and another ten miles to Tupper Lake. The men got pretty hungry by the time they reached Catherine's.

Food was all-important to the lumberjacks. The money they made never seemed to amount to much and was usually spent at bars in town almost as soon as it was earned. But if they did not like the food, they would not say anything; they would just push it off their plates onto the wooden table. The cook generally got the message. If not, and the meals did not improve, the lumbermen would simply leave. They would go down to Tupper Lake, take the train, and go off to White Lake in the western Adirondacks or to Ottawa, where there was always logging work to be had. Often they would not say a word to the job boss but would simply disappear, not even asking for wages that were due them.

"They were a little peculiar, the lumberjacks," says Clarence. "They all wore their hats peaked up and their trousers rolled up. They dressed the same and acted the same. You could tell a lumberman a mile away. It was odd, you know?"

The loggers employed by the Santa Clara Lumber Company were not the earliest residents of the remote Raquette and Cold River regions. The Santa Clara's predecessor, the Dodge-Meigs Company, based at Axton, had lumbered both sides of the Raquette River as far upstream as Raquette Falls. Its main camp, located at the falls, served as the base for as many as three hundred men. They harvested the virgin monarch white pine and spruce, removing the prime softwood along the north and west slopes of the Seward Range in little more than ten years. The Santa Clara Company then began operations on the eastern side of the range, setting up headquarters on Ampersand Pond.

Predating even these hearty timbermen was a woman by the name of Lucy Johnson. A former lumber camp cook from Newcomb, Mother Johnson, as she was called, took up residence at Raquette Falls around 1860 with her husband, Philander. Even at this early date, the secluded spot was a natural location for the distribution of supplies to lumbermen working high on the slopes of the Seward Range.

Mother Johnson remained at the site for many years as a revered cook and innkeeper, and her legendary pancakes were immortalized in Adirondack Murray's book. After her death during the winter of 1875, a hermit by the name of Harney snowshoed ten miles to Hiawatha Lodge to arrange for a coffin for her burial. She was supposedly buried at the foot of the cascade, but there is no sign of her grave. Christine Jerome, author of *An Adirondack Passage: The Cruise of the Canoe "Sairy Gamp,"* notes that a marker bearing the name Lucy Johnson stands among other stones of the same era in the Long Lake Cemetery. The tradition Mother Johnson began of providing lodging at Raquette Falls continued for nearly half a century beyond her death.

Clarence remembers one excellent cook at Raquette Falls, a great big sandy-haired guy who always had a smile on his face. When Clarence's parents first took him to visit the logging operation at the falls, he was only four years old. There were fresh baked rolls and bread to eat. But the thing that really stuck in his mind was taking a ride across the falls, from one side of the river to the other, on a cable car. A few days earlier, they were told, a man had sliced his thumb off while pulling that car across. "I remember looking down," says Clarence, "seeing these big logs go end

The Irish lumber camp cook at Raquette Falls, 1910. Clarence Petty collection.

over end under it, and I kept looking up, afraid the guy was gonna take his thumb off when he was pulling us across."

To reach Raquette Falls in the spring, Clarence and his family had to take a wagon because the river was full of logs. When the dam at Setting Pole Rapids had been built in 1870, it raised the water level some ten feet and drowned millions of trees. That pristine forest that Emerson lauded in 1858 would never again achieve its former glory.

All of these things contributed to making Coreys a magical place for Clarence to grow up. In many ways, it was the hub of the Adirondacks, the place where hard-working and strong-willed men and women came into contact with wilderness. Though life was arduous, those who settled there were drawn by the freedom and independence that characterized the backcountry. It would serve as the perfect crucible in which to develop young Clarence's own independent nature.

CHAPTER 5

Independent Spirits

Clarence's self-reliance is the hallmark of a lifetime of wandering across the Adirondack backcountry and of his conservationist views that put him at odds with many of his neighbors. It is this same quality that led him to make the move back to the old family home at Coreys, where he now lives alone, in his ninety-seventh year.

It is worth noting how Clarence's singular disposition came about, for it grew to a very large extent out of a childhood that would frankly astonish the parents of today's coddled children. As already noted, by the time he was six years old, he was hiking alone through the woods to an isolated bay every day to deliver mail. While he apparently used an established trail and may have encountered the occasional guide, this is clearly not an activity that would be likely to occur today. But being alone at an early age in this still remote and largely untamed wilderness was simply a matter-of-fact part of the Petty children's lives.

One spring, while the family still lived at Putnam's, Catherine decided she would go to Saranac Lake and take the train to New York City to visit her family. Ellsworth was working at Deer Island every day, leaving before dawn and not returning home until well after dark. Clarence and Bill, five and six years of age, were left home alone all day for ten days. That such a thing could happen today is inconceivable. Child welfare would charge the parents with neglect or abuse. The mere idea that a mother, and by most measures Catherine was a superior one, would leave her young children without so much as a second thought illustrates how very much child-rearing has changed in this

Target practice, 1918. Left to right: Ellsworth, Archie, Clarence, Bill, and Ellsworth's cousin, John Young. Clarence Petty collection.

country. It also shows how the isolated existence of wilderness living and the need for hard work forced children to grow up quickly.

The boys did not have the luxury of sitting around watching television, calling friends on the telephone, turning up the thermostat if they got cold, or raiding the refrigerator if they were hungry. They had chores and were expected to do them. They used hatchets to cut firewood and kept a fire going in the stove. Their father was tapping maples in the woods behind the house and Clarence and Bill collected the sap to carry in and put in the boiler in the evening. By the time Ellsworth returned home after dark, the boys had a warm fire going and a dinner of potatoes and venison on the table.

A year or so later, after the family had moved to Coreys, the boys were allowed to use a .22 rifle when they were home alone. Their mother bought the gun and told them, "Now, this is my gun, and you can use it on our land. Don't go off the land." In fact, the boys were still too young to legally handle a gun other than on private property. Catherine said, "Now, we're going to have some target practice, and if I ever see you pointing that gun at someone, whether its loaded or not, you're going to lose it. You're not going to have it."

Clarence and Bill used the gun to shoot rabbits or grouse that came around the house. Clarence's younger brother, Archie, killed his first rabbit with the .22 when he was five years old, barely able to reach the trigger as he shouldered and aimed the weapon. Clarence drove the rabbit for Archie just as he drove deer for hunters.

Neither Clarence nor Bill had learned to swim by the time they moved to Coreys, yet they were allowed to take the boat out and deliver telegrams to other camps. Catherine had been given the Western Union telegram business, and she would get the messages, write them out by hand, and give them to her sons to deliver by boat. Clarence remembers one man who gave them a quarter every time they brought a telegram. This man became concerned that the boys could not swim, and he insisted on taking them down to the water, where he said, "Now the first thing we're gonna do is teach you how to float with your nose down in the water. Hold your breath and hold your feet out like that." And that is how they learned to swim. Catherine never did learn to swim, though she spent much time on the water.

Clarence, age 11, with his first fox, 1916. Photograph by Catherine Petty, Clarence Petty collection.

By the time the boys were ten and eleven, they were taking groups of hunters into the surrounding forests. The family got their first telephone in 1913. Almost every week during hunting season someone would call, often from as far away as Rochester or Buffalo, to see if either boy was available to guide. They became known locally as well.

Bill and Clarence, professional guides, 1920. Clarence Petty collection.

One man named Jenkins, who raised vegetables for market in Saranac Lake, would call them up and say, "Tomorrow morning I'd like to have you make a drive for me up on the Forest Home Road." If it was a school day, Jenkins would pick them up before daylight, and they would make a drive for him and be back when school began at nine A.M.

Clarence and Bill became expert guides before they were teenagers. Sometimes they worked together and sometimes alone. They were the most successful as a team. They roamed all over Stony Creek Mountain, "just like hounds," remembers Clarence, driving the deer down established runways to the points where they had previously stationed hunters to wait for them.

When they were not guiding, young Bill and Clarence ran traplines and became more familiar with the major deer trails. One trip around the trapline might cover ten miles tramping through the woods. Clarence caught muskrat, beaver, fisher, and fox, and one year accidentally caught a marten. He had set the trap for fisher but caught marten instead. The incident contributed to his strong feelings against the leghold trap, because no matter how carefully one set it, one would still catch nontarget species. He came to believe, as well, that it was little short of a torture device.

These were all more or less normal activities for young boys who lived in remote regions at the turn of the century, though the Petty family was clearly more knowledgeable than most, no doubt the result of Ellsworth's lifetime of experience as a guide. It is a tale of boyhood independence nearly incomprehensible to children today, who may scarcely be allowed to walk a block alone to buy a quart of milk by the age of ten, much less roam over hundreds of square miles of wilderness.

Clarence expresses surprise at the lack of discipline in children today. When he went to visit friends with his parents, his mother would say, "When you go in there, you sit down, and I want you to be quiet. Unless you're talked to, don't speak." And he and his brothers would just sit there, Clarence recalls. "Now I have friends come in from downstate somewhere, and the kids are all over the place, just like a swarm of bees."

The discipline that the Petty boys experienced was of an entirely different nature. They were never spanked. It was simply not necessary. They always did what they were told. This grew out of an understanding that ran through not only the family but the entire community as well. People were well aware that they could get into serious trouble if they did not use caution in their everyday lives. It was many miles to the nearest doctor, who did not have much to offer in any event. It was understood that one was responsible for his own well-being. Firemen, policemen, or emergency care workers of any kind were either nonexistent or days away. Clarence once asked the famous hermit, Noah John Rondeau, what would happen to him if he struck his leg with an ax way out in the woods. "You got no business hitting yourself with an ax," was Rondeau's reply.

Before Catherine went off to New York and left her boys alone for ten days, she sat them down and told them, "Now, you can eat this and you can do this and you can't do that." Clarence and Bill followed her instructions to the letter.

This sort of independence was not uncommon among those living on the Adirondack frontier. It was echoed by two childhood neighbors of the Pettys, one of whom the family had a good deal of contact with and one of whom they had almost no contact with at all. Neighbors, in the lexicon of the period, generally meant anyone living within twenty miles.

Bob Marshall, son of Louis Marshall, is recognized today as one of the preeminent figures in the modern wilderness movement. He was also one of the most charismatic. He and his brother, George, spent their boyhood summers at Knollwood, the family home on Lower Saranac Lake, about sixteen miles from Coreys. With their longtime guide, Herb Clark, Bob and George became the first to climb the forty-six Adirondack peaks over four thousand feet high.[1]

Marshall's hiking ability has become the stuff of legend. Daily hikes of thirty and forty miles were commonplace. A few daily hikes of more

1. Technically, only forty-two of the forty-six peaks are over four thousand feet. Also, it bears noting that this was in the days when only twelve of the forty-six High Peaks had trails to their summits.

Climbing partners Bob Marshall and Herb Clark. Courtesy of Adirondack Museum.

than seventy miles were also recorded. It was said that forest rangers kept track of his movements by radio, speculating on when he would reach the top of the next peak. Adirondack preservationist Paul Schaefer described Marshall's arrival at the top of Mount Marcy on July 15, 1932, on his way to climbing fourteen peaks by nightfall: "Here came Marshall, right on schedule, heading for us at a dog trot. He was a stocky, powerful, ruddy man, dressed in a well-worn plaid shirt, blue denims, and sneakers."

During his teenage years, Marshall, who was born just two years before Clarence, roamed all across Stony Creek, Ampersand Mountain, and the region encompassing the Saranacs. It must have been something of a minor miracle that the two boys never met during this time. Marshall's guide, Herb Clark, was good friends with Ellsworth, and the two men often guided together. "Herb Clark was a comical kind of guy and thin as a rail," Clarence recalls. Marshall considered Herb one of the best teachers he ever had and admired his mentor's fondness for "poking the keenest sort of satire at hypocrisy and sham, for twisting up blusterers in their own boastful stories."

Clarence finally met his elusive neighbor in the fall of 1931, shortly after Marshall's return from Alaska. The occasion was a slide show Marshall presented at a Syracuse College of Forestry alumni meeting in New York City. Clarence never did get over the appearance of his long-time neighbor, given his reputation as a hiker. "He looked kind of pudgy. He didn't look like an athletic type at all. But I guess he had legs like steel." This must certainly have been the case to have so impressed Clarence, whose own rambles as a youth were nothing to be ashamed of. Between his round-trip walk to school and at least one ten-mile circuit to check his trapline, Clarence hiked forty to forty-five miles every weekend. The longest single day hike he ever made was *only* thirty-six miles when he was eighteen.

Clarence spoke to Marshall for a while about the Eskimos, and then it was time to leave. Clarence never saw him again. A few years later, the great hiker and conservationist died suddenly, probably from heart failure, at the age of thirty-eight. But that single meeting between the two men contributed to Clarence's lifelong fascination with Alaska.

Another independent thinker became a regular fixture at the Petty dinner table. He led a very different sort of life from the activist, socially involved career of Bob Marshall. Clarence first saw Noah John Rondeau in the spring of 1913. The soon-to-be Hermit of Cold River was walking down Coreys Road, bound for the deep woods. Noey, as the boys eventually came to call him, was pushing a baby carriage loaded down with traps, his gun, and a pile of other belongings. He was not quite thirty years old.

Clarence and Bill were so surprised by the strange apparition that they hid in a culvert. "This was a dirt road back then," says Clarence, "and it was hard pushin' that doggone thing. I don't know why he selected that, but he pushed it all the way from Lake Placid."

Noah stopped at Catherine's post office to arrange for his mail to be held until he could pick it up, something that would happen only a few times a year. Catherine, in her usual conversational manner, soon learned what the strange young man was up to. After he left, she told the boys, "Well, that was Noah Rondeau from Lake Placid. He was a barber and he's going up to live at Cold River."

Clarence did not see Rondeau again

Noah John Rondeau, early 1960s. Courtesy of Ed Petty.

until fall, when the hermit stopped in to see what "Santa Claus" had brought him. There were a few pieces of mail, and Catherine invited him in for dinner. Over the next few years, Noah would stop by regularly, often staying through the evening, and the Pettys came to know him well. "He was considered to be pretty much of an oddity by the local people," Clarence remembers. "They didn't think much of him because he's hiding back in the woods. He was a paradox in a way. He enjoyed the freedom of being out in the woods by himself, and he hated big government or anybody that had any authority. He didn't want anything to do with them. Yet the last years of his life, he was on welfare. The woods life isn't the sort of thing everybody would like, but there's a freedom to it that you don't find anywhere else. I see it up in Alaska. I see it here in the Adirondacks. People that like to get back in the woods by themselves and nobody's telling them what to do."

In the early years, Rondeau spent part of his time in a small cottage at Coreys. The Petty family developed a rapport with the reclusive hermit. Noah's life at Cold River was not unlike the Pettys' former life in their primitive shanty on Upper Saranac: hunting, fishing, trapping, and raising a few vegetables. It was subsistence living.

Over the years, Clarence and Bill often visited Rondeau at his remote camp and joined their friend on hunting and trapping expeditions. Noah named his place Cold River City (pop. 1) and proclaimed himself mayor. Cold River was a thirteen-mile hike from Coreys back into one of the remotest parts of New York State. For the two young boys to head off alone into the heart of Adirondack wilderness to spend time hunting and fishing with this strange character is simply one more example of the extraordinary freedom and independence that the Petty boys enjoyed.

They came to accept Noah's active and curious mind. He had many books, played the violin, and was interested in astronomy and philosophy. He built his own homemade telescope and set his calendar by the stars. He devised a secret code for writing in his diaries, which one friend said resembled "the claw marks of an inebriated chicken." The codes looked like hieroglyphics to Clarence, who caught an occasional glimpse of them.

On one occasion, the hermit expressed an interest in why black bears ate carpenter ants. Clarence had eaten muskrat, beaver, and other animals, but Noah would eat almost anything. Clarence watched in amazement as his friend bit into one of the ants and announced that it had a lemony taste.

Clarence recalls how his mother would have religious discussions with Noah during their evenings together. Noah could talk endlessly on the subject. His own parents were devout Catholics, and their religious demands had been largely responsible for his leaving home at a young age. Catherine had been brought up as a Presbyterian. She read the Bible regularly and took her boys to church down the road at the Indian Chapel, where Clarence and Bill were baptized. Ellsworth, on the other hand, had little time for or interest in religion. He never went to church. By the time the Petty sons were old enough to make their own decisions on the matter, they chose their father's more independent path.

Noah sometimes stayed at abandoned lumber camps up on the Cold River before he began to make his own little huts from boards taken from the old buildings. In later years he tried his hand at log jobbing. As an employer, it was his responsibility to provide his men with food. Before long, the loggers started disappearing. They didn't care for Noah's idea of setting the table. For breakfast he might buy the men oranges instead of bacon and eggs. Eventually the loggers all left, and Noah's short career as a jobber came to an end.

Noah engaged in some highly original woodsmen's techniques that contributed to his reputation. His tiny cabin was set several feet in the ground and was equipped with a wood stove and a stovepipe, in which he would place trout to be smoked for his winter food supply. He had secret caches of supplies and overnight shelters scattered through the woods.

On one occasion, Noah was out with a group of Prudential Life Insurance doctors who used to come up from New York City to fish. Clarence, no doubt with a bemused eye, witnessed the horror of these poor city boys as they watched Noah take a rusted frying pan out of one stump, some lard from another, and a deer heart out of a third and make dinner. "Those doctors were nice fellows," says Clarence. "They wouldn't let on that they didn't want to stay in Noah's shack because he was so dirty. God, he was awful dirty. They camped outside instead."

Noah got his bread from a bakery in Tupper Lake and then dried it in the sun until it was a hard brick, almost like zwieback. On one of their hikes through the forest, Noah walked up to a large tree and said, "I left some bread in this tree two years ago. Let's see how it's doing." He peeled back a piece of bark and there was the bread, still good as new. "He had stuff stashed all over the woods, like some sort of squirrel," says Clarence.

Though he had a gun, Noah did much of his hunting with a bow and arrow. His winter fuel supply consisted of dry sapling poles fifteen to twenty feet in length, which he piled in teepeelike fashion. "He could be a lazy sort of a guy," Clarence recalls. "Instead of chopping firewood, he'd take a long pole and stick one end in the stove and then just keep moving it along as it burned." He ate meagerly, living on game and fish supplemented with wild greens and herbs and whatever else might be handy. He had a habit of draining coffee grounds through an old sock. Few visitors drank coffee when they shared a meal with Noah.

"He had several pairs of deerskin pants," remembers Clarence.

> One time when Noah was still living at Coreys, Bill and I passed by his house and he had a sack of apples. He reached in and pulled out one for each of us, but before he gave them to us, he shined them up on his pants leg, which was this deerskin covered with bear grease. I said, 'No thanks' to that.
>
> He had a regular suit made from deerskins. I watched him put the skins on himself and sew them up just as they were—green—and wear them until they dried out and fitted him. One day when I brought some stuff back in to him, I saw him out there with his bow and arrow crossing a stream. He saw this muskrat, and he shot it and skinned it right there, turned the skin inside out, and slipped it right on his head so it sat up there like a big cone. And he wore it right along with the deerskins."

Noah's distaste for authority of any kind led to his decades-long feud with the Conservation Department. A number of incidents con-

Photo taken by Noah John Rondeau with a Kodak box camera lent to him by Catherine Petty. Note traps and perfectly camouflaged white weasel head poking out of hole, 1925. Courtesy of Ed Petty.

tributed to the conflict, but the best known revolved around a dispute with the game warden during the 1920s. There are nearly as many versions of this famous tale as there were participants in the affair. A relative of the warden's was trapping beaver out of season, according to Noah. Noah wrote a letter to the Conservation Department, informing it of this and recommending that it cut the telephone lines to Coreys and send in a raiding party to find the illegal furs, which it did.

It was apparently as a result of this incident that the game warden later went after Noah, accusing the hermit of shooting at him. Noah believed that the warden, who was trapping along the Raquette River, was stealing muskrats from his traps. Noah decided he would set his own trap for the warden. He cut a *V* in the bottom of the foot of a muskrat so he could identify it, put it in one of his traps, and then hid in the woods and watched as the warden came by and took the bait.

Noah followed the man, who paddled down the Raquette in his guide boat with the purloined muskrat. But Noah's own boat was slower and he could not catch up to the warden. When the alleged muskrat thief reached the oxbow on the Raquette, he pulled ashore. Noah yelled at him to stop. When he did not, Noah fired his gun over the man's head. By the time Noah reached him, the thief had supposedly thrown the secretly marked muskrat into the river, thus disposing of the evidence.

The warden later showed up at Coreys on a Sunday morning and arrested Noah at the Petty home for shooting at him. Noah was kept in jail in Malone for three weeks. Eventually he called Catherine Petty and asked her if she would bail him out. "Noah was strictly honest," says Clarence, "and cared nothing at all about money." Catherine went into Tupper Lake, got money from the bank, and sent it to Malone. However, Noah was acquitted in the meantime, so the bail money was never needed.

This is the story as Clarence remembers it, and it differs in degree from that told by others. Noah himself gave many versions over the years. But the tale reveals how close the Petty family had grown to the strange hermit of Cold River.

Clarence believes that the Petty family related to Noah because of his subsistence way of life. They understood from personal experience what the hermit was up against in his struggle just to survive. But there was a difference. The Pettys understood that they had an obligation to take care of themselves. Ellsworth would frequently say, "You can either go out and work and earn a living, or you can starve in the woods." Clarence, Bill, and Archie, as much as they would have preferred to stay in the woods around Coreys forever, were pushed relentlessly by Catherine to prepare themselves for the future. Noah apparently never gave that a thought. He liked the freedom of the woods but never considered that a time might come when he would not be able to live that life anymore. When it did, he went on welfare. And that was the difference between Noah and the Petty boys.

Dick Beamish, publisher of the *Adirondack Explorer* newspaper, once asked Clarence if Rondeau had served as a role model. "Absolutely not," Clarence replied.

> We could see the difference between his philosophy and ours. But we understood his fascination with the woods, being out there where you had freedom and liberty of action. That's the great thing about

wilderness. It makes a person realize that they're on their own, and it's their responsibility for preventing themselves from cutting their foot off or something with an ax. But one of the main reasons I like wilderness is because it forces people to take responsibility for what they do. A lot of people today are not willing to accept that responsibility. They want to blame whatever goes wrong on somebody else.

Rondeau's life at his Cold River camp has been well documented. Through the 1930s and 1940s he was frequently visited by hikers from the Adirondack Mountain Club. In 1947 District Forester Bill Petty flew over Cold River City and dropped Noah a note, asking him if he would like to attend a sportsmen's show in New York City. Noah tramped out a "yes" in the snow and was picked up the next day by helicopter. With his long beard and deerskin clothing, he became a major attraction in the state's exhibit.

By all accounts, Noah was a less-than-perfect example of a hermit. Jean Freeman grew up on the Indian Carry, and her family was well acquainted with Noah. Her father, Ross, and grandfather, Harry, were both guides on the carry. Ross ran a hunting lodge called Indian Carry

Noah John Rondeau with Clarence and his three sons at Cold River City exhibit at North Pole, Wilmington, N.Y., 1950. Courtesy of Ed Petty.

Lodge, and Harry had been a guide for Theodore Roosevelt. Jean remembers Noah walking by in the early 1940s. He would pull little toys from the pocket of his deerskin suit for her and her siblings. She scoffs at the notion that he was anything approaching a real hermit. "He was the most sociable hermit I ever heard of," she says.

In a letter to Marjorie L. Porter in 1948, Noah wrote, "I came out from Cold River City in late December. Have been at Saranac Lake most of the time. Had 6 days with Saranac Carnival: crowned the winter King and Queen—spoke at Trudeau's, spoke at Marcy Hotel, Lake Placid—at Fish and Game Club—Fish and Game Club dance—Had first flying lesson—and first American Olympic Bobsled ride at Mt. Van Hoevenberg Bobsled Run. And I pose 6 hours per week at Alpine Studio, for aspiring artists, who are painting the cold River whiskers."

Some hermit.

Marshall and Rondeau were early Petty neighbors who, like young Clarence, became infused with the wilderness ethic. They all lived highly independent and original lives. Clarence's early years more closely resembled Rondeau's isolated, living-off-the-land experience (before the hermit's fame took off). But as he grew older and became educated, Clarence's life would take a decided turn in the direction of Bob Marshall's dedication and service to the preservation of the wild.

CHAPTER 6

Bicycles, Planes, and Global Warming

While education was all-important in Catherine Petty's mind, Clarence and Bill were somewhat less enthusiastic. Growing up "like Indians" seemed perfectly acceptable to them. They loved the life of hunting and fishing and could even make pretty good money as guides. But their mother had other ideas, so in 1916 she went to Saranac Lake and made arrangements for the boys to board during the week with Ansel Parsons, who was a guide for the Swensons. Every Sunday Catherine would cook an early dinner at one or two o'clock, and then Clarence and Bill would walk the sixteen miles to Saranac Lake, where they would stay until the following Friday when they would walk home again.

Somehow that walk always seemed to take about four hours. "No matter whether we were on snowshoes or whether it was bare ground," says Clarence, "four hours every time, go down, four hours coming back. We tied our snowshoes on with candle wicking. And of course if it snowed during the week, invariably you had to break trail on the way back."

In winter the trip was usually made in the dark, the pitchiest of black nights, with no thought of such things as streetlights or even the dim reflections on low clouds from nearby towns. The boys had never even seen a flashlight. It was so dark that they would have to find their way by looking up at the treetops and following the path outlined where the tall pines blotted out the stars. One can only imagine the effect such a lonely hike might have on young children, yet Clarence and

51

Bill seem to have hardly given it a thought. The worst time of course was when the blackflies and mosquitos were bad. Then the walk was pure misery.

In 1860 Alfred B. Street described the torture of the infamous Adirondack flies during a hunting trip up the Raquette:

> If you open your mouth, in they go; if you inhale through your nose, up they go; they play an unceasing fife to the drum of your ear, and dart in as if to assault your brain. Just as you motion to slap your forehead, there is a quick sting on your temple, and you don't know which to slap first. If you rub your cheek—w-h-i-z-p—there is a terrific bite on your eyelid. You crush the sight out of your optics with a finger that has three little fiends tacked to it; you try to rub both your prickling hands at once, while your elbows are suffering; you shrug your shoulders and begin to wriggle your back in your shirt, at the same time your legs are twitching as if in a galvanic battery; in short, you are defending the tip of your nose, while the aggregate flesh of your body is creeping off your bones.

A year or two of this was enough. Both boys drew on some of their precious savings and purchased bicycles. Except during snowshoe season, the bicycles transformed their weekly treks to school into little more than one-to-two-hour jaunts. Clarence's used bike cost him ten dollars but came without a mudguard, which he ordered later from the Montgomery Wards catalog. In spring when the roads were bad, they would take the long way around by way of Saranac Inn, for most of that route was paved, with the exception of the short run to the Wawbeek. The best part about their new transport was that it enabled them to outrun the biting flies.

The bikes had thin tires over an even thinner inner tube, and patching materials for the inevitable flats were essential. The roads around Coreys were dirt, and when it was muddy, the boys would have to pedal like mad to get through the wet sections before they sank into the muck. The trail over to Rustic Lodge, on the other hand, had clay soil that was smooth and hard. Here they could fly. Though bike riding had grown in popularity in the late 1800s, Clarence and Bill were probably two of the first true dirt bikers. Most of the old roads were corduroy. The concept of proper drainage, that roads had to be raised up to allow the water to drain away, did not seem to be properly understood in the more remote areas of the Adirondack backcountry. Instead, road workers would come along and throw more fill down where wet spots had gotten out of hand. Of course, this would only be a temporary fix, and before long the entire thing would be a soup bowl once again.

Clarence remembers riding to Saranac Inn one time on top of a Concord stagecoach. He was probably no more than three years old: "I remember looking way down from the top. It was a long way down to the ground. The horses' hoofs were going clip-clop, clip-clop because that was one of the only pieces of stone road around at that time, at Saranac Inn, and I remember thinking how funny it sounded."

By the time Clarence and Bill got their bicycles, there were more stone roads, including one from Saranac Lake to Lake Placid. The hard surfaces were constructed by spraying hot tar onto the road straight from fifty-five-gallon drums that had a furnace roaring away beneath them. The entire contraption was loaded onto a wagon. As soon as the blazing hot tar was down, men would come along and throw crushed stone on top of it. As traffic went over the road, the stone would become embedded in the tar. It made a smooth, hard surface, and the boys would bike to Lake Placid just for the wonder of it.

Bicycles could go almost as fast as automobiles under these conditions. Indeed, the principle involved in the propulsion of early cars was not all that different. Clarence saw his first car in about 1910 while he was still living at Putnam's. They had heard that a wealthy New York family had brought a car up, and Clarence and Bill caught sight of it one day. "It had a bicycle chain that drove the rear wheels of the thing," recalls Clarence. "They sat up real high, and there was a chauffeur who wore one of those tan duster coats and a cap." The vehicle spent much of its time stuck in one mud hole or another (not unlike the bicyclists). The men would then have to climb down and dig themselves out with a shovel. They would go a short distance and then get stuck again.

Clarence and Bill watched this little drama unfold while hidden in the woods, where they often spent their time observing the neighbor-

Saranac Lake High School—the school Clarence and Bill hiked sixteen miles to attend. Located on the site where the Hotel Saranac now stands. Courtesy of the Adirondack Collection, Saranac Lake Free Library.

hood's comings and goings in stealth, pretending to be Indians. During one particularly nasty spell in a mud hole, the car's occupants called on Fred Woods, who was happening by with a wagon and a team of horses. Fred hooked his team up to the car, pulled it free, and watched it head off once again. The boys came out of hiding to talk to Fred, who sat up in his wagon and lit his pipe. He stared after the car and said, "Those things will never amount to anything."

The central school the boys attended was a three-story building located where the Hotel Saranac now stands. Clarence entered the fifth grade, which was on the first floor, and Bill went into the seventh grade on the second floor. The high school was on the top floor. The superintendent was Professor H. V. Littell, who had come to the little village, like so many others, because he was tubercular. Saranac Lake was the home of the Trudeau Sanatorium, the leading facility in the country for treating tuberculosis, which doctors believed could be cured by a regimen of rest and clean mountain air. Littell, however, was a chain-smoker, a habit that few related to lung problems at the time.

Professor Littell stood out among educators, Clarence remembers, because he expected his students to go on to higher education, an expectation that was quite unusual at the time. Every week Littell ordered a convocation, during which he would bring in all sorts of people from the professions—doctors, dentists, and so forth—who would talk about their jobs. When America entered World War I in 1917, the superintendent volunteered for duty and was gone for the duration of the hostilities. After he returned Clarence's graduating class dedicated their 1925 yearbook, the *Mazda*, to this progressive educator.

In that same yearbook Clarence was remembered for the ages in a series of both flawed and accurate descriptions written as a class history by Charlotte Kennedy. For some reason, it was felt that Clarence did not like girls, though this was most likely the result of another characteristic: he was voted "most bashful." Also described, however, as "most handsome," it is likely that his years living a decidedly masculine existence in the woods had left him tongue-tied in the presence of female classmates.

Bill Petty with trombone, Saranac Lake Boys Band, 1919. Clarence Petty collection.

"Clarence," Kennedy wrote, "is to be just as polite in the future and yet as retiring as he always has been. [He] will receive his clients into his place of business with great courtesy and a pleasant greeting. He will offer them a chair and converse with them in a friendly manner. He will never snub anyone. He will be very solicitous for their feelings and he will by no means do anything to hurt them or cut them. If he does so he is very sorry. Clarence is going to be an excellent barber, you see."

This is a delightfully accurate analysis in many ways, with the exception of a career as a barber, which Clarence would leave to his friend Noah Rondeau. His politeness and unwillingness to snub anyone fits perfectly with his own analysis of how he always attempted to deal with issues rather than personalities. During his many years of involvement in a variety of intense Adirondack controversies, Clarence never wavered from a respectful and courteous approach. But "retiring" and "bashful" could never be words that one would associate with him in later years. He was to hold strong opinions and to be respected for his willingness to promote them in public forums and on the many committees and boards to which he would one day belong.

The war years brought changes even to the remote regions of the Adirondacks. Clarence remembers most of all the food rationing. His landlady had to buy cereal in order to get permission to buy a pound of flour, which was in great demand. She also bought a great deal of rolled oats, and they ate rolled-oat biscuits until they nearly burst. Sugar, too, was in short supply, which led to one memorable family incident. Ellsworth, who did not like cats, had nevertheless allowed Archie to have a cat of his own. The animal promptly decided to use the family sugar supply as kitty litter. The contaminated sugar was carefully scooped out so that the remainder of the rare delicacy could be saved.

Another peculiarity was the saving of nutshells. Clarence did not know why at the time but later learned that the shells were ground up and used in gas masks to neutralize mustard gas. It must have been quite a procedure, for the masks were enormous, requiring a pack and a large separate breathing device. Mustard gas was one of the most lethal substances used during WWI, resulting in over one million casualties, including seventy-nine thousand deaths.

The years surrounding World War I were an exciting time, even for boys living on the edge of the wilderness. All sorts of technological advances were being made, and occasionally one of them would make an appearance. In October of 1912 George Gray of Boston became the second man to land an airplane in the Adirondacks.[1] He had taken off from Malone in a Burgess-Wright biplane. Encountering high winds while flying over Whiteface Mountain, Gray was forced to land in a wheat field near Bloomingdale. He eventually flew on to Saranac Lake, where he stayed for several days, giving rides to thrill seekers.

It is likely that the Petty boys heard about Gray, but they would not have another chance to see a plane for six years. Near the end of the war, Clarence and Bill learned that a plane was going to be flying from Lake

---

1. The first was pioneer aviator Robert J. Collier, who hauled a Curtiss-Wright biplane to Raquette Lake by freight train. The seaplane flew briefly over the lake on July 1, 1912.

Placid to Tupper Lake. They climbed to the top of Panther Mountain and stayed all afternoon, looking for the aircraft. It never came, and Clarence's opportunity to see his first flying machine was again put on hold. One could speculate that these missed opportunities whetted his interest all the more and presaged what would become a lifelong passion and profession.

Just a few months later, in 1919, Clarence finally saw his first aircraft when a man by the name of Chapin flew a float plane to Saranac Lake Village and landed on Lake Flower. He proceeded to take people up for rides, and in the process hit a stump and put a hole in one of the floats. The float partially sank, tilting the plane over onto one side. Undaunted, Chapin sat smoking a cigar until someone came to tow him ashore. Clarence's first ride in a plane would not come until 1925, when he was a new student at the College of Forestry in Syracuse. At a place called Amboy Field, just west of Syracuse, he took a ten-minute ride in a Waco biplane.

But to a high school student, trekking to school in the winter, planes were still little more than a fantasy. Snowshoes were the more traditional mode of transport. Occasionally a ride might be scared up from someone who had a sleigh, but otherwise the boys got a healthy workout each weekend. There was snow on the ground from before

Clarence and Bill exhibit their racing form on a shoveled track on First Pond, 1920. Clarence Petty collection.

Thanksgiving until well into April. Clarence is astonished by today's moderating winter climate, with snow often failing to appear until Christmas, and the spring melt coming in March or even February. In the past, there was nearly always a January thaw around the middle to the end of the month, but that was usually it until the spring melt. Now winter thaws occur frequently and, come February, it is hard to tell if one is experiencing a brief thaw or an early spring.

Safety on the ice has always been a major concern for Adirondack residents. The traditional cold winters of the early twentieth century meant that ice skating was possible by Thanksgiving. "We would always skate either the day before or the day after Thanksgiving," remembers Clarence. "It wasn't thick, the ice, but the Stony Creek Ponds were all frozen over. And we used to skate on what we called 'rubber ice,' because you could see the wave going ahead of you when you went. We stayed close enough to the shore, so if we broke through, we wouldn't go in over our heads. Where the little brook comes in down there, you could see muskrat swimming under the ice. They'd come right up under our feet."

Today it is considered unwise to go out on the ice before New Year's, and there is generally a degree of danger throughout the winter because of the warm breaks in the weather. People on snowmobiles are always falling through the ice, and more than a few have gone through while attempting to drive their cars the length of Saranac Lake, all the way from Rustic Lodge to Saranac Inn. Clarence first began to notice

Retrieving car that fell through the ice on Upper Saranac Lake, killing the occupants, 1940s. Clarence Petty collection.

the change, perhaps the first signs of global warming, back in the 1930s, after he returned from college at Syracuse. The Pettys could no longer count on skating at Thanksgiving. And where they used to cut ice to put in the icehouses in January, the blocks were no longer worth cutting until February or March.

Ice harvesting was one of the major winter chores for guides and caretakers such as Ellsworth in the early part of the century. At the Adirondack Mountain Reserve property known as the Ausable Club, located at St. Huberts near Keene Valley, an average of fifty horses and thirty men were kept busy for a month filling the club's icehouses. Harold Weston, who spent his childhood summers at St. Huberts, described the intensity of the effort in *Freedom in the Wilds:*

> Back of the old Inn were two large icehouses which together held 8,000 cakes, more or less, according to the thickness of the ice cut that year. The Adirondack Mountain Reserve had a good-sized icehouse holding around 600 cakes by the home of the superintendent. Each privately owned cottage, some twenty-five of them, and the ten year-round residences had their own smaller or larger icehouses averaging at least 300 cakes apiece. The same was true for the three club camps and the eleven private camps at the Upper Ausable Lake. Thus the total number of cakes of ice to be harvested each winter was at least 25,000 cakes 16″ x 16″ square ideally and thirty-six inches thick. Some winters the average yield was nearer twenty-four inches thick, but then the number of cakes cut had to be considerably increased. In the twenties, one year the ice from the Lower Ausable lake was forty-seven inches thick, but that was not desirable and much harder to handle.

Clearly the days of such incredibly thick ice have long since disappeared. Whether the change is from global warming or from some other cause must be left to the scientists. But Clarence was surely one of the earliest to note the first subtle changes in Adirondack ice.

One of the pastimes that Clarence enjoyed the most came right after the January thaw. He could skate the length of Saranac Lake from the Rustic Lodge all the way to Saranac Inn and back, a round-trip of sixteen miles. "It was glare ice all the way," Clarence remembers. "And

New York State Ice Skating Relay champions—Saranac Lake High School, February 9, 1924. Clarence holding trophy. Clarence Petty collection.

you'd be totally alone. It was the same way down here on the Stony Creek Ponds. These ponds would be just glare as a bottle. You could skate anywhere. You don't see that anymore. But you always knew, every January after the thaw, you'd have smooth and clear ice. It would last that way for maybe three, four, five days, and then all of a sudden you'd start getting snow on it." It is hardly surprising to see Clarence's picture of himself holding a trophy in 1924, the year he and two friends were New York State relay ice skating champions for Saranac Lake High School.

Another picture that emerges shows Ernest Stowe's ice boat resting on that same incredible glare surface in front of the Rustic Lodge about 1905. Stowe was a well-known rustic furniture maker who worked out of a small cabin at the lodge from the 1890s until about 1911. That year he moved to Florida and never returned, writing to tell Ellsworth that he could have his cabin and carpentry tools. The cabin was hauled the length of Indian Carry and skidded across the ice to the Petty home. An exhibit of some of Stowe's meticulously carved and designed furniture is on display today at the Adirondack Museum.

Ellsworth used to walk the three miles to Deer Island in the winter to do his caretaking chores. He would always try to keep walking in as late as possible into the spring. As a result, he fell through the ice nearly every year. The technique for getting out of the water was an essential skill, one that Ellsworth taught the boys at a young age.

Ernest Stowe's ice boat in front of Rustic Lodge, Upper Saranac Lake, 1905. Photograph by Catherine Petty, Clarence Petty collection.

Most people tried to get out as though they were getting onto a dock. This did not work, as the ice would keep breaking off from the concentrated weight. The secret was to let one's feet rise to the surface. If one had snowshoes on, this would happen naturally, since the wooden shoes were lighter than the water. Then one should spread one's weight along the edge of the ice and *just* roll out. A person needed to understand that the ice might break off a few times before this worked. But if he kept at it back in the direction from which he had come, he would eventually reach the ice that supported his weight on the way in.

Clarence and Bill both fell through the ice a number of times in the winter. Clarence sometimes crossed the Raquette River, which had a strong current. This was especially dangerous, for his snowshoes could be caught by the current and pull him under. To deal with this, he was taught to cut a ten-foot pole and hold it as he walked across. If he went through, he used the pole to pull himself back up.

On two or three occasions, Clarence fell through while he was out alone, trapping in minus twenty or thirty degree temperatures. He was only fifteen or sixteen at the time. Fortunately, he dressed entirely in wool. This not only hastened the drying-out process but also gave him a minute or so of protection from the initial shock of cold until his clothes became saturated. Wool also insulates to a degree, even when wet. But once he was out, he had to keep moving or he would freeze.

Eventually he would dry out on the inside, but a crust of ice would form on his clothes on the outside.

One of the closest calls Clarence ever had came much later in his life, while he was leading George Davis into remote areas to do ecological studies for Governor Nelson Rockefeller's Study Commission on the Future of the Adirondacks in 1970. Davis, who became planning director for the new Adirondack Park Agency the following year, and much later served as executive director of Governor Cuomo's Commission on the Adirondacks in the Twenty-First Century, describes the event thirty years later:

> Because I had a previous engagement on Monday, Clarence started our Monday through Wednesday field trip without me. He was to check OK Slip Pond and see how much development had occurred on its shores with some rustic hunting cabins we thought were there. And, in addition, he wanted to check the boundaries of the private land in that area and the extent of any logging that might have happened on this private land.
>
> Of course, it was extremely cold and a good deal of snow on the ground, being the middle of an Adirondack winter. On Monday afternoon after my appointment in Albany, I came up to North Creek to meet Clarence at the motel. When I got there, Clarence was already back from his field trip, which struck me as strange, since he normally stays out until dark. As I arrived, it was twenty below zero and dropping. I learned from the desk clerk that it had been thirty-four degrees below zero that morning. I also learned that he thought something might have happened with Clarence because of the way he came in earlier that afternoon, but he had no details. I checked with Clarence, and this is the story that resulted.
>
> It did take some teeth-pulling to get it all out of him, because I think he felt a bit embarrassed by the whole thing and wasn't sure he wanted to acknowledge it. But after seeing his room with the clothes and boots and stuff hung up the way they were, I kinda had him trapped, so that he had to "fess up" a little bit.
>
> He had headed from the motel on up to the edge of the proposed primitive area at the Upper Hudson, to where he would snowshoe in to OK Slip Pond. He checked the boundaries as he went along and it was

a beautiful day, but clear and still way below zero. When he got to the pond, he went out on the ice and was looking things over, when he did something that he knew full well he shouldn't have done, but it just didn't occur to him in time. He stepped too close to a broken log jutting up through the ice. Of course, if there's going to be thin ice anywhere, it's along or next to such an object jutting through the otherwise very secure ice. Well, the next thing Clarence knew he was more than waist deep, nearly chest deep in icy cold water, and all alone about four miles from his car. He was able to get himself out, which was not an easy trick with snowshoes on, get his snowshoes up onto the ice, and pull himself out.

The only reason he was so successful undoubtedly is that the ice was so thick, because of the cold winter we had had, and except for that one small area next to the log, it was stable, so he didn't break it off when trying to pull back onto it. Being the woodsman he is, he knew that the first thing to do, when something like this happens, is to get your boots off immediately and wring out your socks and get your socks back on and your boots back on. He bent over to do this, but just in the time it took to bend over, his boots and laces and everything had frozen solid, and there was no way to unlace them. So he started back toward the car.

At this point, I interrupted him and asked why in the world he didn't break into one of the cabins on the shoreline of OK Slip Pond and get a fire started immediately. That's the first thing I would have done if I was able to even survive to that point, and I think the first thing that most people would've done, but not Clarence. He would not consider breaking into someone else's property. So instead he backtracked in his own snowshoe tracks, moving as quickly as he could to keep from freezing to death. His clothes from a line somewhere below his chest and above his waist froze up immediately as his boots had, and it was only by a jogging action, keeping the knees bending, that he was able to keep them flexible enough to allow him to get out to the car. By then he had built up body heat and was able to get into his car and get the heater going.

I've always sworn that if this had happened to anyone else but Clarence, they certainly would've died if they hadn't broken into a cabin and gotten a fire going. I know myself, if it had happened to me, and even if I had got out of the water, I would've just curled up on the ice and said goodbye to this world. But not Clarence. He's tough as any old duck I've ever run across.

The next day Davis walked back in to OK Slip Pond and found Clarence's trail. He photographed the tracks Clarence had made coming in and that he had backtracked out on. Where he fell through, the tracks ended abruptly. Davis marked the picture "The end of the trail."

CHAPTER 7

Expanding Horizons

throughout their high school years Clarence and Bill continued to guide during summer vacations and on weekends. They were becoming accomplished woodsmen and were always in demand. At Catherine's insistence, school took precedence, but whenever the opportunity presented itself, the boys headed for the woods. This pattern persisted during their college years as well. If they had a vacation, like as not, they could be found deep in Cold River country, fishing and visiting with their friend Noah Rondeau.

"Until the late twenties and early thirties, that was fabulous fishing up there," Clarence recalls. "It was a fast-running stream, Cold River was, and you could throw a spinner or worm out there and out from under the bank would come brook trout that weighed four and five pounds."

There are still trout in Cold River country, but the big ones are long gone. The five-pounders Clarence and Bill caught had to survive for five or six years to reach that size. They became that large because no one was going in there to fish in the early part of the century. Another factor affecting trout size may have been the change in water temperature. In those days, the water would be so cold in June that a person could barely put his hand in it. Nowadays, says Clarence, the water in June is much warmer, "just like milk."

An interesting peculiarity of the fish in the Cold River, Clarence notes, was how they would disappear under the bank after a few casts were made and not reappear for forty-five minutes. Ellsworth had first commented on this phenomenon with regard to the fish in Panther Pond, which he said did the same thing. He thought it might take the fish that long to circle around the pond back to where you were. But the Cold River trout followed the same pattern, forty-five minutes, almost to the minute, every time. Clarence's theory is that it took the trout that long to forget their fear before they would emerge again. Sometimes a single cast would be enough to spook them.

In about 1923 an incident occurred that would forever make the boys more cautious during their guiding. Bill had taken a group of four or five hunters into the woods beyond Panther Pond. As Clarence was returning home from Bartlett's, he ran into guide Arlow Flagg, who told him that his brother had been shot and his mother had gone for the doctor. Clarence rushed home to discover that Bill had had the top of his big toe shot off. Hiking in to Panther Pond, one of the four hunters accompanying Bill had put a cartridge up in the barrel and pulled the hammer back, ready to fire in case he saw a deer. The trigger caught on some brush and the gun went off. After that, Clarence and Bill never took a group out without first going over basic gun safety. Many of their city-bred clients had virtually no experience with firearms.

The boys were not particularly good students, but they worked hard and consistently. Math was the subject that gave Clarence the most difficulty. Given his subsequent career in fields that required a great deal of math, his later success is no small tribute to his lifelong ability to apply himself in the face of a challenge.

One of the moments that always stood out in Clarence's mind as pivotal in his life came when he entered the seventh grade. He had the choice between taking a basic commercial course or the more difficult classical science course. Always anxious to spend less time studying and more time out in the woods, he chose the easy class. But his advisor took him aside and told him he should take the classical science course because if he did not, he probably wouldn't be able to get into college. Clarence told her he could not do the math, but his teacher said she would help him, and though it was a struggle, he managed to complete the work. If he had not chosen that route, he would not have had the

Saranac Lake High School graduation, 1925. Clarence is fourth from right, top row. Clarence Petty collection.

necessary credits to get into the College of Forestry, and his entire life path would have been changed.

Given his backwoods upbringing, it was almost ordained that Clarence would choose forestry as a career. He wanted to spend time in the woods. If his mother would not let him live like an Indian or at least as a full-time guide, then he would become a forester. If he had known at the time how much of his life would actually be spent behind a desk, he might have had second thoughts. But in 1925 he entered the State College of Forestry at Syracuse (later called the SUNY College of Environmental Science and Forestry). Bill had also taken to forestry and was studying at Cornell. By attending the state school at Syracuse, Clarence avoided having to pay tuition, which he would not have been able to afford. As it was, he worked at various jobs throughout his school years to help defray costs. He joined a fraternity, and in exchange for performing various duties he received free board.

Clarence found the discipline and the coursework difficult. He longed for the freedom that had for so long been ingrained in him. In his

Clarence (right, hand in pocket) at Axton Plantation with College of Forestry Class of 1930. Clarence Petty collection.

sophomore year he made the mistake of going out for the football team. His grades fell, and he dropped out for a semester. When he came back, and without the distraction of football, he was able to keep up with the work. Math continued to be a struggle, but in his junior year he was offered a job as an assistant instructor of civil engineering. He was paid thirty-five cents an hour to grade papers and take students out for instruction in the use of transits and survey equipment. Clarence was surprised to be given the job, since he could barely understand the courses himself. But teaching helped him to better comprehend the work and gave him a lifelong feeling for how instructing others could benefit oneself.

For many of the forestry students, this was an entirely new way of life. They came from all over, some straight out of New York City. One of Clarence's roommates was from Brooklyn. The boy had no experience in the woods. Yet the regimen maintained by the college was demanding and was designed to give students the flavor of life as a lumberjack. They were awakened at six A.M. to form work details. For an hour Clarence and his roommate sawed wood for the stoves until the breakfast bell rang at seven. Other groups engaged in various cleanup details or helped the cook prepare sandwiches for students who were going out into the field. Clarence enjoyed cutting wood with the cross-cut saw. It was good practice for the annual competition with the Ranger School at Wanakena.

Every morning at eight o'clock, rain or shine, they were out in the woods, studying dendrology, silviculture, entomology, ecology, pathology, mensuration, and surveying. The city boys grumbled at first about having to go out in the pouring rain or bitter cold. But after a few weeks, they became accustomed to it, and the grumbling stopped. This was how the lumberjacks lived, after all, and the emphasis at the school in those days was on timber production.

While Clarence enjoyed this immersion in the out-of-doors and even spent his summer vacations working at various jobs in the Adirondacks, the draw of the wilderness was also beginning to expand his horizons.

During the summer of 1929 he and a friend, Art Selzer, took a trip out West. They traveled in Art's 1925 Buick, camping as they went. The trip across Canada on the trans-Canada highway was exactly the sort of adventure they were looking for. In those days the highway was little more than two wheel-tracks through the grass. They crossed into the United States and visited Yellowstone and Glacier National Parks. They climbed Pike's Peak at night to avoid the summer heat and stayed to watch the sun rise the next morning. The young adventurers immersed themselves in their wild surroundings, fishing, rock climbing, and hiking.

Upon reaching Art's home in Portland, Oregon, Clarence was left to hitchhike home. Many of the rides he got came from people wanting him to share in the driving. He first headed south to Sacramento in order to pick up the main east-west highway. He crossed the Great Salt

Art Selzer with the Buick used on his Western trip, 1929. Clarence Petty collection.

Clarence at Mount Rainier in Washington State during his Western trip with Art Selzer, 1929. Clarence Petty collection.

Lake desert and caught one ride from a Mormon who told him all about his religion, and another from a man driving an enormous Lincoln Continental, who turned out to be the president of the Miami Jockey Club. This western trip became one of the sterling memories of Clarence's youth.

Back at school, part of the four-year course of study that led to a bachelor's degree included a "summer camp" of field work at Barber's Point on Cranberry Lake. The site for this camp, which was to become a college tradition, first began to take form in the spring of 1915 at a location near the mouth of Sucker Brook. Faculty and students worked together to clear the site and to build a storehouse and, of all things, a tennis court. In the early years students lived in tents, with a larger tent as the dining hall and classroom.

One early neighbor of the camp at Barber Point was Fay Welch, whose lifetime association with Cranberry Lake began in 1902 and included time spent as guide, naturalist, forestry student, teacher, and conservationist. He recalled exciting water meets, canoe and swimming races, and nighttime songs around a roaring campfire in which neighbors often joined in. "In 1903," wrote Welch, "Cranberry Lake was largely a wilderness, an untouched and exceedingly beautiful area, its waters abounding in trout and its numerous bogs and impenetrable bays—blocked by standing and fallen tree trunks and driftwood—a haven for wildlife."

One of Clarence's professors was Nelson Brown, who had been an ad-

visor to Franklin Roosevelt, working
with the governor in reforestation at
his Hyde Park estate and again, later,
after he became president. Brown
credited Roosevelt's work at Hyde
Park, along with his jobs as chairman
of the New York Forest, Fish and
Game Commission and as governor,
for later giving the president the
background that would lead to the
creation of the Civilian Conservation Corps (CCC). A bit of a showoff
and a terrific "bull-thrower," as
Clarence describes it, Brown nevertheless was liked by his students and
went out of his way to help them
whenever he could. He had traveled
to Italy a number of times during
World War I to advise the king on the
war. "He always used to say, 'My
friend, the king of Italy,' " Clarence
remembers.

*Clarence climbing in Glacier Park,
1929. Clarence Petty collection.*

Another teacher was Bill Har-
low. He was the summer-camp instructor during Clarence's stay at Barber Point. About a year after Clarence graduated he wrote to Harlow,
asking if he had any slides of Adirondack vegetation that Clarence
might be able to use in public presentations. Harlow replied regretfully
that he did not. But a year later when Clarence ran into his former
teacher, Harlow told him that Clarence's letter had made him think
that creating slides would be a good thing to do, and so he had begun to
take pictures of the flora. Evidently, the photography seized Harlow's
imagination, for he went on to work for Walt Disney and to make films
for Encyclopedia Britannica that used time-lapse photography to show
how flowers and other plants grew.

Clarence graduated in June of 1930. Thrust into the working world at the starting bell for the Great Depression, he nevertheless found his first job almost at once, beginning a long and steady string of occupations that would not end until his retirement (in name only) some forty years later.

While still at the College of Forestry, Clarence attended an interview with a personnel director from Western Union who came up to recruit. Nine students were interviewed. The first thing Clarence told the man was that he did not want to get stuck in New York City, because he loved being in the outdoors. That would be no problem the man assured him, since Western Union men were always doing fieldwork. The company representative went back to New York City, and Clarence took off on a vacation for a week at Dawson Pond. When he got back, there was a telegram informing him that he had gotten the job.

So Clarence headed for New York City. The first thing the company did was to send him to Seabright on the New Jersey coast for an orientation course. After two weeks of what was essentially a vacation as far as Clarence was concerned, the rest of the men returned to the city to work in the company's laboratory. Clarence was sent out to Oklahoma to work with an engineer named Perkins, who was doing electrical conductivity studies on telegraph poles. The company's lines ran along the railroad tracks, and Clarence was given a pass to ride on virtually any railroad in the country.

Western Union wanted a survey of the potential of different kinds of wood for the construction of telegraph poles. They were paying a premium price for southern yellow pine and wanted to see if other species would work as well. Clarence traveled to Salt Lake City and surveyed a number of forests in the area. He made an extensive study of lodgepole pine. The tree was very limby and full of knot holes, which caused problems for the linemen who had to climb the poles using spikes on their boots. Upon finishing this, he returned to Oklahoma and worked some more on conductivity studies until, in October, he was told to come back to New York.

It turned out that the company's income was dropping drastically as the Depression settled in. They could no longer afford field studies. Clarence suddenly found himself face-to-face with his worst nightmare: he was stuck in an office on the sixteenth floor of 60 Hudson Street in downtown Manhattan, with a tiny lab next door to work in. His days were spent staring through a microscope, examining cable boxes and other equipment, and trying to determine why and how they decayed. "It was highly technical stuff," he recalls, "but I was ready to get out of there by any means possible."

As it turned out, Clarence's desperation to escape from the city led to one of the most important decisions of his life. He was living at Valley Stream on Long Island and commuting into New York every day. Right next to his apartment was a Curtiss-Wright Flying School, one of a number of such flight-training schools that were springing up all over the country. The Curtiss-Wright schools had been established by Casey Jones, a famous World War I pilot. Clarence decided to learn to fly.

The course cost six hundred dollars, which was a huge amount of money at the time. Clarence took a big risk by using up a large portion of his savings at the beginning of the Depression to get his pilot's license. Even the flight school was experiencing hard times and was actually in the process of closing down; there were only a handful of instructors left. Clarence met the famous Casey Jones a number of times as the World War I ace desperately tried to keep the flying program alive in the deepening Depression.

The training program lasted five months, from October 30 to March 31. Once a student gradu-

Clarence in front of Jim Gann's De Havilland Moth at Curtiss Field, Valley Stream, Long Island, 1933. Clarence Petty collection.

ated from the school, he could take the pilot's exam after as little as eighteen hours of total flying time.

The planes Clarence learned to fly in were Curtiss Fledglings, heavy two-place biplanes with Challenger engines. They had been used for training WWI pilots during the final stages of the war. The only instruments the Curtiss Fledglings had were a magnetic compass, an altimeter, oil pressure and temperature gauges, and an airspeed indicator. It was all visual flying. There were no brakes or tail wheels, only a steel spring bar. In order to slow down after landing, a pilot relied on the tail skidding along the ground. Takeoffs and landings were from a sod airstrip.

On the far side of the field, the navy had a twelve-hundred-foot diameter landing pad that it used to train pilots for carrier landings. In carrier landings the ship was always headed into the wind. To simulate landings at sea, the field had a huge windsock to tell pilots which way the wind was blowing, so they could fly into it during practice takeoffs and landings. As many as a dozen planes at a time would use the pad, and accidents were common. Clarence never had to land on a carrier during his career, but he practiced landing on the twelve-hundred-foot navy pad under all sorts of conditions, day and night. At night the landing lights would be cut back in order to simulate landing in combat areas. Small smudge pots were used to provide a bare minimum of light.

Clarence never regretted not having to try one of those landings on a real carrier. "When you see how a carrier will roll, bucking those big waves, and that ship is moving up and down like that, it's a tricky business to land there and get your tail hook in the arresting gear. Otherwise you'd go right over the side. There were a lot of deaths that way in World War II."

Some of Clarence's fellow students told him to stick with just one instructor in order to make the best progress. But he found the reverse to be true and felt he learned something from each of them, bomber pilots and pursuit pilots alike. After just five hours of flying time, during which he was required to demonstrate stalls, recovery from left and right spins, emergency landings, slips, and vertical banked turns, he made his first solo flight, consisting of six takeoffs and landings.

The instructors treated the students "like dirt," that is, in a very strict, military fashion. They would swear a blue streak at their charges if any of them made a mistake. One of the instructors was an alcoholic, "a real wino," Clarence recalls. A lifelong teetotaler, as was his father before him, Clarence has little tolerance for alcohol abusers. This occasionally leads to some exaggeration on his part when he labels someone a "wino."

By the end of February Clarence had taken the required physical examination, passed the ground school written exam, and was signed off to take the flight test. The CAA flight examiner, a WWI veteran by the name of Weems, appeared at the field March 2. Examiners were not allowed to fly with students because there were so many crashes. Weems gave instructions and then went out and stood on the field to view the results.

The day Clarence took his flight exam was sunny and extremely cold. The temperature was below zero, and the planes they used had open cockpits. There were four students taking the exam at the same time. Weems gathered the men around and said to one, "You go over there, circle around that coal plant, and you go up to four thousand feet. I want to see you do a two-turn spin to the right and then you go back up there at four thousand feet and you do a four-spin turn to the left." Then he would turn to the next man and tell him to do another series of maneuvers and so on for all four of the men taking the test. They also had to do maneuvers for different emergencies—pulling the power back until the engine could not be heard, simulating a dead engine, making a certain kind of pattern, coming in and landing within a certain dis-

Jim Gann's De Havilland Moth at Valley Stream, 1933. Clarence Petty collection.

tance, and so forth. Weems stood out in the middle of the field, smoking his cigar and exchanging humorous remarks with the flight instructors.

Clarence passed the exam and was awarded his pilot's license in 1931. He was subsequently required to fly at least ten hours every year to get renewed for the next year. When he went back for his first renewal, he met Weems sitting behind a desk at a hanger in Newark. The examiner said, "God, you're still alive?" Clarence asked him if he was flying. Weems replied, "Oh hell, I wouldn't fly with the students."

The Curtiss-Wright Flying School at Valley Stream folded two years later. Clarence managed to continue to fly by renting a series of planes, beginning with a new Kinner Bird that he was able to rent for fifteen dollars an hour versus the thirty dollars required for the Fledglings. He also rented an Aeromarine Klemm low-wing craft at Newark Airport for twelve dollars an hour and a Curtiss Junior, equipped with a three-cylinder radial engine, for nine dollars an hour. At that time, there were four types of certificate issued: private, limited commercial, commercial, and transport. Holders of commercial or transport pilot certificates were allowed to give flight instruction.

These were Depression days in New York City, and Clarence saw evidence every day of the hard times. He could look out his window at 60 Hudson and see long lines of people going to the soup kitchen. Banks were foreclosing on all people who could not pay their mortgages, throwing entire families out onto the street, furniture and all. People in despair were jumping off the Brooklyn Bridge and out of office buildings. "People that didn't go through that big Depression have no idea what it was like," says Clarence. "Today you've got a net that catches people. But there was no such thing then. If you were out of money, there was no way of getting it from anywhere."

Many businesses were feeling the pinch as well. The chairman of the board of Western Union demanded that the company reduce salaries to ninety-five dollars a month. Clarence, who had to spend ten dollars a month just to commute into the city from Valley Stream, found his budget very tight. At the end of the year Western Union declared that it would have to dismiss all employees hired within the last three years.

Clarence did what he always did when he had a little free time: he headed back to the woods. On the way he stopped off at the College of Forestry at Syracuse. Here he met Nelson Brown, who told him to get his name in for a big new job opportunity. The Civilian Conservation Corps was going to be established by the Roosevelt administration, and it was going to need a lot of foresters. So Clarence put his name on a list and then went home, loaded up a pack basket, and headed straight into Cold River country for eight days.

"I was glad to get back to the woods and away from the demoralizing signs of the Depression," he remembers. "And I'd had my fill of the racket of trains, screeching brakes and milling crowds heading to nowhere. I wanted to be back where the only sounds were of a beaver slapping his tail or a barred owl hooting in the distance. It was a great relief."

Clarence in New York City was like an animal in a cage. Throughout his life he would never feel comfortable surrounded by such masses of humanity. Flying had offered one method of escape from this imprisonment. His sense of release when he finally returned to the woods was overwhelming.

But the Depression had taught Clarence one valuable lesson. He needed to prepare himself for any eventuality by learning more than one trade or profession. An alternative means of making a living was clearly going to be valuable in this uncertain economy. Accordingly, he vowed to earn his commercial pilot's license. It would serve to either supplement his work in forestry or allow him to go full time in another direction.

When he came back from Cold River there were five telegrams waiting for him, four from the Forest Service and one from the state Conservation Department in Albany. It was an amazing thing, and his family was stunned. No one ever received so many telegrams. One of the telegrams was from Georgia and a couple were from the Midwest. They offered salaries comparable to the hundred thirty-five dollars a month he had been earning in New York City prior to the cutbacks. The message from the Conservation Department in Albany was from Bill Howard, the director of the Division of Lands and Forests. He offered

Clarence a position as forestry foreman at one of the CCC camps for one hundred two dollars a month. It was the lowest offer he got. But the camp would be near Tupper Lake at a place called Cross Clearing, where Bernhard Fernow had once set up a landing for his logs. This was only five miles from the Petty home, and it was precisely where the reluctant city dweller wanted to be.

In the spring of 1933 he got another telegram, which told him to go down to Cross Clearing and meet Ernest Sterling. Sterling was a Yale graduate who had been a vice president of the James H. Lacey Company, a big timber-cruising firm in Chicago. Like many well-established business executives, Sterling had found himself out of work as the Depression took hold.

Clarence and Sterling began work at their first CCC camp right there at Cross Clearing. For Clarence, it was all beginning to come together. He was finally on his way in the profession that would dominate the rest of his working life.

CHAPTER 8

Leadership and the CCC

Clarence's return to the Adirondacks was a great relief. City life was clearly not for him. But it would not take long for him to realize that the CCC would test him in ways that he could never have imagined.

The young forester's first camp was quickly filled with men from eighteen to twenty-five years of age who had been recruited from New York City. The camps were a curious mixture of military and civilian control. While state Conservation Department personnel planned and carried out the projects, the U.S. Army was responsible for setting up the camps, supplying food and shelter, and supervising the various recreational, educational, and physical training programs.

The commanding officer at the Tupper Lake Camp was Captain John. He and his lieutenant arrived and set up tents for the men. Though funding was tenuous, and there were no supplies of any kind at the beginning, the camps were nevertheless established quickly. At first Clarence thought Cross Clearing would only operate in the summer. But in September carpenters came in and started building barracks, and it was clear the camp would operate straight through the winter.

The first day Captain John came to Clarence, who was considered the employee with the most local knowledge, and he said, "Petty, if we're going to have anything to eat this noon, we've got to have some wood for these fires. Where are we going to get some wood for the cook?"

Clarence replied, "Well, there's lots of wood around here. What tools have we got?"

"I haven't got a damn tool," Captain John answered.

Clarence went home and got a double-bladed ax and a crosscut saw and was back by nine A.M. Captain John was the perfect caricature of an army officer. He wore puttees and marched about, striking his leg with a riding crop, a huge cigar planted firmly in his mouth. He told his lieutenant to line the men up, and when the lieutenant blew his whistle, one hundred eighty men lined up. Forty-four were selected to go with Petty to cut wood.

So Clarence began his CCC career cutting firewood with forty-four men, one ax, and one saw. Fortunately, there was plenty of downed, dry wood that could be gathered up by hand. The men were completely inexperienced in the woods. They called every tree that was a conifer a Christmas tree. They referred to each other as "Spics" and "Spans." The Spics were Italian and the Spans were Spanish. Not surprisingly, there was tension in the camp. Several weeks after that opening day of wood cutting, there was a riot, and troopers were called in to bring things under control using tear gas. Afterward, the men's identities were checked thoroughly. Six were found to be escaped convicts, wanted for murder and other crimes in New York City.

After this experience, one of the other foresters said to Clarence, "You know, this is a great chance for us to learn how to handle men." But the men they had dealt with so far were angels compared to what was in store for the young forestry leaders. When spring came, Ernest Sterling recommended Clarence for superintendent of the next camp to be formed. This turned out to be at Brasher Falls, where Clarence soon found himself face-to-face with the most unruly bunch he had yet dealt with.

Just twenty-eight years old, Clarence was now in charge of one hundred fifty men, most in their forties and fifties. These were the Bonus Marchers, unemployed and financially desperate WWI veterans who had marched on Washington, D.C., a year earlier, in the spring of 1932. Demanding passage of a bill providing for immediate payment of their WWI bonus, they called themselves the Bonus Expeditionary Force.

Camping in vacant government buildings and open fields, the veterans lived in squalor, though they generally conducted themselves in a

Clarence at the Brasher Falls CCC Camp Forestry Headquarters, 1934.
Clarence Petty collection.

peaceful manner. But when the Senate defeated the Patman Bill that would have met their demands, they refused to go home. On July 28, President Hoover ordered the army, under the command of General Douglas MacArthur, to evict them forcefully. By this time most of the real veterans had left, leaving behind a hard core that the FBI declared to be mostly hardened criminals with records of murder, rape, and drunkenness. MacArthur had their camps set on fire and drove the veterans out of the city. President Hoover was widely criticized for the severity of this response and MacArthur was denounced (falsely, he always maintained) in the press and before Congress.

"They were some gang to work with," Clarence recalls. "After the first payday, I drove down there, and they were all lying by the side of the road drunk. They were all winos. We didn't get a single man out to work for two days afterwards." The men were complainers by nature. Some of the so-called veterans had only been in the army for a week or two but were already trying to get extra pay from the military. In one instance, some of the workers did not like the lunches they were getting. They gathered together some rotting fish sandwiches, packaged them up, and mailed them off to Eleanor Roosevelt.

Clarence was getting a rapid education in how to "handle" men. In later years, he reflected that "handling" was the wrong term. The secret was to accept what you were given and learn to work within the capabilities of the men you had. On-the-job training was essential. Most of the veterans had few skills, though there was one well-known piano player who had performed on Broadway. This was not a skill in demand, however, in a wilderness CCC camp.

The entire program was brand-new and everyone was feeling his way, trying anything that seemed to work. At first, Clarence believed the men were never going to amount to anything. "We were just spinning our wheels. I'd have them out sawing wood and so on and they didn't seem to give a damn what was going on." But over time he changed his opinion. Former teachers were brought in as "educators" to provide evening classes where workers could learn to read and write. Many of the men gained valuable experience and work skills, as Clarence relates:

> We had a program where we taught them how to drive. I had a mechanic and put him in charge of that and getting the men licenses so we could put them to work driving the trucks. It was a formative thing all the way along. I had seven foremen, each with twenty-five men, and there were leaders and assistant leaders. The leaders got forty dollars a month, the assistants thirty-five, and the regular guys thirty. If we found somebody that was particularly good and could handle a few men, we would recommend them for assistant leader or leader.
>
> We had charge of the forestry work. The army had charge of discipline, housing, and all that stuff. It was a two-headed monster, and oftentimes, we would conflict. The army was allotted twenty men to run the camp, but they often took many more and as a result, we'd see them just sitting around doing nothing. We needed all the men we could get, because we had a host of programs that took a lot of work. We were doing blister rust control and digging fire lines, constructing trails and building roads and bridges and doing reforestation—we planted over six hundred thousand trees at the Brasher Falls Camp alone. So when the CO wouldn't turn the men over to me, I told him I would only record the ones I got into the field. Well, he wanted me to record the men he had hanging around in camp and charge them off to my project, and I wouldn't do it. So we had a lot of words, but it was an interesting experience.

At the end of the year, Clarence had to submit a plan for the following season for two hundred men, one hundred eighty of whom would be in the field. He worked closely with the district forester in charge of the region. The Forest Service often did things differently from the way the state was used to operating. In the past, when the state wanted to build a truck trail into an area, the men they hired plotted it out by eye and went straight in. But the Forest Service wanted truck trail locators and someone who could do civil engineering, someone who would go out with his transit and plot the course for the road so there would not be any sharp curves, just like the highway department had.

In another example, culverts for roads had been built in the past for the state Conservation Department out of hemlock and cedar. These were good woods to use because they lasted a long time in the ground without rotting. But the Forest Service decided that it would use no more wood in culverts. Metal or concrete became the preferred materials. In Clarence's opinion, these sorts of changes illustrated how far ahead of the state the Forest Service was in planning and improving the quality of the work that was done. The money was coming from the federal government, and New York was glad to get it. This probably accounted for the state's willingness to go along with the Forest Service's suggestions.

After a year at the Brasher Falls camp, Clarence was transferred again, this time to the CCC camp at East Dickinson (sometimes called the Brushton Camp because mail came to the Brushton Post Office). This would be the camp he would stay at the longest. It was also a move that would be fortuitous in another way.

Prior to his actual move to East Dickinson, the authorities arranged for Clarence to receive room and board at a farm owned by a family named Hastings. The Hastingses had four sons and two daughters, Annabelle and Ferne. Ferne caught the eye of the young camp supervisor. She was just a year younger than Clarence and was employed teaching school in St. Regis Falls. For the next four years the two dated steadily, going to the movies or skiing whenever they could steal time away from their jobs.

They were married without fanfare in Vermont in 1938. The wed-

Shady Hill Farm, East Dickinson. Ferne's grandparents seated in front of their home, 1898. This was the house where Clarence boarded while working for the CCC and where he met Ferne. Clarence Petty collection.

ding was a secret, because women teachers were not allowed to be married. It was felt at the time, deep in the Depression, that if a woman was married, she had a means of livelihood in her husband. There were not enough jobs for wives. Clarence and Ferne were married in the fall, and in order for Ferne to finish out the school term, they told no one about the marriage until the following year.

All of the CCC men were trained in fire fighting, for fires were an ongoing concern in the Adirondacks. The year 1941 was unusually hot and dry. The Boot Tree Pond fire, south of Massawepie Lake, turned out to be one of the worst blazes. It was caused by sparks from a train and began during a windstorm that went on day and night, spreading the flames viciously.

Clarence was still at the East Dickinson Camp when he received a call from Bill Foss, who was the head of the CCC camps. He told Clarence that Moses LaFountain, the district ranger at Cranberry Lake, was having serious trouble with the fire, and he wanted Clarence to go up and see what he could do to help out. When he arrived, Clarence discovered that LaFountain was having heart trouble and had been unable to contain the situation. Clarence was stunned by the state of affairs. "He hadn't any idea where the hell the fire was, where the margin was or anything. It was a going fire, running, so I said I'd go out and look it over. Well, that fire was all over the woods, several thousand acres burning at least. The smoke was so thick you could hardly see anything. I knew that if we were going to do any good, we were going to have to cut the point of it off, where it was blowing."

Clarence got on the phone and called in everyone he could find to work on the fire. By the next day, he had one hundred eighty men divided into work crews of twenty-five each. With workers from two CCC camps and the help of local people, he eventually had eleven hundred men fighting the flames.

Fire control in the days before aerial water dumping and smoke jumpers was a hands-on operation. "At that time," says Clarence,

> the Forest Service was just getting into a system called the 'one lick' method. They would take a line of men and give each one a tool. One might have an ax and another a saw or spade. The whole idea was to get a fire line down to mineral soil as quick as possible. The first man would take one whack and then the next guy would take another and by the time the whole troop had gone through, the line would be done.
>
> This wouldn't stop a crown fire, of course. Then we had to take a different tack. After we'd made our line using either the one-lick or a bulldozer if we could get one in, then we'd make a line fire, which is often called a backfire. We'd wait till nightfall when the wind went down and then burn out a section from our line back a quarter mile toward the fire. We used portable pumps also, which had to be packed in of course, along with the fuel to operate them. We called them backpack pumps. You couldn't use them for a running fire, though, because you couldn't get them in there quick enough. They were mainly for mop-up operations.

After three or four days Clarence's troops began to control the run of the Boot Tree Pond fire, but the work continued for another three weeks, with men trying to stamp out small brushfires all along the fringes of the outbreak. Finally, Clarence was able to return to his job at East Dickinson, but the fire continued to smolder away underground until Christmas.

"In fires out West you get situations that are often more critical than we have in the Adirondacks," says Clarence.

They have huge areas of soft woods and a crown fire, boy, it'll just go. On my trip out West in 1929, we built a campfire one night and in the morning we thought we'd put it out. But then I saw some smoke coming from it. We were close to a stream and I went down with a pail and I bet I put fifty pails of water on that thing and then dug it out because it had gone down so deep. When I scraped all the stuff away, it looked like mineral soil, but it wasn't. It was actually humus—real black-looking stuff. That stuff was still burning like a furnace. They've got a lot of that out West. It's pretty rare here, but you get it sometimes. That's why the Boot Tree Pond fire burned till Christmas.

The East Dickinson camp was closed down not long after the fire, and Clarence was shifted over to the Mannsville Camp, the fourth camp that he worked at during his years with the CCC. This was an African-American camp, segregated from the others.

Despite resistance from southern legislators, Roosevelt had insisted on minority participation, for he saw the camps as an opportunity to advance black leadership. Though he was unable to keep the camps from being segregated, Roosevelt authorized hundreds of African-American reserve and education officers, as well as chaplains and medical officers. Eventually, more than two hundred thousand African Americans became members of the CCC.

Clarence was only at Mannsville for a few weeks before it too was shut down. By this time, in the spring of 1942, the war was raging and Congress, against the wishes of President Roosevelt, abolished the Civilian Conservation Corps. Clarence personally closed three camps, Brasher Falls, East Dickinson, and Mannsville. It was a big job, because there was virtually no one left, and all of the tools and records had to be packed up and trucked down to Albany.

During its nine-year history, more than three million men in over four thousand camps participated in the CCC. Members spent six million workdays fighting forest fires, cutting sixty-eight thousand miles of fire breaks, constructing thirteen thousand miles of foot trails, building thirty-four hundred fire lookout towers, and planting more than two billion trees. It has been said that the CCC helped win World War II by pro-

viding a huge pool of trained officers for the army and giving millions of men a taste of military
discipline and job training.

Clarence worked with the
CCC through its entire run, including most of the Depression.
They were productive years in
which he learned how to organize and lead large groups of men
and how to provide all sorts of
backwoods services, from fire-
fighting to road building, from
blister rust control to reforestation. They were years that pro-

Ferne Petty holding son Donald, 1940.
Courtesy of Ed Petty.

vided him with a wife and his first child, Donald, born in 1939.

But for all of this, there was one more thing that took up a good deal
of his time during these years. It was something that would lead to the
final, and in some ways most essential, piece of the puzzle that would
contribute to the success of his forestry career. It would also be signifi-
cant in the formation of his uniquely independent character.

CHAPTER 9

A New Passion and a Dual Career

Clarence's interest in flying did not spring wholly out of his distaste for his desk job at Western Union in New York. In fact, flying had taken America and the world by storm ever since the Wright brothers' first flight in 1903. Clarence took to the air just twenty-seven years later, at the age of twenty-five. It was a young man's adventure, an exciting new pastime that was sweeping the nation.

The public was captivated by flight. In 1910 former President Theodore Roosevelt exchanged his Adirondack hiking boots for helmet and goggles and went aloft in a plane flown by Arch Hoxsey at a worldwide flying meet at Belmont Park. Hoxsey had to caution TR against waving too exuberantly to the crowd below for fear of unbalancing the plane. The following year a single meet in Los Angeles attracted more than thirty thousand people.

At the beginning of World War I in 1914, the Aviation Sector of the Signal Corps had fifty-five airplanes (mostly trainers) and thirty-five pilots. The navy and the Marine Corps had fifty-four planes, three balloons, and forty-eight pilots. But by the end of the war in 1918, over eight thousand aircraft were active on the western front. In Britain alone, the number of people employed in the aircraft industry between 1914 and 1918 grew from several hundred to 350,000 and over 50,000 planes were built. The military usefulness of the airplane had been established.

The effect the war had on the advancement of aviation was huge. In addition to improvements in the design and maneuverability of aircraft, the public had become much more widely aware of the potential of the new invention. And boys such as thirteen-year-old Clarence had become hooked for life on the glamour and excitement of flying.

Further contributing to the rapid increase in postwar aviation was the sudden availability of government surplus planes. The most popular and cheapest in 1920 was the Curtiss JN-4, known as the Jenny. It was a tandem cockpit biplane produced as a WWI trainer. It cost the government five thousand dollars, but was sold as surplus for a few hundred dollars. Thousands of people got their first plane rides in these "flying gypsies" at a dollar a minute.

The service veterans of WWI became the barnstormers of the 1920s. The loop-the-loops and Dutch rolls performed by their prewar counterparts no longer satisfied the more sophisticated plane-watchers of the twenties. New thrills were demanded, and the airmen complied by offering wing-walking, feigned falls, hanging from rope ladders by their teeth, and riding bicycles and roller skates off the wings and parachuting to the ground. One flier, Slats Rodgers, dressed a dummy to look like an aviator, went aloft, and performed a loop during which the dummy would fall out and plummet to the ground where an ambulance would race to the scene. The zanier the stunt, the more the crowd loved it.

New uses for planes were being invented on an almost daily basis. The 1920s witnessed the beginnings of aerial crop spraying and forest—fire spotting. In the years following WWII, Clarence would become engaged in each of these pursuits.

The 1930s was the decade of record setting. Newspapers were filled with the exciting exploits of aerial adventurers, and Clarence paid as much attention as anyone. Ever since he had climbed Panther Mountain as a boy of thirteen in the vain hope of seeing his first plane, he had been unable to resist anything to do with the newfangled technology. In 1927 Clarence, his brother Bill, and a friend from college traveled down to New York City to witness Charles Lindbergh's triumphant ticker-tape parade through the canyons of Wall Street.

As the 1930s unfolded, brand-new pilot Clarence avidly followed the achievements of Wiley Post, who piloted his Lockheed Vega, the *Winnie Mae*, around the world in less than nine days. Another dashing figure was business mogul and motion picture producer Howard Hughes, who set a world speed record of 352 miles per hour in a plane of his own design.

In 1932 Amelia Earhart became the first woman to make a solo flight across the Atlantic. She was the first person to fly alone from Honolulu to California in 1935, a trip that Clarence would make repeatedly during the Second World War. Two years later she and her copilot, Fred Noonan, disappeared somewhere between New Guinea and Howland Island during an attempt to fly around the world. On his World War II missions, Clarence often flew across the flight path where Earhart had so mysteriously disappeared.

All of these risk takers kept aviation before the public eye throughout the decade. They also kept Clarence's own interest high, as he continued to work on improving his skills and flight ratings.

"They were experimenting with instrument flight but it still wasn't in practical use in the early thirties," Clarence recalls. "Airmail pilots were flying open cockpit Pitcairn Mailwings on their runs between Cleveland, Pittsburgh, and Newark, pushing through bad weather, and a lot of them ended up splattered against the Appalachian Mountains. That section of the route became known as the graveyard of the air mail pilots. The pilots had the option of canceling a flight, but almost none of them did because they had bought into the 'mail must go through' logo. The result was a kind of Russian roulette that left mail, airplane wreckage, and dead bodies strewn all over the mountains."

In 1934, while working at the CCC camp at Tupper Lake, Clarence received a notice from the Civil Air Board that all pilots had to take a special check-ride in order to keep their licenses. He took a week off from work and went down to New York City, where he took his test at Roosevelt Field. Only a few pilots still had the money and desire to show up during the depths of the Depression. The exam mainly covered emergency procedures, such as precision spins and recovery.

Clarence was recertified in February of 1934, during one of the coldest New York winters on record. Temperatures of fifty and sixty below were recorded in the Adirondacks. MGM and Pathe News cameramen were in the city, shooting pictures of the many dispossessed and freezing people who were forced to live on the streets during the depths of the Depression. Clarence flew over Long Island Sound, which was frozen solid for the first time on record.

Flying in a small, open cockpit plane in the 1930s could be a cold, brutal business. Padded flying suits, leather helmets, and heavy boots and gloves gave a modest amount of protection. Clarence did not fly a plane with a radio until the middle of the decade. There were no weather reports once a pilot was aloft. He got his weather information on the ground if he was going to get it at all. A pilot had to be ready to land on a moment's notice if conditions changed.

"You had a better chance of making a reasonably good landing with the old airplanes because they had a much slower stall speed than modern aircraft," says Clarence.

> Between Malone and Syracuse, God, I landed in half the fields there with an old E2 Piper Cub, because I'd get into headwinds and the damn thing would only cruise about seventy miles an hour. There'd be a thirty-mile headwind, and I'd look down and the garbage trucks would be going by me. I'd run out of fuel—the Cub only held about ten gallons—and I'd have a little two-and-a-half gallon tank that I kept in

The first plane Clarence owned, a Piper Cub. He landed it on its skis on Second Pond on glare ice, the only plane that ever landed on the Stony Creek Ponds, March 1935. Clarence Petty collection.

the baggage compartment. I'd land at one of those fields and walk to a gas station. They had what we called marine gas—it was clear gasoline. I'd use that in place of the aviation fuel, and it seemed to work just as well.

That E2 Piper Cub, single magneto, with copper tubing for the fuel line, was the first plane Clarence ever owned. It had a thirty-seven horsepower engine. He bought it for just six hundred dollars. "They called it a forty horse, but it really had only thirty-seven," says Clarence.

He kept the plane at Malone, and whenever he had time off from the CCC, Clarence would go over and fly with students who wanted to learn:

> In order to fly during the winter the plane had to be equipped with skis, and I discovered that the U.S. Civil Aeronautics Authority (CAA) had not yet approved them for the Cub. But I received word in October from Air Associates of Roosevelt Field that they had just got authorization to sell approved wooden skis and that they could furnish me with a pair including fittings for about seventy dollars. I purchased them and made a tail skid of exactly the same weight as the tail wheel unit I removed so the fuselage wouldn't sink into crusted snow and damage the fabric.
>
> When the engine on the Cub began to approach its TBO (total before overhaul), I crated it up and sent it to the Continental factory for reconditioning. With little more than a hundred hours on the reconditioned engine, I was returning from Syracuse and had to land at Rotundo's Field near Governeur because of darkness. One of the Rotundos helped me tie the plane down and refuel it. There was a dance being held in a place near the field, and sometime after midnight a group was seen under the plane's wing, after which the plane caught fire and was destroyed. I dismantled the remains, sold the engine, and gave the fuselage to someone who wanted to use it for an iceboat.

In about 1938 a man named Mack Rogers, who ran a radio shop in Potsdam, told Clarence that there were a lot of people in Potsdam who wanted to learn to fly. Rogers said he would build a hangar for Clarence if he would bring his plane over and give lessons. So Clarence bought a new plane, a Taylorcraft, brought it to Potsdam, and began teaching the first of what would prove to be many hundreds of students, extending over a period of more than sixty years. Potsdam did not have a real airport at this point. Instead, a farmer's field owned by a man named Peck was used until World War II started.

Clarence remembers how a number of small, northern New York towns got their first airports:

> The federal government decided to build airports along the northern border for the use of military aircraft in the event that the war in Europe expanded and it became necessary to guard against invasion from the north. Officials in various towns near the Canadian border were contacted by the federal government to see if there was interest by local government for an airport in their area.
>
> The mayor of Potsdam opposed the construction of any airport near the village. Occasionally, he would send one of the village police to Peck's field to tell me that the mayor did not want any plane flying around Potsdam early in the morning because it interfered with his sleep.
>
> The village of Massena was willing to support the construction of a federally financed airport, so an area suitable for the purpose was selected and construction began. A large hangar was built on the west side of the field, and a number of flight students that were coming to Potsdam asked me if I would occasionally go to the Massena field and fly there, even before the work had been completed.
>
> I was given permission by the town supervisor to leave my Taylorcraft in the hangar even before the doors were installed. He was about to run for higher office and asked me if I would be willing to fly over villages in northern St. Lawrence County and drop leaflets for his campaign. I contacted the CAA and they told me they would approve it if each of the communities over which the leaflets were to be dropped gave me written approval. When I told him this, the town supervisor laughed and said he would have to abandon the idea, because the officials in each of the villages he had targeted were of the opposite party and there was no way they would give approval.

After the airport at Massena was completed, it was decided that air mail should be initiated. A pilot from Watertown was to fly to Massena and pick up a sack of mail for the first air mail service out of the new airport. But the day was rainy and very windy with gusts up to fifty mph, so the pilot sent word he would not be able to come that day. Well, the officials had all the plans made for the historic event and were determined the mail would fly. They asked me to put the sack of mail in the Taylorcraft and fly it around the field a couple of times. After fifteen minutes in the air and much picture taking on the ground, the mail was sent by rail to Syracuse.

Years later, in 1967, Clarence would open his own flight training school at Potsdam. He stayed in business for more than thirty years, until he finally stopped teaching at the age of ninety-five in 2000.

Another early flier in the North Country was Dwight (Dippy) Church, who would become well-known in later years for his aerial photography. Clarence met Dippy in about 1935, when Dippy flew into Malone in a Monocoach and said he had a problem with one of his cylinders. Clarence said, "Well, you know, there's only one aircraft mechanic that's licensed around here, and that's Clarence Dufort." But Dippy said he would just go find an engine mechanic in town and have him work on it. "He was going to get a guy with no experience working on airplanes," says Clarence.

But that was Dippy. He began flying before I did, back in the 1920s. He kept his Velie Monocoach in a hayfield west of Canton.

Once I let him take an Aeronca because he said he was going up into the Adirondacks to take pictures. He was gone about two hours, and when he came back, he said, "You know, you shouldn't rent out an airplane like that. That thing kept cutting out on me. I was right over Oswegatchie, taking pictures and the thing would cut out."

I asked him, "Did you have the carburetor heat control on?"

He says, "What's that?"

What he was doing, he was closing the throttle back in a glide, leaning out to take a picture, and of course it was picking up ice, and he didn't even know there was a carburetor heat control. You're supposed to put the heat control on when the engine is idling. When you close that throttle, you always put the heat control on first. Here was a guy been flying all those years, and he says, "What's that?"

Dippy was renowned locally for his pictures of the Grand Canyon, usually taken with one hand or foot on the steering mechanism of the plane while he leaned out the cockpit door and took a picture with his other hand. "Once he hit the pole that the windsock was hung on at Potsdam and another time he made a crash landing near Lowville while carrying the mail. He was in more damn scrapes like that," says Clarence, "and he always walked away. I was just amazed he could do it. He lived a charmed life."

The Taylorcraft that Clarence had taken to Potsdam to store in Rogers's hangar was the second plane he owned. He purchased it in December of 1938 from the man who ran the airport in Glens Falls. Bringing this plane home required an elaborate procedure, as Clarence describes:

> There was snow at the time in the Adirondacks but the ground was still bare at Glens Falls. My brother Archie drove me down with the skis that I'd used on the Piper Cub, because I knew they would fit the Taylorcraft. What I had to do was fly on wheels up to Lake George, which was almost all bare ice, except they had about half an inch of snow on it. I landed there with wheels. Then Archie came along in the car with my skis and I put the skis on right on the bay on Lake George. I flew off the ice just as snow began falling over the High Peaks. By flying over Lake George and Lake Champlain, I was able to sneak through the notch north of Giant Mountain and over the Cascade Lakes to the Lake Placid airport just as the snow blotted out visibility.

Clarence shared the Lake Placid hangar with Fred McLane's Stinson aircraft. McLane had come to Lake Placid in the late twenties. He began carrying passengers out of a field near the Chubb River, which is now the Lake Placid airport. He attempted to establish a CAA—approved airline between Lake Placid and Albany, but the CAA apparently believed that such service should be initiated by one of the airline companies then in existence. However, the 1932 Olympic Winter Games brought more people to Lake Placid and gave McLane's flight operations a boost.

Clarence spent a week in Lake Placid in 1932, attending the Olympic Games. The games had been engineered primarily by Melvil Dewey, the owner of the Lake Placid Club, and his son, Godfrey.

"It was the warmest winter I ever saw," remembers Clarence. "There was water running down the streets and green grass was coming up. They had to bring in snow in freight cars from Canada and truck it up the mountain in order to have the ski jump competition. That winter seemed like it was designed to destroy the Olympics. The day after the games ended and they were giving out the medals, it started to snow and it snowed steady all day. Eighteen inches fell the last day. Melvil Dewey was just about shot, because we never had a winter like that before."

Clarence saw famous figure skater Sonja Henie and speed skating champion Jack Shea. This was before the speed skating oval that was built for the 1980 Olympics. Shea won his competition on Mirror Lake. Clarence remembers watching the future star practice when Shea was very little. The skater's father was grooming him to be a champion and would meticulously oversee every facet of his son's practice sessions. One of the Japanese ski jumpers at the Intervale site, south of Lake Placid, evidently had little experience; he landed in the bleachers and was seriously injured. The bobsled run at Mount Van Hoevenburg was quite primitive in 1932. Clarence believes one of his high school classmates, Henry Homburger, took the first run.

By this time Clarence had his commercial license. But in 1939 the Civil Air Board (CAB) sent a message to all commercial and transport pilots telling them that if they wanted to instruct, they would need an official instructor's rating. Before that, a pilot could instruct with just a commercial or transport license. Clarence believes this came about because of the war starting in Europe that year. The government wanted to increase the numbers of instructors available in case the United States was drawn into the conflict. Clarence went down to Buffalo where the CAB had a special training base and got his newly instituted flight instructor's certificate, which enabled him to increase his commercial ventures, as he details: "On weekends and holidays I was able to use the Taylorcraft for passenger carrying out of many locations such as Lake Placid, Tupper Lake, and Saranac Lake. A surprising number of people took their first airplane rides. On Lake Flower at Saranac Lake, I often flew from early in the morning until dark with only time to stop for fuel."

After the bombing at Pearl Harbor in 1941, everyone who owned an airplane received notice that they either had to put the plane under twenty-four-hour armed guard or store it with the wings removed in a padlocked storage area that had to be inspected at regular intervals. Clarence had no place to store his plane, so he was forced to sell it to a flight school in Ogdensburg that had a full-time guard on duty. He would not own another plane until after the war.

What the 1930s had made clear to Clarence was the unique manner in which his two careers, forestry and aviation, had begun to synchronize. They complemented each other perfectly, allowing him to perform each at a much higher level than he could have if he was only proficient in one. His lifetime in the woods, his education, and his work with the CCC had already made him an expert in forestry. He was also a skilled flyer and about to become more so, courtesy of the emperor of Japan.

CHAPTER 10

A Woodchuck Goes to War

When the CCC folded, Clarence still had six weeks of paid leave. With full-scale mobilization for the war, he knew he might be called upon at any time. Nevertheless, in his usual hyperkinetic manner, rather than take a vacation he began to look around for other employment.

He noticed that the U.S. Army Corps of Engineers was putting in an airport at Lake Clear, just a few miles from Coreys. He stopped in to talk to the people in charge and found that they needed someone with experience in civil engineering to be an inspector of the construction work. Men were being hired quickly, for the push was on to install airports around the nation in preparation for the war. He signed on and for a few weeks received two paychecks until his back leave from the CCC was paid up.

Clarence and Ferne rented a home on Lake Clear. Work at the airport was on a shift basis, twenty-four hours a day. He would work for two or three days from eight to five and then be on a night shift. It was on these night shifts that he began to discover some shady dealings by the subcontractors. One man from Glens Falls was trying to beat the fee by dumping fill over logs and brush in violation of the contract and by putting in metal culverts that had been damaged. Clarence clamped down on the illegalities and quickly became a target of complaints by the contractor: "They were after me and any of the others that caught them doing stuff. They operated out of a headquarters in Glens Falls, and we knew they'd try to shortcut things whenever they could. The fellow in charge would come down here and just go wild, yelling at me, calling me an old woman for making them correct things they'd done. But that was what we were there for, that was our job. There were five of us inspectors in the construction unit, which was a good thing. There were enough of us that we could find safety in our numbers."

While making tests on batches of new macadam for one of the forty-four-hundred-foot runways that had just been constructed, Clarence looked up one day to see three huge, single-engine Fairey Battle airplanes with Canadian Air Force markings. These were the largest single-engine planes built at the time. The planes circled the airfield and landed on the new macadam runway. They were Canadian Air Force students from Trenton, Ontario, who had become lost during a formation flying exercise. Their leader had crossed both the Ottawa and St. Lawrence Rivers without recognizing that he was going in the wrong direction. The pilots called their base in Trenton and were ordered to remain until the following day, when a twin-engine plane brought three flight instructors to fly the planes back to base.

It was while he was working at Lake Clear that Clarence's brother Bill gave him the notice from the navy that it wanted flight instructors who qualified for navy standards. Clarence was ordered to report at once for a physical. This was in May and nothing happened all summer. Then, on the first of October, he received a telegram telling him to re-

Pensacola flight instructor course, 1942. Clarence is sixth from right, front row. Clarence Petty collection.

port within four days. He was commissioned as a senior-grade lieutenant in the navy on October 12, 1942. His name had been listed at the draft board in Malone, and some time after he received his navy commission, the army tried to draft him, but it was too late. He was already a navy man.

Clarence was first sent to Pensacola, Florida, for his navy flight instructor standardization. Years later, he learned that he was getting his wings at the same time and place as the future astronaut and senator John Glenn, though the two never met. Already a civilian instructor, Clarence did not have to go through the same lengthy training that was prescribed for cadets. His group of about seventy men had to learn everything in just four weeks. They were pushed through as quickly as possible. "There was a navy regulations book that was as thick as a dictionary," Clarence remembers. "We had to study everything that was in it and pass a written examination before we got our wings." As one of the oldest trainees, Clarence was appointed company commander. The training program represented a new level of intensity for Clarence:

> Each of the specified stages of flight standards—precision emergency landings, night flying, formation flying, aerobatics, and so forth—had to be completed in specified hours. If you didn't meet the proficiency required by predetermined standards for each stage, you were dropped from the program.
>
> For a woods hick coming from northern New York where the air was free of most everything except birds, it was a jolt to enter airspace swarming with thousands of airplanes doing inverted spins, falling leafs, snap rolls, and nine-plane close formations. Anyone who didn't develop a swivel neck in a hurry . . . well . . . the results were fatal.

The push to train pilots quickly led to numerous accidents. Some sixty planes a month were lost during the Pensacola training. One squadron of nine planes became disoriented at night and mistook a light on the water for a star. The entire formation flew straight into the ocean. In his book *The Wild Blue—The Men and Boys Who Flew the B-24s Over Germany*, Stephen E. Ambrose records that eight hundred and fifty planes of one type were lost in 1943 alone—eight hundred and fifty airmen lost in just B-24 training accidents.

Clarence's ingrained self-discipline helped him to survive this slaughter and the great conflict itself. Everything was alien to this man who had lived most of his life in the remote Adirondack backcountry.

> All the military mumbo jumbo was new to me too. We had to get up at five o'clock in the morning and go out front for exercise in the dark. They had guys inspecting how clean the barracks were and checking for dust with white gloves and using a square to check corners on the beds. All this stuff. The first time I had to line my guys up and march them to our exercise site, I walked right off and one of the staff members came running up to me, waving his arms. He says, "You're walking too fast." Well, I thought I was walking a normal pace and I looked back and there were all the guys way back there. I hadn't paid any attention, and they were all a long ways back. He says, "These guys don't walk that kind of a step." Well, I'd done plenty of walking in my time. I thought I knew how to walk.

Pensacola was the first in a long string of training assignments that would vastly increase Clarence's flight ability and ratings. He was next transferred to the navy base at Bunker Hill, Indiana, where he instructed for about ten months. Then he was made a flight supervisor at a school in Bloomington, Illinois, where they were training navy and marine pilots as fast as they could turn them out. After a few months of this, he was sent to Atlanta for a specialized instrument training course with multiengine aircraft. This was followed immediately by a trip to Fort Worth, where he went through American Airlines Plane Captains School.

Ferne must have felt like she was on some sort of assembly line of her own during this period. Like most military wives, she bounced around from base to base. After Pensacola, she moved to Bunker Hill Navy Base where they rented a house. Later, she went out West and lived in a hotel while Clarence went through American Airlines Plane Captains School. When her husband was sent to Honolulu to fly four-engine transports at the height of the Pacific war, Ferne returned to stay

with her parents. She would not rejoin Clarence until he was transferred back to a navy transport base at Olathe, Kansas, for a rest and re-
cuperation break from flying in combat zones.

Clarence heard that the head of United Airlines had been given a
commission as a vice admiral and had been told to set up a naval air
transport service. This was how he came to be sent through plane captains school and to find himself shifted out of training command to
naval transport, flying R5D planes out of Honolulu. Once again
Clarence faced new challenges in new surroundings:

> I flew into all of the Pacific Islands, Guadalcanal, Guam, Tarawa,
> Saipan, Midway. Just as soon as they'd take one island, we'd come in
> with the blood plasma and all the rest of the stuff. It was quite a change
> from being in San Francisco walking the streets one day and forty-eight
> hours later being out in the jungle with all the parrots and monkeys up
> in the trees.
>
> We had three pilots onboard because the flights were so long,
> sometimes fifteen hours. Two guys would stay up front while the third
> slept for four hours. Every so often we had to change the blowers.
> Above a certain altitude, the air is so thin, you have to have blowers to
> push the air in. These were four-engine aircraft, and there was a blower
> for each engine. Every hour you had to change the blower; otherwise
> they'd get clogged up. I never could sleep very well because I'd be
> thinking about what was going on up front.
>
> Navigation was done with star shots at night and sun shots during
> the day using a theodolite.[1] The tropical front, where there was always
> severe thunderstorm activity, lay across our route to Guam, Saipan,
> and other bases. It often kept us from celestial navigation for hours at a
> time and resulted in being blown off course by one-hundred-mile-per-
> hour winds.
>
> Radio silence was mandatory due to the threat of enemy aircraft
> and ships. If we happened to be flying in daylight below the cloud deck,
> we were occasionally requested to keep watch for sea marker dye, in-

---

1. A theodolite is a surveying instrument used to measure horizontal and vertical an-
gles with a small telescope that can move in horizontal and vertical planes.

dicating possible survivors from a sunken ship. The eyestrain in such a search made it necessary to change places about every half hour.

I never saw any Japanese aircraft, but we would get shot at every now and then. I flew the first trip the navy made out of Guadalcanal to an island called Manus, which is just north of New Guinea. We flew right over Rabaul, which was still active. There was fighting there, though they'd pretty much shot down all the Japanese Zeroes. There was plenty of antiaircraft fire, and we were dodging in and out of the clouds. Kind of a helpless feeling, because we were flying unescorted and didn't have self-sealing fuel tanks.

Usually, our guys had got rid of most of the antiaircraft guns before they sent us in. One time, on my first trip to Saipan, the navy was still dive-bombing the Japanese who were dug in up on the cliffs. Every once in a while there'd be bullets come zipping around, we'd see tracers and so forth. The Japs were shooting out of the caves at the marines and they were also, I suppose, shooting at us.

We were flying with three, four thousand gallons of fuel onboard. The wings were just loaded with gas. I mean, they were gas tanks. Then we had two tanks inside that were just back of the crew's quarters. There was an eight-hundred-gallon tank over here and another eight-hundred-gallon tank over there. We'd use the wing tanks first, and then we'd use up the inside ones. We were flying a bomb. We knew it. If we got hit with flak—even a single tracer—it would've been over real quick.

We didn't wear parachutes. All we carried was a pistol and a weighted book of codes. Everything we got was in shortwave codes, and when we'd cross the International Date Line, the code would change. And every day was different. It was very difficult—that was one of the most difficult things I had to do. We had to decipher what the hell the message was we were getting. Because say on Monday over here you crossed the Date Line and you'd be on Tuesday, or vice versa, depending on which way you were going. It was always a question when you interpreted the shortwave stuff you got, whether it was correct or not.

Living a strangely parallel existence in the Pacific at the same time as Clarence was Charles Lindbergh, then a world-famous celebrity.

Lindbergh had been one of the leaders of the prewar pacifist, isolation-ist, and allegedly anti-Semitic group, the America First Committee. As such, his reputation had suffered considerably. But after Pearl Harbor he supported the war effort.

In 1944 Lindbergh spent several months touring the Pacific as a civilian observer studying the single-engine Corsair fighters. He flew into many of the same islands as Clarence, ran numerous troubleshoot-ing flight tests, and participated in fifty "unofficial" combat missions, often to the heart-thumping fear of his superiors, who could only cringe at the prospect of the celebrated flyer going down in the Pacific from a stray Japanese antiaircraft gun.

From Lindbergh's meticulous wartime journals, we can get some of the flavor of the sort of flying that Clarence was doing. On a fifteen-hour flight to Hawaii aboard the R4D (the navy designation for the commercial Douglas DC-3), he wrote:

> A new moon and clear night except for scattered clouds at about 3000 feet. We took turns flying. There was no heat in the plane, and as the outside temperature was close to freezing and the tail end rather drafty, we spent most of the time forward, even though it meant stand-ing up for two men . . .
>
> We flew at 8,000 feet during the night, with scattered to overcast clouds rising as high as 6,500 feet. The sky was clear at all times. Food at intervals from boxes and cans—and lukewarm black coffee—good only for keeping awake.

Of course, the similarities to Clarence's Pacific sojourn ended as soon as the great Lindbergh touched the ground. He remained a super-star on par with the movie idols of the day, despite his prewar isolation-ist activities. Wherever he landed, commanding officers came out to greet him, generals, admirals, and commodores alike. He was invited to dine sumptuously, to go spear fishing, to be entertained by rich planta-tion owners and at traditional native celebrations. His companions in-cluded Douglas MacArthur, General Teddy Roosevelt Jr., and virtually every other military figure of import in the South Pacific, all of whom wanted to meet the pioneer aviator. Lindy's war was unlike anyone else's, even though he often tried to avoid the attention.

Clarence's own roster of famous Pacific encounters was decidedly less encompassing. He did see Betty Grable during one of her trips to Honolulu to entertain the troops. And there was a man named Eddie Peabody who was billed as the Banjo King. But the occasion that stood out the most was glimpsing Franklin D. Roosevelt as he toured the island during the Honolulu Conference in July 1944.

Roosevelt had sailed from San Diego aboard the stripped-down cruiser the *Baltimore*. The trip was made under wartime conditions, the ship showing no lights and accompanied by air patrols and six destroyers. FDR had just been renominated for president, and some thought the trip was little more than a political stunt. Certainly Douglas MacArthur thought so. After keeping the president cooling his heels onboard for half an hour, the general finally appeared in an enormous open car behind a screaming motorcycle escort.

FDR, relishing his role as commander in chief, presided over meetings in which MacArthur and Pacific fleet commander, Admiral Chester W. Nimitz, argued over their conflicting Pacific strategies. Eventually, Roosevelt agreed with General MacArthur that the Philippines should not be bypassed.

During his time on the islands, the president reviewed the Seventh Infantry Division, watched combat exercises, and had himself wheeled through a naval hospital filled with amputees in order to show them how they might overcome their plight, as he had.

Roosevelt invited Nimitz and Admiral William D. Leahy to join MacArthur and him for a ride around the island in an open car. Despite Secret Service fears of a possible bomb threat, the occupants of the motorcar waved and returned the salutes of the cheering servicemen who lined the streets. One of the men waving to the leader of the free world was a thirty-eight-year-old pilot from the backwoods of New York named Clarence Petty.

Meanwhile, continuing his tour through islands that Clarence was growing more familiar with, Lindbergh instructed pilots on how to increase the combat radius of the P-38s by almost two hundred miles. By raising manifold pressure and lowering revolutions per minute, less gasoline was consumed, and the planes began surprising the Japanese with attacks deeper into their territory than expected. A grateful MacArthur gave Lindbergh authority to fly any plane anywhere in the Pacific theater. The international hero Clarence had once glimpsed parading triumphantly down Wall Street was again cheating death on the opposite side of the globe. On one occasion, Lindbergh came close to a head-on collision with a Japanese plane. Afterward, he said that he could feel the impact of the air pressure as the other plane passed a hair-breadth away.

Lindbergh worried about the casual way in which suitcases, tool boxes, and other heavy equipment were routinely piled, unlashed, in the tail of the transports. If there was a forced landing, he suggested, all of this stuff would come flying down on the pilots. But an officer explained that in case of a forced landing, the policy was to throw everything overboard before hitting the water anyway. With the very long flights required over the Pacific, it was not uncommon for planes to run out of fuel, especially if they bucked head winds most of the way. On such occasions, everything moveable was jettisoned, cargo and personal effects alike.

Lindbergh flew over Rabaul as Clarence had, though in a fighter rather than in a transport. The city lay on the edge of a volcanic harbor and showed few effects of the massive bombardment it had suffered. Once U.S. forces had destroyed Rabaul's airfields, the one hundred thousand Japanese troops were isolated and considered harmless. The decision was made to bypass the island. Occasionally, planes would attack to keep the airfields from being repaired. The Japanese responded by firing at the planes, as Clarence had experienced. Lindbergh's description of his sortie gives a good idea of the conditions that Clarence must also have witnessed:

> We circle overhead for a time—at 10,000 feet. A "strike" is scheduled for this morning, and before long a formation of TBF's appears, coming in from the west. . . . The smoke and fires from magnesium clusters spring up from a grove of coconut palms below us. The TBF

formation has broken up, and planes are everywhere amid the ack-ack—the blue silhouettes of TBF's, the black bursts of the antiair-craft—all against a background of jungle green. Several planes have accomplished their mission and are making their getaway low over the water. Great splashes of water follow them far out from shore. The Japanese antiaircraft gunners at Rabaul are considered the most accu-rate in the South Pacific. They should be; they have had constant practice.

Clarence saw some strange things during his time in the Pacific, the sort of anomalies that one comes to expect during wartime. On one of his trips to Saipan, he came across a hangar with the entire roof shot off. Inside was an enormous snowplow in a place that had never seen so much as a snowflake. The plow had apparently been on its way from San Francisco to Alaska when the ship was needed elsewhere in the war effort. The plow was off-loaded and sat out the war in the tropics.

From a military point of view, one of the craziest things that Clarence witnessed was actually planned by the navy. He was assigned to fly the entire headquarters unit that was going in to take over after the recapture of the Philippines. Clarence took the men on the first leg of their journey, as far as Guam. There were some thirty officers, in-cluding army and navy personnel, an admiral, and several generals on-board. "It was absolutely crazy," recalls Clarence. "If we'd been hit, they would have lost the entire command"

Clarence flew out of John Rogers Airport in Honolulu, which was right across the bay from Pearl Harbor. In visits to Pearl, he saw the re-mains of the bombed ships still in the water. The harbor had been re-opened, but some of the ships were never removed. The *Arizona* has since become an underwater memorial to the thousands who died on December 7, 1941.

Clarence remembers Honolulu as a quaint little place, despite the new military presence. The most posh building on the whole island was the Royal Hawaiian Hotel. After the attack on Pearl Harbor it was taken over by the navy and used as a rest center by more than two hun-dred thousand troops. Clarence and his friends sometimes used the

Clarence in navy uniform, 1943.
Clarence Petty collection.

hotel to change clothes so they could swim on Waikiki Beach during their off-duty hours.

Many airmen and sailors tried to get transferred to Hawaii, which, along with the Philippines, had a reputation as a Pacific paradise. In addition to the sparkling beaches of Waikiki, there were numerous bars, such as the Black Cat near the Honolulu servicemen's YMCA, where brawls were frequent. The islands were filled with beautiful and friendly women. Clarence, married and a teetotaler, saw little of this side of things. One suspects he stayed away from comrades who indulged in this seamier element of military life.

During one leave, Clarence visited a pineapple factory (hardly a typical airman's leave destination). Here he watched the manufacturing process from start to finish, surprised to learn that the pineapple juice was all produced in the same factory and simply given different labels for Libby or Dole on the assembly line. He was amazed to see how completely the pineapples were utilized. The tops were cut off and returned for planting in the field; the outsides were peeled away, with the peelings getting squeezed for juice before going through a dryer, where they were chewed up and made into cattle feed.

"It was a complete utilization of a product—they even let us drink as much pineapple juice as we wanted," remembers Clarence, who must certainly be the only serviceman to ever brag about the amount of pineapple juice he drank while on leave in one of the hottest R&R sites in the Pacific.

After many months flying in combat zones, pilots would be given a break and returned stateside for a while. As a result, after nearly a year in the Pacific, Clarence returned to meet Ferne in Olathe, Kansas. He received his promotion to lieutenant commander and resumed flying DC3s from Olathe to Phoenix, Arizona, back and forth, almost every night. He became so familiar with it that he called it the "milk run." He would haul personnel and equipment, come back empty, and then go out again. He finally received orders to return to the Pacific, but on his last flight to Olathe, with his new orders in his pocket, the war ended. "I was flying over Albuquerque," Clarence recalls. "It was about four o'clock in the morning and I called the controller because we kept reporting from each station. It's different than it is now. We had to report over each station and then we estimated the time to the next. The controller said, 'Did you hear the news?' And I said, 'What news are you talking about?' And she said, 'Japan has surrendered.' When I got into Phoenix it was about five A.M., and the whistles were blowing and the streets were filled with people celebrating. That was the end of the whole business right there.

Clarence kept right on flying the Olathe to Phoenix run, only this time the whole flow was reversed, with the troops and all the equipment coming back from the Pacific. One group he flew home was a collection of shell-shocked victims: "They were all tied down in cots and there was a man assigned to watch every two patients to make sure they were all right and belted in and so forth. I took them from Phoenix to El Paso through a helluva storm with thunder and lightning. We were flying by sound at that time, and our route took us through some real mountain peaks. You had a signal you had to listen to that was very faint. If it was on one side, it would go dot, dot, and if it was on the other, it would go dot, dot, dot. You had to be right on that to go through those places, or you'd end up crashing into one of the mountains. It was an awful tough flight for those poor guys."

While Clarence was flying the "milk run" into Phoenix, he received a telegram one day from Bill Foss, the director of lands and forests back in New York. Foss asked if he wanted to take the written exam for the district ranger position. Never one to pass up a job opportunity, he agreed. Foss sent the exam to the civil service people in Kansas City, where Clarence took the test and became number one on the list.

On January 1, 1946, Clarence went on inactive duty, though he would continue in the U.S. Naval Reserve for the next thirteen years. When the war ended, uncertain if a district ranger job would be immediately available, he once again looked around for something to do right away rather than take a vacation.

It was one of the patterns of his entire life. When one job ended, he always seemed to find another at once. One can almost hear his mother Catherine's directive: one thing a person could not do was waste time in this life. Clarence never wasted time.

Though his first postwar job would be a brief one, it would take him into one of the new lines of work that was opening up in the field of aviation. And it would allow him to meet a fascinating new employer.

CHAPTER 11

Cat Drops in Borneo

The first thing Clarence did after getting out of the navy was call Bill Foss to check on the district ranger's job. It still was not available, but Foss told him about a Dr. Frank Craighead who was looking for a pilot who was also a forester to work on developing a spraying program to control the spruce budworm. Once again, Clarence's ability to mix two skills provided him with a job, though it would be one he would regret in later years.

Craighead was the entomologist in charge of the Division of Forest Insect Investigations for the U.S. Department of Agriculture. His sons, Frank Jr. and John, would become famous in the 1960s and 1970s for their work with the grizzly bears of Yellowstone National Park. The Canadian government had asked Craighead to organize a spraying program to control a spruce budworm outbreak in the forests of New Brunswick.

The last serious outbreak had occurred from 1910 to 1920 and was estimated to have destroyed 40 to 70 percent of the timber in Maine, Ontario, Quebec, and New Brunswick. Balsam trees were the mainstay of the pulp and paper industry, and now the old-growth trees were once again under heavy assault from the budworm.

The insecticide of choice as far as the Department of Agriculture was concerned was DDT. Clarence first became aware of DDT while he was flying in the Pacific Islands during the war: "We had a lot of mosquitos in the South Pacific. When I flew into Saipan, I was awful glad they had something to knock those mosquitos down, because that

111

place was just full of them. They had all kinds of diseases out there, and DDT was used all over the islands."

Dr. Craighead was attempting to develop a system for spraying and delivering on target the most cost-effective dose of DDT possible. The substance was so lethal that it worked at quite low dosages and the idea was to use as little as possible over the huge northern forests. Clarence was hired in early 1946 to help develop the delivery system. He would work, initially, out of the U.S. Department of Agriculture's research center in Beltsville, Maryland, just north of Washington, D.C.

At first they did not have an aircraft to use. Clarence was sent up to Greenfield, Massachusetts, where there were two aircraft that one of Dr. Craighead's units had been using for spraying gypsy moths. Clarence flew one of the planes, a navy-made N3N rigged with spraying booms, down to Washington. The N3N was a tandem aircraft built for training pilots during the war. The front cockpit of this plane had been converted to hold the tank containing the DDT solution. There was a small, engine-driven pump that forced the chemical, which was under pressure, out the booms all along the underside of the wings. Clarence controlled the release from his rear cockpit. As he had in his years with the CCC, Clarence was once again innovating in a new occupation:

> We were experimenting with different things. I was carrying about a hundred gallons of stuff at a time, and we were running these test strips, trying to determine the best height to spray from and so on. I generally sprayed at treetop. I had to be real careful to watch out for snags that might clip the plane. There was always a problem with the wind affecting drifts, and we could only fly when the wind was below five miles per hour.
>
> The idea was to spray as soon as the larvae hatched, which occurred at certain times in the spring. You had to time it pretty carefully. If it rained right after you sprayed, that would wash away the spray and you had to spray again. I worked in the laboratory when I wasn't flying, so I got to know pretty well what the chemists were doing. But it was all DDT spray. I'm not proud of spraying that stuff.
>
> I remember one time, Dr. Craighead called us into his office and said, "I can't reveal this to the public just yet, but DDT is now being

found in mother's milk. There's a possibility that we may have a real problem with this stuff." Shortly after, Roy Nagel, who was our chemist, came to me and said, "You know, we were using fruit flies as one of our test insects—spraying the DDT into an area and then turning a bunch of fruit flies loose in there to see what happened." And he says, "It's a funny thing, that stuff that we sprayed last week, now the flies are walking over it." And sure enough, those flies were walking right on the DDT. That was the first time we both recognized we were producing a resistant bunch of insects. This was about April or May of 1946.

The phenomenon of resistance had been known since 1908, when the San Jose scale insect developed resistance to lime sulfur applied to apple trees. As early as 1945 entomologist E. H. Strickland had published an article entitled, "Could the Widespread Use of DDT Be a Disaster?" A report in 1946 stated that houseflies in Sweden were no longer killed by DDT. The failure was blamed on improper use or an inferior grade of insecticide. This explanation was short-lived, however, as similar reports began to come in from all over the world.

The initial success of DDT spawned a host of new lethal compounds. Total production of DDT itself by U.S. firms rose from ten million pounds in 1944 to over one hundred million pounds in 1951. One characteristic of the potent insecticide was its residual effect, its ability to continue to be deadly long after its initial use. While some thought this staying power made it even more desirable as an agricultural control, it was soon discovered that DDT could be found in the atmosphere, in the rivers and oceans, on the land, and in virtually every living thing.

Exquisitely insidious, the insecticide was capable of working its way through the food chain in completely unpredictable ways. In the 1960s the World Health Organization (WHO), in an attempt to control malaria in Borneo, sprayed houses with DDT. Mosquitos were killed and the incidence of malaria decreased. But the side effects were not long in showing up. House lizards ate the dead bugs. Cats ate the lizards and died from the accumulated insecticide. Without cats, the rat population exploded—rats that carried plague and typhus. The WHO, working with Singapore's Royal Air Force, came up with a novel solution: Operation Cat Drop. They packed cats into perforated containers and parachuted them into upland villages.

In a Department of Agriculture publication entitled *Insect Enemies of Eastern Forests*, published in 1949, Dr. Craighead pointed out the positive results that he had obtained by spraying in New York and Canada from airplanes. But he went on to warn: "DDT is poisonous and should be labeled with care. . . . The use of DDT on ornamental plants growing close to fish ponds or streams should be avoided since there is danger of killing fish and other aquatic life. DDT in oil solutions and emulsions may be absorbed through the skin of man and animals. Persons using it in these forms should take special precautions to avoid repeated or prolonged exposures."

Bill Foss told Clarence that he was being pressured to spray DDT over all of New York State in order to protect it against the gypsy moth. They had already been spraying in selected areas, including portions of Long Island. But Foss refused to spray across the state, saying there was not enough known about the insecticide to justify the action. He took the controversial stance despite the fact that he had himself used DDT regularly to spray the screens at his camp and had never experienced any negative effects.

"It was real common stuff," recalls Clarence. "Everybody used it. We had no problem with it. I never had any negative effects, and it used to be on our hands and everywhere else. But Dr. Craighead, when he heard about it showing up in cow's milk and mother's milk, he was real concerned about it."

Clarence continued to spray around Beltsville; then he moved up to Watertown and sprayed there and around Bloomingdale, where they had an infestation of budworms. There was also a problem with the white pine weevil in the Watertown area. Craighead wanted to see if the spray would work on these insects as well as the budworm, so Clarence worked there for several weeks. But it was difficult to find a large enough stand of white pine to measure the effectiveness of the treatment.

During my time in the CCC, we found that if you didn't mix your plantings so that you had a combination of other species, then you'd get a heavy infestation of white pine weevil. So they started doing what they called mixed-bucket plantings. They planted spruce along with the pine. That made it real difficult to find a solid block of white pine. We finally did find two or three small stands of young trees south of Watertown in the state forest and we sprayed them. It was effective to a certain extent, but it was expensive, and you had to spray when the weevils came out, which was in June or July when we usually got a lot of rain, so then you had to go right back in and spray it again.

After six months with Dr. Craighead, Clarence learned that Moses LaFountain, the district ranger at Cranberry Lake, had died. The position was Clarence's if he wanted it. He was more than ready to leave his job with Dr. Craighead, even though it would mean a sizeable cut in salary. The reason had nothing to do with DDT. Clarence simply hated living in a big city. Washington, D.C., was no better than New York had been back when he worked for Western Union.

After his years in the military and his work for Dr. Craighead, Clarence's wanderlust was all used up: "It just wasn't the kind of a deal I liked. I would've done anything to get back to the Adirondacks. Looking back, it's kind of interesting for me to realize that here was a time when they were just starting to understand that DDT was not the cure-all for everything. It took a long time before they finally stopped using it though."

Clarence's experience with DDT occurred right at the beginning of the insecticide age. Throughout the 1950s and 1960s, DDT would continue to be widely used, despite the early suspicions about its safety. But not until the publication of Rachel Carson's groundbreaking book, *Silent Spring,* in 1962 did the alarm begin to be spread seriously. Carson Wrote: "Our attitude toward poisons has undergone a subtle change. Once they were kept in containers marked with skull and crossbones; the infrequent occasions of their use were marked with utmost care that they should come in contact with the target and with nothing else. With the development of the new organic insecticides and the abundance of surplus planes after the Second World War, all this was forgotten. Although today's poisons are more dangerous than any known before, they have amazingly become something to be showered down indiscriminately from the skies."

Clarence's foray into the spraying of DDT for the U.S. Department of Agriculture was fortunately a brief interlude. He had found a new way to combine his forester and aviator abilities. His treetop spraying increased skills that he would later find useful in aerial fire fighting and fish stocking in the Adirondacks—if not for cat drops in Borneo.

Like a homing pigeon, Clarence kept returning to his roots. He would spend the rest of his working life in the forests where he grew up.

CHAPTER 12

A Ranger at Heart

Clarence's acquisition of the district ranger job at Cranberry Lake marked the true beginning of his career as a conservationist. Up to this point, he had maintained a practical, hands-on relationship with the Adirondacks. He and his family had lived off the land or earned a living guiding, cooking, and doing chores for summer residents and sportsmen.

The love for the land instilled by this upbringing, along with Catherine's insistence on education, led Clarence to forestry school. Now that education would enable him to continue to live where he wished, in the mountains where he grew up. Brief forays into the alien worlds of New York and Washington, D.C., reinforced this desire, while the CCC gave him his first adult taste of what living and working in the Adirondacks could be like. It was a taste he never forgot. And despite the interlude of the war, there was never any hesitancy once the opportunity to return to the Adirondacks presented itself.

His passion for flying only enhanced his love for the mountains, allowing him to admire them in an entirely new way, one that members of his father's generation could only have dreamed about as young men. Over the next quarter century, Clarence would become one of the most knowledgeable men alive on the Adirondack region. Even well into his tenth decade of life, his opinions would be sought after by bureaucrats, politicians, reporters, environmentalists, foresters, and recreationists. He would be appointed to innumerable committees, boards, and commissions. The old family home on Coreys Road would maintain a well-

117

beaten path to its door, trodden by newspaper men, writers, *National Geographic* photographers, and television producers. In articles written about Clarence's move back to the family home in his ninety-fourth year, some worried that he would be alone on the edge of the wilderness. But the guru of the Adirondacks was rarely alone.

Clarence is different from others who philosophize about the out-of-doors. He is different from writer-naturalists, bureaucrats, and the native-grown property rights and environmental activists who have their own drums to bang regarding the Adirondacks. His life is a blend of real, hands-on experience combined with his own conservationist ethic of being responsible for what one does. He is as his parents created him, independent *and* responsible, with an abiding love for his surroundings and a fierce desire to see the mountains survive the onslaughts of the industrialized world.

Edward Abbey, whom many consider the father of the modern environmental movement, once wrote: "Human needs do not take precedence over other forms of life." This is how Clarence, who never could understand why a man would want to catch a fish just to throw it back again, also views the world.

When he took the position as district ranger at Cranberry Lake, Clarence was beginning not just a new job, but a personal journey that would, over time, set him apart from his neighbors and even strain relations within his own family. Many would see him as an outsider, perhaps the worst sort of traitor because he was a native son; they could not abide his willingness to accept and even enforce restrictions on what people could do with their land. As the resistance to such restrictions increased through the 1960s and exploded in the 1970s, people with Clarence's views were expected to hail from New York City or the suburbs, not from the Adirondack heartland. Clarence was an embarrassment, a native son who was not afraid to speak out in favor of protecting the wilderness.

The Ranger Corps that Clarence was joining had its genesis in the establishment of the Forest Preserve in 1885. The commission formed to oversee the preserve authorized the appointment of fire wardens to be in charge of fighting forest fires. But the huge fires of 1899, 1903, and

1908 soon demonstrated the ineffectiveness of the fire warden system. Tourists and "sports" who had begun flocking to the Adirondacks were alarmed at the numbers and size of the seemingly ever-present conflagrations. Of the 1903 fire, Clarence later wrote in his foreword to Louis C. Curth's *The Forest Rangers*, "The guests at the Wawbeek Hotel on Upper Saranac Lake kept my father and other guides busy transporting them to Saranac Inn by guideboat where they planned to take the train south and out of danger. But they were thwarted in this attempt because the train could not reach Saranac Inn station due to burned out wooden trestles."

The fire of 1908 was even worse. It cast a cloud across much of the northeast from Washington, D.C., north into Canada. For days New York City residents walked about gasping and wheezing, tears streaming from their eyes. It was so dark that streetlights were kept on all day, and the strange light of midday was compared to that of a total eclipse. In a 1981 account in *Adirondack Life* magazine, Robert Bernard described the arrival of the Cunard liner *Mauretania* off Sandy Hook on its regular run from Southampton to New York: "Lookouts reported a dense and entirely unexpected bank of fog over New York City. By the time the huge liner reached the Narrows, at the mouth of the harbor, visibility was so reduced that the captain ordered foghorns sounded as the ship, barely moving, crept toward a rendezvous with its waiting tugs. But it was not fog that stopped the *Mauretania*. It was smoke. For the second time in five years, the Adirondacks were burning.

The superintendent of forests, William Fox, who had been in office since 1891, had long been dissatisfied with the fire warden system. In his annual report in 1897, he concluded that "Rain is the best Firewarden we have" and called for a change. But it would require an extreme fire year to provoke action. It came in 1899 when fires burned some eighty thousand acres, the worst loss since the Forest Preserve had been created. Fox used the grim statistics to recommend sweeping changes, including a proposal for a force of forest rangers.

The superintendent got the name for the new group from Rogers' Rangers, which had been formed in 1755 to fight in the French and Indian War. Under the command of Major Robert Rogers, the rangers joined Sir William Johnson's command near Lake George. Ranger tactics, which utilized knowledge of the woods and Indian fighting techniques, later influenced the American soldiers who stymied the British in the Revolutionary War. The bravery and woodsmanship of Rogers' Rangers would become the hallmarks of the men who would share the title "ranger" one and one-half centuries later.

But it would take over a decade, two more bad fires, and the help of conservationist Louis Marshall, among others, before the present ranger system was finally established in 1912. William Fox, who died three years earlier, never saw the fruits of his long battle to establish the force.

The early rangers were greatly influenced by the Adirondack guides, emulating their independent and resourceful ways. Men such as Clarence Petty, who had actually come out of the guiding tradition, were highly respected by their fellow rangers. Eventually, as the science of forestry took hold, degrees for forest rangers would be offered at the Ranger School in Wanakena and at Paul Smith's College.

By 1947 the starting salary for a ranger was 1,920 dollars a year, and the title of "forest ranger" had become a competitive, civil service position. But the job remained a difficult one, as Clarence later wrote in Louis Curth's *The Forest Rangers*: "The Forest Ranger, often working alone in remote areas, under adverse conditions of weather, rugged terrain and travel, sometimes lacking needed equipment, also requires self-reliance and the ability to improvise under stressful circumstances that few other occupations demand."

When the Adirondack Park was created in 1892, the original intent was to demonstrate the state's interest in everything that happened within the Blue Line.[1] Historian Philip Terrie wrote, "both legislators and Governor Flower appeared to have been assuming that the state would eventually own all the land in the newly defined park."[2]

---

1. The Forest Commission published a map of the Adirondacks in 1890, setting a historic precedent by circling the proposed State Park with a "Blue Line," that has since become synonymous with the park's area.

2. For descriptions of Conservation Department history, I am indebted to Philip Terrie's concise histories, *Forever Wild: A Cultural History of Wilderness in the Adiron-*

Early conservation agencies and leaders such as William F. Fox saw forest management as their main function. They believed that selective logging improved the forest. Coincidentally, it also provided money for the state's coffers. Early plans to dam the Saranac and Raquette Rivers were promoted as ways to regulate flow (which helped in the transport of logs) and to improve the aesthetics of the rivers by eliminating unsightly swamps and wetlands. If something was not useful, it could not be perceived as beautiful in the utilitarian sentiments of the day.

The Forever Wild provision of the state constitution, passed in 1894, was an anathema to this way of thinking, for it locked up the forests. Most of the state's conservation employees believed that Forever Wild would eventually be abolished.

The Conservation Department that Clarence joined in 1946 had already gone through several name changes. It had begun as the Fisheries, Game and Forest Commission, established in 1895. In 1900 it became the Forest, Fish and Game Commission. In 1911 the name was changed yet again to the Conservation Commission. At about this time the members of the conservation bureaucracy began to feel that an emphasis on the recreational functions of the preserve might be an acceptable focus in addition to the traditional concentration on tree harvesting and forest management. What they had in mind was hunting and fishing, since these pastimes were growing in popularity, especially among the well-to-do citizens of the state. The *Report of the Conservation Commission* for 1919 marked a clear and abrupt shift in attitude toward a greater willingness to begin building dams, trails, open camps, and fireplaces in order to allow more people to use "the most important public vacation grounds in the United States."

The Conservation Commission's[3] efforts over the next several

---

dacks and *Contested Terrain: A New History of Nature and People in the Adirondacks*, and to Frank Graham, Jr.'s *The Adirondack Park: A Political History*. Also extremely informative is Louis C. Curth's *The Forest Rangers: A History of the New York State Forest Ranger Force*.

3. In 1926, the name was again changed to the Conservation Department, the moniker still in use when Clarence joined in 1946.

decades to "improve" the Forest Preserve for recreation grew more controversial. Terrie writes, "the shift of emphasis from timber harvest to
recreation did not eliminate the hostility either to Forever Wild or to
the idea of wilderness as such. . . . An impoundment dam, even if only
a few feet high, or an interior Ranger station violates a wilderness aesthetic nearly as much as does logging or a dam built to generate power."

The Conservation Department's progression from supporting timber production to emphasizing recreational promotion proved to be a
direct threat to the sort of wilderness that the preservationists had in
mind. Recreational enhancements threatened the wilderness in many
ways, and the leading source of this threat in the 1930s was a group that
Clarence Petty was aligned with, the Civilian Conservation Corps. By
1940 the CCC was listing scores of improvement projects, from dams
on remote rivers and streams to the construction of fire-truck roads.

The wilderness aesthetic of the preservationists found itself in direct conflict with what the CCC was doing. "As early as the 1930s,"
Terrie writes, "men like Paul Schaefer, John S. Apperson and Robert
Marshall were going to court, lobbying the legislature, arousing public
opinion, and doing everything they could to keep dams, truck trails,
and highways from compromising wilderness in the Forest Preserve."
This earliest of wilderness lobbies relied upon article 7, section 7 of the
state constitution as its chief lobbying tool.[4]

The clash between the Conservation Department, with its continuing efforts to provide the "improvements" that recreationists wanted,
and the preservationists, who were calling for absolute protection of the
wilderness, has continued to ebb and flow down to the present day.

Clarence arrived on the scene precisely in the middle of this whole
controversy. As an alumnus of a forestry college that emphasized timber production and a former CCC camp leader who had supervised
many of the recreational improvements of the 1930s and 1940s, he now

---

4. After the Constitutional Convention of 1938, the Forever Wild clause became
known as Article XIV. It reads: "The lands of the State, now owned or hereafter acquired,
constituting the Forest Preserve as now fixed by law, shall be forever kept as wild forest
lands."

found himself a member of a Conservation Department that was continuing to "improve" the wilderness for recreation, even as it fought rearguard actions against the preservationists.

It would not take long for Clarence to establish where he fit in the scheme of things. He intended to enforce the conservation laws and to protect the wilderness that he had loved since his earliest days living in a tent on the shores of Upper Saranac Lake. He would become a part of a new conservation leadership that was moving relentlessly toward ever-greater protections for the Adirondack preserve.

CHAPTER 13

Odd Man Out at Cranberry Lake

Cranberry Lake in the late 1940s had begun to see a growing influx of people. In a perfect example of unintended consequences, angling on the lake and the Oswegatchie River was excellent immediately after World War II due to the lack of fishing pressure during the conflict. This phenomenon was echoed on a larger scale because of German U-boats, which helped restore marine life in the North Atlantic by scaring fishermen back into port.

The abundance was short-lived, however. The fishing deteriorated rapidly as a result of beaver dams on the streams and the introduction of yellow perch, which forced out the brook trout.

One of Clarence's rangers, Bill Doran, told him, "You know what's killed Cranberry Lake is that road. They paved the road [in the 1920s]. That's what brought the people in. That's when they started getting trash fish in Cranberry Lake, and it killed the brook trout fishing."

Paul Jamieson arrived in Canton, New York, in the summer of 1929. His introduction to the Adirondacks came aboard the mail launch *Helen,* which circled Cranberry Lake, delivering mail to summer camps. In a 1992 *Adirondac* essay entitled "The Embowering Woods," he reminisced about those early days before the tourist hordes of later years overwhelmed the quiet of the mountains:

> Sometimes I look back with nostalgia to the Great Depression. It was a fine time for visitors in the Park, though a disastrous one for natives dependent on tourism. Visitors were a tiny fraction of the nine

Ellsworth with the day's trout catch from Cranberry Lake, 1930s. Clarence Petty collection.

million of today. The pre-crash animation of Cranberry Lake yielded to the silence and solitude of an almost primeval forest. What is now heavily traveled Route 3 between Tupper and Saranac lakes was then, from Wawbeek Corners east, an overshadowed one-lane dirt road where you rarely met another car. If you did, you or it had to back up as much as a quarter-mile for space to pass. You could climb Ampersand or Algonquin without meeting another hiker. Trails in the High Peaks were uneroded and free of hog wallows. The silence on Middle Saranac Lake was profound, for there were no powerboats in summer, no snow-mobiles in winter, no jets overhead; often not even another canoe. The forest was a fine and private place. You were enclosed in it like a fetus in the womb.

Despite that early mail launch, there were still relatively few camps around Cranberry when Clarence arrived. He patrolled the lake in a small motorboat and searched for lost hunters or hikers. Some-times his son Richard went hiking with him when he inspected trails. Richard recalls always wanting to run ahead, though his father coun-seled on the importance of keeping an even pace. "By the end of the day, I usually knew what he was talking about," says Richard, "but that didn't seem to stop the practice."

Sometimes the need to deal with a nuisance bear would arise. Though black bears almost never attack people, cabins and campsites are another matter. Some bears become habituated to humans and the garbage they invariably leave behind. Then the creatures can be unpredictable. "The thing about bears," says Clarence,

is that you don't know where they're going to run. The black bears in the Adirondacks don't attack people, almost never. But there was a case where a bear broke the shoulder of the observer up on Ampersand Mountain. He was coming down out of the tower and there's a kind of a little cleft where you go around a corner. Well, he was just trying to go through there, and the bear happened to be coming the other way. The bear got scared and when that happens, he'll just go straight no matter what. He tried to get out of there, and he struck the guy and broke his shoulder. Some people said it was a bear attack, but it wasn't. The bear was just scared and wanted to get out of there. Instead of turning around, the bear just went straight—straight through the guy.

There was another time at Jenack's Landing when a guy was camping there and his kid was across the way in a canoe. The bear began swimming across toward the campsite, and the kid went out with the canoe to try to head it off. Well, that bear went right over the canoe, tipped it over, and threw the kid in the water. The father was scared to death, because he thought the bear was attacking his boy, but he wasn't attacking. The bear was just afraid and went straight through the canoe.

Years ago, the ranger down at Oswegatchie issued a permit for a tent platform at Wolf Lake, south of Cranberry. We used to be allowed to do that. The permit holder leaves it up all winter with a tent and canvas cover on it. The sides go up three feet and they're allowed to put boards on it. This was my first winter on duty there, and I suggested to the ranger that we snowshoe in and look those platforms over because no one had been in there in years.

So we went in, I think it was February, and there was a new snowfall. But when we got there the first thing we noticed was that the three-foot boarded section had a hole right through it, like a cannonball had burst through. We went inside and the whole floor was scattered with knives and forks and pieces of metal and pots and all kinds of stuff. And here was this hole right through the side. We started looking around, and we found a can of pressurized insect repellant with teeth marks on it. So we knew what happened. When the bear bit into that, because it was under pressure, it kind of exploded a little and the bear went right through the side of the building. That's typical of a black bear. He's scared, he'll go straight, bang, just like that.

When Clarence first arrived in Cranberry Lake, there were eight rangers in his district. He was on the job barely a year before the Forest Practice Act of 1946 stimulated a reorganization of the field operations of the Division of Lands and Forests, dividing the state into fifteen administrative districts. The activities of forest rangers, district rangers, and all other personnel were brought together under the administrative supervision of a district forester.

This new plan allowed for the pooling of the workforce when and where it was needed and helped the rangers during emergencies. The area Clarence supervised was changed from parts of Hamilton and Franklin counties to just St. Lawrence County, which was the biggest county in the state. So in 1948 his office was moved to more centrally located Canton, though he retained the title of district ranger for Cranberry Lake.

As district ranger, Clarence expected his forest rangers to have complete control of their area for trail maintenance, fire suppression, and illegal logging, and to generally know what was going on in their region. The game laws were another matter, however.

"We didn't get mixed-up with the game law violations," says Clarence, "because some of our best fire fighters were some of the worst damn violators of the game law, shooting deer out of season and so forth, so we kept pretty much away from that. We cooperated with fish and game law enforcement, but we didn't try to get too close to them."

Illegal loggers were sometimes caught, but violations were usually the result of not knowing where the lines were. There were thousands of miles of state boundary lines in the Adirondacks. When property was sold, it was often done without a survey, simply taking the records as they were because there was not any money for resurveying or marking out lines. After a while, nobody knew exactly where the lines were.

Many years after Clarence left his position at Cranberry Lake, the system was changed in ways that he felt destroyed much of the pride the rangers took in their jobs, as he explains:

> I'm glad that I wasn't involved with it, because the way it was, each forest ranger was responsible for his area, whether it was trespassing on a forest preserve or whether it was keeping the trails maintained. Every spring I would go out with the rangers, and we made sure that all those trails were kept up. As soon as the season was over in the fall, we'd go over all the trails to make sure they were in good shape. Each ranger felt he had responsibility for it.
>
> Now they've got a new system where nobody's responsible for anything. It happened when they took away the authority of the forest rangers from the Division of Lands and Forests. Always the forest rangers used to be under Lands and Forests. Now they take them out, put them under a different law enforcement group, the Office of Public Protection, which is the same as the conservation officers. So now the rangers are going up and down the roads with their big hats and a gun on their hip, and they don't go into the woods.
>
> I've talked with some of the surveyors, and they say they can't get one of these guys to help them in a survey. I always sent my rangers out to help the surveyors. But no, they're union people now. They belong to the union, and they're not going to dirty their hands with an ax or a saw. So this is the sort of thing that's happening now, and it needs to be changed if the public is going to have the services that they're paying for.

Clarence's view of the rangers' predicament was echoed at a June 2000 meeting of environmental leaders at St. Lawrence University's Thirtieth Annual Adirondack Conference. Peter Bauer, of the Residents' Committee to Protect the Adirondacks, deplored the change in the duties of rangers from primarily backcountry educators to "gun-totin' cops." And David Gibson, of the Association for the Protection of the Adirondacks, felt the rangers' status was the lowest it had ever been: "Their job should not be simply enforcement. They have a long and distinguished tradition as interpreters and educators. Forest rangers are the eyes and ears in the field for the Department of Environmental Conservation (DEC), and we need to return them to that tradition."

Pat Whalen is a senior forester in the Division of Lands and Forests. He, too, feels something has been lost by the administrative changes in the rangers:

> The old guard believes in the old definition of rangers. Some don't even think the six-shooter is needed. Unfortunately, those guys are retiring now. At the last academy, I've been told only a couple of guys even had hunting or fishing licenses. I can understand a few people not hunting or fishing, but not a majority, if they are folks who are truly interested in nature.
>
> In 1996, when the department was developing mission statements and goals, the rangers complained that they thought it was unfair that they were led by a group of foresters. They preferred to be in a group that was more police oriented. The new director is a former city cop, a political appointee, and he pushed the rangers even further toward their police orientation. The old guard, maybe 10 percent now, aren't happy with the changes. They rarely get into the woods anymore. They have a very defined, rigid structure, and the interpretive, educational function has been lost. But the new guys love it.

Clarence had encountered a similar lack of respect for nature among some of his colleagues as far back as the 1940s and 1950s. Many, in his opinion, were less than diligent when it came to protecting the Forest Preserve:

> We had a guy who became head of Lands and Forests who had been a forester. He was a forester when I was a district ranger, and we used to clash on things. He couldn't care less about what happened in the Adirondacks. One time he let a bunch of guys that were working on a campsite at Meacham Lake cut a whole stand of hemlocks down for a parking lot without letting anyone know about it. That was a strict violation, and he really should have been clobbered for it, but he got away with it because the commissioner didn't press it. But that's the sort of thing that's always bothered me. I was always in controversy with some of these guys. One of the things I wanted the Division of Lands and Forests to do was to work with the people down in Albany who make up the competitive exams, because maybe they could have

found out that way whether an individual was in favor of article 14 or whether he was against it.

Clarence was considered something of an odd man out at this time by many of his contemporaries in the conservation bureaucracy who were still looking for ways to get around the Forever Wild Amendment. The Conservation Commission was building and maintaining millions of dollars worth of facilities in the Forest Preserve in support of recreation. But the constitutionality of what they were doing was in question due to article 14.

One of the last major attempts of the conservation bureaucracy to get around the constitution came after the "Big Blowdown" of November 25, 1950. On that Saturday, winds of one hundred miles an hour rocketed in from the east. Braced defensively against the prevailing westerlies, the root systems of many of the region's oldest remaining trees gave way. More than four hundred thousand acres of Forest Preserve and private lands were devastated.

The state had to decide quickly what to do about the wind-blown timber. The Conservation Department, still abiding by its old utilitarian philosophy, wanted to allow private companies to harvest the wood before it rotted, which would have avoided a proliferation of pests and an increased threat of fire once the wood dried. But this was in direct opposition to the constitution, which prohibited the removal of trees from the Forest Preserve, dead or alive.

The Conservation Department solicited and received an opinion from the state attorney general that permitted the salvage operation. The department advertised for bids, and over the next few years the cleanup went forward. Thus encouraged, the department decided to try to determine if the public would consider removing permanently the constitutional ban on logging in the Forest Preserve. This, they argued, would create healthier forests, would promote wildlife (of the game variety especially), would provide revenue to the state, and would expand recreational opportunities. The old bureaucracy was still unable to imagine a forest best left to its own natural processes. Its leaders did not want to see intensive logging in the Forest Preserve, but they felt the

Forever Wild clause was interfering with their ability to promote recreational uses.

The response from the public was immediate and furious, and was led by Paul Schaefer, a leading preservationist since the early 1930s. The reaction to the Conservation Department's proposals has been known ever since as the "Big Blowup." Rather than weaken the constitution, Schaefer said, what was needed were *more* regions such as the Forest Preserve "where one can walk among forest giants and sense that tranquility obtainable only in the wild forest, away from the sights and sounds and hustle of this mechanized civilization."

By the time the windstorm of 1995 struck the northwestern Adirondacks, the attitude of state agencies had changed radically. After a comprehensive review, the DEC concluded that logging on Forest Preserve lands was not justifiable either ecologically or economically. Governor Pataki agreed with the study. He allowed trails and roads to be cleared, but no commercial logging was permitted on state lands in the park.

Ed Ketchledge is professor emeritus of the State University College of Environmental Science and Forestry at Syracuse. He summed up the effects of the great windstorms of 1950 and 1995, as well as the ice storm of 1998, in a December 1999 *Adirondack Life* article by George Wuerthner: "I welcome all these natural events. . . . People see the aftermath of the ice storm during one summer and they think it's terrible. But they are seeing it as one might view a single frame in a long movie. If you don't have insect epidemics, ice storms, blowdowns, wildfire and other natural processes, we would not have the dynamic, beautiful forests we have here today."

The controversy surrounding the Big Blowdown led to the formation of a Joint Legislative Committee on Natural Resources in 1951. Its purpose was to investigate the management and future course of the state's protected lands. Over the course of the decade, the committee began to formulate the idea of zoning the Forest Preserve. Eventually, Clarence would be asked to help the committee determine which parts of the preserve would be suitable for wilderness classification. Land designated as wilderness would be distinct from the rest of the Forest Preserve, primarily in that motors of any kind would be prohibited.

This work would later influence the Temporary Study Commission of 1968–70 and the State Land Master Plan of 1972. But in the immediate aftermath of the Big Blowdown, Clarence's duties as district ranger were much more specific. He began that windblown day on a hunting trip:

> It was an overcast day, and the wind was just roaring like the devil. Of course I didn't know it at the time, but it was the side of a hurricane coming up the coast.
>
> It was the last day of hunting season. I left home at daylight and got pretty high up on Stony Creek Mountain when I saw a buck. The wind was blowing and there were trees falling and limbs coming down all around. I had to look up all the time to keep from getting hit by something. But it was a beautiful day to hunt because it was so noisy that you could walk right up to a deer and he couldn't hear you coming.
>
> The next morning my brother Bill, who was the regional forester, said, "All the telephones are down, everything's blocked, and there's a survey crew stuck up along the Cold River." He was real concerned because logs and everything were across the roads and you couldn't begin to get a car up in there. So Bill headed out to start work getting that road open.
>
> I went up to the Five Ponds, because I had charge of the whole area. One of the things I had to do right away was to get the trails to the cabins and the fire tower opened up for fire control. But we got hit with snow soon after the hurricane and that knocked the fire hazard down.
>
> I had rangers working on the lines up to Cat Mountain and Tooley Pond. I went into Five Ponds by myself to see how things were in there. I took a bow saw and a hand ax with me. Soon as I crossed the bridge at Five Ponds, I found a bunch of little tamaracks that had fallen across the trail. Further on there were a lot of big hemlocks down, but I started by cutting the tops off those little tamaracks with the bow saw. Pretty soon, I got hot. I was wearing a jacket I'd used in the navy, my flight jacket. So I took it off and laid it on one of those trees I'd cut.
>
> Well, I worked my way into Five Ponds, and I was gone about three or four hours. After crawling around through all that downed timber, I

figured it would take a crew of four about three days of work to clear out that trail. Coming back, I got almost to the bridge and I said, "God, what did I do with that jacket?" I'd laid it down on a tree, and I looked all over, and I couldn't find it anywhere—thought I must be losing my marbles. I wondered if someone had come along and taken it. Then I was looking down and noticed one of the trees I'd cut was starting to lift up—you know—spring back up again. So I looked up and there was my jacket, thirty feet in the air, stuck in that tree. I had to take my bow saw and cut it down to get my jacket back. That was a good jacket. I didn't want to lose that.

I had responsibility for checking on the guys who had gotten the bids for salvaging the downed timber. There was a bunch of bonded Canadians up there cutting on Pine Ridge. One day I found one of the lumberjacks about to cut down a good pine tree simply because a branch had been knocked off by a tree that had fallen down next to it. I said, "You can't cut that tree. That's a good tree." He spoke French, only a little English. He says, "The tree is damage, the tree is damage." Well, I said, "There's nothing in the contract that says you can cut it." I stopped him from cutting it.

As it turned out, it went down later from another blowdown anyway, but that was the sort of thing that went on. I later found a huge white pine right on the Oswegatchie River that had been cut down. Of course no one would admit to cutting it. But that's what was going on. They were only interested in getting the volume of timber out, and there were a lot of violations. State foresters were supposed to be checking up on those guys, but a lot of them didn't care about what was cut or not.

The Great Blowdown of 1950 resulted in the closure of vast stretches of the most affected parts of the Forest Preserve. With trails hopelessly blocked and the perception of increased fire potential, some remote areas, such as Cold River, were not reopened until 1955. The storm precipitated the end of Noah John Rondeau's time at Cold River, since he was sixty-seven in 1950. Seven of the forty-six High Peaks were closed. Many aspiring forty-sixers, some needing only a single peak or two to join the coveted list, had to wait years to complete their task.

Clarence's years as district ranger were busy ones. It was also a crucial time for the Adirondacks. People's attitudes toward the Forest Preserve were hardening into two factions: those who wanted less government interference and those who wanted more controls and protections for the park. Clarence fell soundly into the latter category. He believed in the necessity of rules to protect the preserve from just the sort of violations he had come across after the Blowdown. And once a rule was made, he believed in enforcing it.

CHAPTER 14

Ranger at Large

Clarence was about to enter his most productive and influential period as a conservationist. From the close of his eleven years as district ranger at Cranberry Lake in 1957 until several years *after* his first retirement from government service in 1971, he would hold a bewildering number and variety of positions.

His particular blend of skills was in such demand that he was constantly being "loaned" from one department to another, and his job title underwent numerous inventive alterations. As pilot, member of the Inter-State Fire Compact, liaison to the Joint Legislative Committee on Natural Resources, and forest preserve specialist on the staffs of Governor Rockefeller's Study Commission on the Future of the Adirondacks and the Adirondack Park Agency, virtually anything of substance that went on in the Adirondacks had Clarence Petty's hand in it.

By the end of the 1940s the Conservation Department had an array of aircraft. There was a Ryan Navion (low wing) used for forest fire control, two Stearman N2S-4s used for aerial spraying, a Stinson L-5 for the Division of Fish and Game, and an amphibious Grumman G-21 "Goose," which was used for everything from fish stocking and hauling freight to transporting executives around the state.[1] As a pilot with considerable experience, Clarence's advice was often sought concerning

---

1. Information on Conservation Department aircraft comes from Louis C. Curth's *The Forest Rangers: A History of the New York State Forest Ranger Force.*

such things as aerial fish stocking of remote lakes and forest fire spotting and control.

In 1947, after a huge fire burned much of Bar Harbor, Maine, the United States Forest Service decided it had to have a different system for fighting a fire of such magnitude. During the war, conservation had been one of the first areas to suffer severe cutbacks. Virtually all activities of the state's Division of Lands and Forests had been put on hold as resources were diverted for military purposes. The one exception was fire control. Faced with the specter of sabotage, the fire control system so laboriously put into operation over many years had to be maintained. As a result, forest rangers and fire observers had been deferred in most cases from military service.

In the aftermath of both the war and the fire in Bar Harbor, it was now clear that this fire control system needed updating. "A big fire is just like a combat operation," says Clarence.

> You've got to have a lot of personnel, not only to fight the fire but to man a headquarters unit to administer the whole operation. The Forest Service said what you need up here is a combined effort of the northeastern states, so that if you have a fire in any one of the states, the others would come in and help.
>
> In 1949 the Northeastern Interstate Forest Fire Protection Compact was approved. I had to go up to the unit at Upper Darby, Pennsylvania, every year where the headquarters of the Forest Service was and spend two weeks writing up procedures for the big fires. We'd take what we learned back to Laconia, New Hampshire, and put on training for the eastern states.
>
> Then Canada heard about it and they started sending representatives from New Brunswick, Quebec, and Ontario. They invited us up to one of their training sessions at Smoke Lake in Algonquin Park where they had their headquarters, and that's where I learned what they were doing with aircraft up in Canada.
>
> They had such huge areas that they had virtually no choice but to fight fires with airplanes. They were using water in five-gallon sacks that they'd roll out the back of the plane. When it hit the trees it would

splatter, and that was their initial phase. Then they developed amphibious planes with tanks mounted on each float to pick up the water.

Clarence explained the new technique to the conservation commissioner, who then contacted the De Havilland Aircraft Company in
Toronto. The company sent an Otter aircraft down to stage a demon-
stration. The commissioner purchased one of the planes and sent
Clarence to Toronto to fly it back.

"I used that plane to dump water on a lot of fires," Clarence remembers. "Instead of landing, I got so I could just skim the surface and
the snorkels would fill the tanks in a few seconds and I'd be off again."
Clarence was the first person in New York State and probably the entire
eastern part of the country to use planes to fight fires in this manner.
Many years later he would receive an award from St. Lawrence University in which he was cited for being the first aerial fire fighter in the
state.

Around the same time that Clarence was flying on fire duty and
performing assorted other functions in the Adirondacks, another opportunity presented itself. In about 1957 Fred McLane, the pilot for Governor Averell Harriman, had flown the state comptroller to New York
City. On the return trip, somewhere near Poughkeepsie, both engines
on the plane quit. It went down hard, landing in some trees, and
McLane was hurt so badly that he had to stop flying.

Clarence was asked if he'd like to replace the veteran pilot. The job
was noncompetitive, unlike the district ranger position, and Clarence
hesitated, for he knew he would be subject to politics and possible dismissal from the pilot's position. But it paid more, so he finally resigned
as district ranger and became a full-time pilot for the state, working
under the Division of Lands and Forests.

Clarence continued performing various flying duties for the division, including firefighting and fish stocking. In addition, he was called
upon to perform inspections of various department activities around
the state in his capacity as forest preserve specialist. But now he was
also on call at a moment's notice to fly Governor Harriman wherever he

wanted to go. It was the worst possible assignment for someone like Clarence:

> If it was anticipated that the governor might need a plane, we would have to be in the Albany hangar all day waiting for a call. There wouldn't be anything to do, but we had to be there. All of a sudden, the phone would ring at four thirty, five o'clock. It would be the governor's office, and he'd want to go to New York or Buffalo or someplace.
>
> One night he wanted to leave for New York at eight o'clock and return at eleven. There was thunder rolling and lightning flashing all around, and Hank Evans, who was also a pilot for Harriman [the governor required two pilots on his planes], said, "Well, we might get held up over New York because of all that traffic coming in." You couldn't just go in there anytime you wanted. You had to take your turn. If we were delayed at all, it would have made more sense for him to take a limousine. He would have gotten there faster after all the waiting and getting transported to and from the airport.
>
> But no, the governor wanted to fly, so at eight o'clock, up we went into the storm. We ended up sitting up there with a lineup of planes below us. We'd get held up for ten minutes, do a procedure turn, wait, go down another thousand feet, then another thousand. Forty minutes we were holding up there. We got in about an hour later than we figured. The governor and his people went into town to do their business, and we were left waiting in the hangar again. One of his men said they'd be back by eleven. Well, eleven comes, twelve o'clock comes, one o'clock, two o'clock. Finally, two-thirty they came in and we flew back to Albany, getting in about four in the morning. That kind of stuff can get pretty stale, I can tell you.

Not long after Harriman became governor, the "suggestion" came down that the Conservation Department needed to buy a twin-engine Beech 18 for fire control. The Grumman Goose that crashed had been the only twin-engine plane the department owned. Now the governor wanted the Beech for his personal transport.

"This was supposed to be an emergency expenditure," says Clarence. "They charged it up to fire control, but it wasn't needed for that. I remember a notice appearing in the paper, and we were all kind of snickering about it, because the governor said the Beech was going to be used for fire control and fish planting. Well, using a twin Beech for those kinds of things is like using a telephone pole for a fish rod. They spent more money on stuff like that. It was really amazing."

Clarence found Harriman to be something of a cold fish: "He had a real gruff attitude. He treated the people around him pretty shabbily. We had set up a table for him so he could work while he was flying. But when he got through with whatever he was working on, he'd tear it up into little pieces and throw it on the floor." Clarence was the one, of course, who later had to clean it up. This sort of waste of time did not endear the governor to his pilot: "It was the sort of thing that disgusted me with the guy. He didn't care a damn for the people around him. He was a little dictator."

It was unfortunate that Harriman and his pilot were unable to connect personally, for they might have discovered that they had at least one interest in common. Like Clarence, the governor had been fascinated by aviation since the earliest days of the new technology. Before World War I he financed his wife's brother, who was developing an air-cooled aluminum engine in hopes of being able to carry passengers hundreds of miles. One of those engines, the Wright Whirlwind, powered Lindbergh's *Spirit of St. Louis* on its journey to Paris.

Harriman's interest in flying continued throughout his life. He invested in a company manufacturing bombers and amphibious planes for the army in the mid-1920s and became one of the original investors in a forerunner of Pan American Airways. All of this was possible, of course, as a result of the Harriman family fortune.

But any sort of cordial relationship between Clarence and Harriman was not to be. Averell was not an easy man to know, and certainly not for someone he considered an employee. Robert Meiklejohn, who was Harriman's personal secretary for more than a decade, said he hardly felt he knew the man. "He was not inconsiderate," Meiklejohn recalled. "He was just no good at human relations—naturally aloof. God only knows how many thousand hours I spent alone in his company, but I do not know one interesting anecdote about his personal life."

Clarence, who spent considerably less time in Harriman's presence, had several anecdotes to tell. During the years that Harriman was governor, 1955–59, he insisted on personally handling any legislation having to do with the development of skiing in the Adirondacks. Harriman had been interested in skiing since the mid-1930s, when he founded a resort in Sun Valley called Baldy Mountain.

On one of Clarence's flights, in January of 1958, he flew the governor into Lake Placid, where he was going to open a new ski run and chairlift on nearby Whiteface Mountain. Clarence recalls:

> The people at his office said he wanted to leave at eight o'clock at night and fly into Saranac Lake. Well, Saranac Lake didn't have instrument-landing equipment. They had a little weak signal over there, but you couldn't get in if it was instrument conditions. My copilot, Hank, told them they'd have to leave an hour early in order to get in there; otherwise we'd have to land at Plattsburgh and drive up from there. Well the governor arrived at eight o'clock anyway, and it was just starting to snow in good shape. We barely made it in to Saranac before things socked in. After we landed, Harriman looked over my shoulder and said, "You see, it isn't so bad."
>
> Well he was going to stay overnight, open this run, and then fly back. So Hank says, "Why don't we go over to the ski run early in case he wants to come back suddenly or changes his plans." So we went over and went up the chairlift onto Little Whiteface. We got out there and I told Hank I was going to walk down. Hank wanted to ride, so he did that while I walked down and met him at the bottom.
>
> By that time the governor had come up with his bodyguard, and they started up the lift. But something happened to the cable, and it stopped. Harriman and his bodyguard were trapped up there, thirty feet off the ground. It was below zero, and the damn cable had come off the wheel or something. I was real amused by the whole thing, because they were sitting up there with no place to go and they couldn't get him down for an hour and a half. They had to call in a cherry picker from somewhere to get up there to reach him. It made all the papers.

Newspaper accounts of the incident differed slightly from Clarence's. The *Watertown Daily Times* suggested the problem with the chairlift was simply a matter of someone pushing the wrong button. There was no mention of how long the governor was trapped or of his being rescued by a cherry picker, though he was stuck long enough to "be fully photographed and widely publicized." It is possible that North Country publications did not want to raise any doubts about dangerous problems with the new and highly touted ski lift, which was to be, it was hoped, an economic boost to the entire region.

Clarence remained on call to the governor for almost two years, by which time he was so disgusted with the job that he was looking around for any way to get out of it. Once again Bill Foss from Lands and Forests came to his rescue. He told Clarence that if he wanted to keep flying but be based in the Adirondacks as much as in Albany, Foss had a job that suited his skills. It came with yet another new title: liaison officer between the Conservation Department and the Joint Legislative Committee on Natural Resources.

The committee had been established in 1951 under the chairmanship of Assemblyman (later Senator) Wheeler Milmoe. It studied a wide range of problems associated with the management of the state's natural resources.

Now the committee was under the new direction of Assemblyman (later Senator) R. Watson Pomeroy, one of the leading legislators on environmental issues. The enormous growth in the recreational uses of the Adirondack and Catskill forests was producing problems of overuse and degradation of scenic values in many places. The invasion of some remote areas by four-wheel-drive vehicles, both homemade doodlebugs with big tires and the more conventional jeeplike vehicles, had already caused alarm in the minds of many backpackers and other backcountry users. These kinds of threats to the wilderness would be the subject of the first studies undertaken by the Pomeroy Committee.

Clarence, the reluctant aerial chauffeur, leapt at the opportunity to leave Governor Harriman's personal service. The move marked the beginning of what would become a signature achievement of Clarence's long career: his work classifying and mapping the Adirondack wilderness.

CHAPTER 15

Into the Fire

Clarence signed on to the staff of the Joint Legislative Committee with an almost audible sigh of relief. No longer would he be subject to any whim of the governor. He was once again his own man. Though he as yet had little inkling of the political winds that would buffet him over the next fifteen years, to be free of Averell Harriman was its own reward. In the years ahead, however, he would often wonder if he might not have stepped out of the frying pan and into the fire.

Bill Foss, director of the Division of Lands and Forests, had asked the Joint Legislative Committee to address the problem the Conservation Department was having with administering the Forest Preserve under the strictures of Forever Wild. His hope was that the committee would recommend zoning the Forest Preserve. He saw this as a way to partially bypass Forever Wild by specifying areas where development could occur.

But Foss's plan would have unexpected consequences, as Philip Terrie explains:

> This scheme, part of the Conservation Department's strategy for weakening the grip of Forever Wild, nonetheless contained elements key to the eventual official acceptance of a wilderness aesthetic. One of the zones would be "Restricted Areas . . . to include scenic, wilderness and roadside areas with outstanding natural features. Development within these areas to be permitted only to the extent necessary for the construction of primitive facilities such as trails, lean-tos, fire-

places, etc." Although even this amount of interference still violated the purest definition of wilderness, the conservation bureaucracy was for the first time declaring its willingness to minimize the development of at least some part of the Forest Preserve. It was a major step toward admitting the legitimacy of wilderness.

Under the committee's direction, members of its staff began to map and identify those parts of the Forest Preserve that possessed important wilderness characteristics. It was a job tailor-made for Clarence.

Watson Pomeroy's appointment shortly after Nelson Rockefeller became governor in 1959 was "an odd thing," Clarence recalls,

> because Watson was born in Chicago, and he told me that when he was a kid, he and his friends would drive all over the city looking for something to do. Then his family moved and he and his father established a brokerage business in New York City. So he came out of those big cities, but he got to travel in the Adirondacks enough that he got interested in it, and that's how he became an environmentalist.
>
> You see, the Forest Service had already established wilderness areas out in the west, and this is where Watson got his idea from. He said, "We've got a huge area of public lands up here. The Forest Service is already setting up their wilderness. We ought to be doing something with ours."

Working closely with Clarence during his years on the staff of the Joint Legislative Committee was Neil Stout. Pomeroy appointed Stout to be his executive director and charged him to meet with Clarence to make a professional inventory of potential wilderness areas in the Adirondack Forest Preserve. Stout could not have been more pleased to have Clarence assigned as his full-time associate: "Clarence brought to the assignment years of Adirondack experience plus a genuine interest in the goals of the committee. His aircraft expertise and friendly relations with many natural resources and forestry professionals were extremely helpful."

Clarence had first met Neil through the Society of American Foresters, to which they both belonged. Now the two men would spend much of the next three years together, exploring the Adirondack wilderness by canoe, foot, snowshoe, and plane. Clarence had been chosen for the assignment because of his vast knowledge of the Adirondack backcountry. He had visited the remotest parts of the region, knew the high peaks intimately, and had detailed knowledge of the facilities, campsites, lean-tos, trails, and so forth. From a lifetime of trapping, hunting, guiding, working as a ranger, and flying across the northern forests, he was the most knowledgeable person around.

"We had a meeting with the committee members," Clarence recalls.

It was an assembly committee, but there were also members of the Senate brought in, because Watson wanted the Senate people involved. We would have meetings up in the commissioner's office and Bill Foss said, "Out West they're having a minimum of five thousand acres for wilderness areas. That's too small. I think we ought to double that and have ten thousand acres." Well, that made it simpler for Neil and me, because then we wouldn't have to go to anything smaller than that. We started on that basis and spent most of the next three years out in the woods, which was where we both wanted to be anyway.

We had this big map in red. It was red wherever the Forest Preserve was. That simplified things. We picked out twelve areas in the Adirondacks and four in the Catskills. Some were marginal areas that didn't quite make the size cut but were close enough that we thought we ought to check them anyway.

Ten thousand acres was the minimum, but many were much larger. The High Peaks area was the biggest and then there were some very small ones like the Putnam Pond area. It was a lot of work. We tried to do the office work in the winter and then go out other times of the year.

One trip made by Neil and Clarence was into the West Canada Lakes region. They flew south from Long Lake aboard Herb Helms's air service on a crisp autumn day in October. If Helms had had any inkling of what the outcome of their work would be, that is, the designation of wilderness lakes that he could no longer land upon, it is doubtful he would have flown them.

"Herb was very bitter about being restricted in his flying," Clarence recalls. "But he and other flyers were taking hunters back into remote lakes, setting up semipermanent camps, and hauling in bedding and mattresses and supplies. These places became real junkholes. People began to think they owned the camps, and it's one of the things that spurred creation of the wilderness areas." Helms later spent years suing the state over the restrictions that were imposed.

Neil Stout and Clarence on trail from Pharaoh Lake to Crane Pond, 1959. Photograph by Assemblyman R. Watson Pomeroy, courtesy of Neil Stout.

Snow was already capping the High Peaks as Clarence and Neil arrived. They made their base of operations at the ranger station at the end of West Canada Lake. "Our inspection revealed several problems," Stout recalls.

> Trail littering was evident as well as the excessive use of fire roads and old logging roads by motorized conveyances. We also inspected the zones where land exchanges between the Department of Conservation and the International Paper Company [IP] were made based on legislative action during the earlier Milmoe Committee period. Generally, these exchanges had improved the management of lands which had previously existed as a checkerboard pattern of state and private land ownership. The logging of older trees by IP had allowed a new forest to come in, and evidence of the use of the cutover lands by deer was striking. Much more browse was now available in proximity to blocks of state land.
>
> Heavy winter snows had damaged the lean-to shelters in this area,

a problem we had noticed in several wilderness areas. This type of problem may have been a factor in the general de-emphasis of providing such shelters for recreational users in the Forest Preserve. We discussed the matter of permitting aircraft use of certain bodies of water, at the same time reducing the widespread general use, i.e., motorized use, of many remote lakes and ponds.

Deliberations of such matters by the Legislative Committee, followed by further analysis and study by the Conservation Department, resulted in the evolution of a policy statement in April 1965 on the administration and use of Forest Preserve wilderness areas. West Canada Lake in Hamilton County was the major water body within an otherwise inaccessible zone where aircraft landings were permitted. The policy recommendations also restricted the use of motorized vehicles on many fire trails and forest roadways. Similarly, many bodies of water were to be kept free of power-driven boats and available only to users of canoes and rowboats.

The low clouds and rainy weather kept the Helms aircraft from returning to pick us up on the scheduled day of return. We had to pack out all of our gear on the trail. Mr. Helms arranged for our pickup and return to Long Lake. That was a long day of hiking on wet and muddy trails, but we believed it had been a very successful excursion.

Throughout my days in the forest with Clarence, I felt privileged because of his familiarity with the Conservation Department's phone and radio network at ranger stations and fire towers. I was always impressed, too, with Clarence's smooth walking style. It often appeared that his feet barely touched the ground. His stride may have benefited from his ice skating skills developed in earlier years. His field assistants were often so amazed that they were quick to suggest that Clarence must have embedded roller bearings in the soles of his shoes, or some other such speed-inducing feature.

This, of course, was the same hiking ability that had so impressed Clarence's comrades in the military. On that memorable occasion when he had set off briskly at the head of the troops, only to leave them far behind, Clarence had been told that the men did not walk that kind of a step. "I thought I knew how to walk," he later commented. Over the years of the Adirondack wilderness studies, few of Clarence's lagging colleagues ever questioned his walking ability.

On another expedition Clarence, Neil, and the Tupper Lake forest ranger climbed Street Mountain south of Lake Placid to the site where a Conservation Department aircraft had crashed several weeks earlier.

"An inexperienced pilot had headed in the wrong direction into the pocket for a fish drop into a backcountry lake," Stout recalls.

Unable to gain the altitude necessary to go over the summit, the plane smacked into the upper slopes of Street Mountain.

It was October 25, 1959, the opening day of deer season, when we started up Roaring Brook. We found a suitable downed tree for crossing the turbulent stream and then encountered snow. Along the way we saw fresh bear tracks. The purpose of the trip was to check on the status of the radios located in the rear of the wrecked plane. Clarence had been instrumental in having the additional radios installed and was not sure, when viewing the wreckage from the air, if the fire which followed the crash had scorched the tail end of the Otter.

Our packs were heavy and the terrain was rugged. It took us until late afternoon to reach the crash site. We learned that fire damage was extensive. Radios were burned and the interior of the plane was severely damaged. Spruce trees more than a foot in diameter had been sheared off by the wings as the plane, heavily laden with fuel and fish tanks, crashed into the mountainside.

A small site below the wreckage and along a stream afforded the only overnight camping spot. Darkness was coming on fast. Gathering firewood of dead stems was an urgent task. In my quest for wood, I crossed the stream by stepping on boulders and, as darkness took over, slipped on an icy rock and wound up completely submerged in the freezing water. With my clothes soaked and the temperature around zero, my companions were quick to recognize the need for my stripping off the wet clothing and getting into a sleeping bag in order to avoid hypothermia. The fire was smoky but provided warmth, and my clothes dried overnight. Nobody got much sleep, but with the fire we were able to keep from freezing. Clarence worked all night at maintaining the flames.

On our return the next day, we stopped at the ranger station at Duck Hole, built a fire in the stove, and prepared hot soup. I guess it was "just another day" in the life of forest rangers, who were often called on for search and rescue missions.

On several occasions Clarence and Neil stayed overnight in Paul Schaefer's cabin. "We always had our sleeping bags," Clarence recalls.

We stayed all over the Adirondacks and a lot of times, everything was closed down. You couldn't find anyplace where there was a hotel or motel, and we had to bring our own groceries. Otherwise, you'd end up starving to death. We slept outside a lot of the time. But when we were working up in the Bakers Mills area, outlining the region for the Siamese Ponds wilderness, we stayed at Paul's place.

It was just a little shack, and I guess it's pretty much disintegrated. Then he built another one, later on. We used to joke about it, because you could see the lines were out of skew, not plumb, just by looking at it. 'Course he probably intended it to be that way on purpose, because he was a building contractor down in the Schenectady area. He was a very good builder.

One guy I knew said that Paul often wouldn't send a bill out. Everybody was always owing him because he'd never get around to settling his accounts. It was amazing. I don't know how he could get on and buy stuff, because he was always so close to the cushion.

Schaefer's wilderness home consisted of two "cottages," located a couple of miles from Bakers Mills under a spur of Eleventh Mountain. They looked out on a distant view of Crane Mountain. This wild place would figure prominently in the eventual protection of Adirondack, and indeed of all American wilderness. The story revolves around one of the greatest figures in twentieth-century wilderness preservation, Howard Zahniser, the author of the federal Wilderness Act of 1964.

In 1945 Zahnie, as his friends called him, left his job in the federal government to become the director of the Wilderness Society's one-man office in Washington, D.C. For the next eighteen years he would lead the struggle begun by Bob Marshall. In a speech before the Joint Legislative Committee in 1953, Zahniser urged the members not just to set aside wilderness, but to protect it from overmanagement as well. Zahnie's words had a powerful effect on Assemblyman Watson Pomeroy, who would later chair the committee. With this speech Zahniser effectively initiated the movement to designate wilderness areas in the Adirondack Forest Preserve.

Zahnie was driven, in large part, out of a love for the Adirondacks that was nurtured by his relationship with Paul Schaefer. Sensing a kindred spirit, Schaefer invited Zahnie and his family to visit him at Bakers Mills. That trip, in August of 1946, introduced the new Wilderness Society leader to the Adirondacks.

Schaefer and guide Ed Richard took Zahnie to see Adirondak Loj. From there they hiked to Avalanche Pass, Flowed Lands, and Hanging Spear Falls on the Opalescent. The two families, including their combined six children, stayed at Schaefer's cabins. Impressed with the beauty all around him, Zahnie expressed a desire to have his own piece of land in the Adirondacks. Almost at once, Schaefer located a nearby lot that was for sale and suggested the deal to his new friend.

For the next eighteen years, the Schaefers and Zahnisers would be friends and neighbors. Zahnie's cabin was named Mateskared, after his four children. It was here that his love for the Adirondacks grew, providing him with the inner spirit and fortitude necessary for the long battle that led to the passage of the Wilderness Act, a bill Zahnie had to rewrite innumerable times before it was finally enacted.

In one of life's sad injustices, Zahnie died just four months before the bill's final passage on September 3, 1964. The National Wilderness Preservation System, created by President Johnson's signature on the bill, has today grown to over one hundred million acres and is responsible for spurring similar movements around the world. The wilderness movement got a big boost from Paul Schaefer's little cabins, one of which Clarence and Neil had used while surveying the Adirondack wilderness.

◆　　◆　　◆

Jay Hutchinson worked with Clarence and Neil during the summers of 1960 and 1961, while Jay was working on his master's degree at the State College of Forestry at Syracuse. "The aim was to identify areas with potential wilderness values, describe their natural features, and map any illegal jeep roads and structures on them," Jay recalls.

It was a wonderful way to see the best of the Adirondacks and spend the summer hiking.

Sometimes we worked separately, following illegal jeep trails in the Forest Preserve, but often we'd spend a long day hiking together up Snowy Mountain or walking what is today the Silver Lake Wilderness. After work, we'd eat supper at the local greasy spoon and return to our small hotel, our rough-and-ready cabin, or our "tourist home" (they still existed then). One time, in 1960, we listened to the radio in amazement as Swedish boxing unknown Ingemar Johansson knocked out America's Floyd Patterson in the first round.

Clarence was always dedicated to maintaining and furthering his flying knowledge. And he seemed to be indefatigable following the day's work. Tired after our exertions, I would write up my notes, eyelids sagging, and soon be ready to turn in. Clarence—twenty-five years my senior—would still be going strong, intently studying a Federal Aviation Administration (FAA) correspondence course to keep his piloting status current, or reading a flying magazine. Then on Friday afternoon he'd get in his car and drive back up to Canton to work all weekend long on the house he was building that summer.

Jay was just one of many who worked with Clarence over the years who could only marvel at the remarkable stores of energy that drove him. Time was not to be wasted. As a young boy, hiking sixteen miles home from school every Friday, Clarence would turn around the next day and walk another ten or twenty to maintain his traplines or to guide a group of sportsmen. A regimen of walking Adirondack wilderness all week only to drive to Canton to spend weekends building a house was simply the way of things.

Improving his flying ratings and abilities was an ongoing responsibility that Clarence never shirked throughout his seventy years as a pilot. It was this dedication that led him, in 1951, to use some of his GI credits and take a ten-day leave. He traveled to Providence, Rhode Island, to obtain his helicopter rating.

"The FAA didn't have any helicopter examiners," says Clarence, "so they designated the chief helicopter pilot of Wiggins Airways to give me the required flight test. The craft we used was only the tenth helicopter ever made by Bell Helicopters. The main rotor blades were not metal. They were wrapped with a fabric that had a tendency to peel off in the rain, so I was fortunate in finding ten days with no snow or rain."

Jay Hutchinson had taken a few hours of flying lessons and had been a light aircraft mechanic in the army. He was always keen on listening to Clarence's flying stories. One he remembered was about the time Clarence flew to remote Lake Colden to stock trout from the air: "His Conservation Department plane was loaded with a tank of trout fingerlings as he swooped down low over Lake Colden. Unfortunately there was a glitch somewhere, and the wildly waving Lake Colden ranger in his rowboat below got a surprise shower of hundreds of flopping fingerlings."

Shortly before Jay's time with Clarence, in the fall of 1958, *Albany Times-Union* staff writer Jerry Cartledge went along with Clarence and his two assistants while they stocked a series of remote ponds with fingerlings. (The earliest such stocking attempts had been made in the Fourth Lake area by Bud Windhausen and Harold Scott. While one man flew the plane, the other braced himself in the door and poured fish from milk cans. Even this primitive technique was an improvement over the laborious carrying of fish into remote areas in backpack tanks, as was done years earlier. Later, Scott designed a tank with a dump pipe that extended through the fuselage. On a test drop into Sacandaga Lake, a net placed under the water's surface enabled them to determine that only about one out of every five hundred fish was injured by the drop.)

Cartledge's trip was made in the department's new Canadian-built, amphibian Otter. The little plane bucked and tossed in the air currents as it sank low before each drop, causing the *Times-Union* writer to drop his breakfast along the way. "In the rear section," wrote Cartledge, "we passed buckets of water and fish from the carrying tanks to the drop-hopper. The floor was sloshing with water jerked and spilled from the buckets. . . . Trying to dump a net-load of jumping trout into a hopper in a bucking, sliding airplane is like trying to stuff melted butter down a wildcat's throat with a hot awl."

By the late 1950s the Conservation Department was air-dropping half a million fingerlings a year into hundreds of remote wilderness ponds. Cartledge, suitably impressed by Clarence's piloting ability, called him "an Adirondack-seasoned flier with ice water in his veins."

Clarence and Jay used the Conservation Department's unusual twelve-foot, forty-five-pound cedar-ribbed guide boat, to check out ponds and trails accessible only by water. "On a trip from the south end of Lake Placid to the north end and back, he let me take the oars," Jay remembers. "I soon learned the wonderful speed and power advantage of oars over a paddle—but at the cost of bruising my knuckles on the overlapping oar handles, until the trick of keeping one hand constantly elevated over the other became second nature."

Other times, the two used Clarence's more standard, seventy-five-pound guide boat, crafted in the Hanmer workshop in Saranac Lake. Jay recalls:

> Portaging this boat required less finesse but more brute strength and presented a real challenge to my one-hundred-forty-five-pound frame. On one hot, sticky Adirondack day, I got my initiation into carrying Clarence's guide boat when we went in to check on the circle of connecting ponds north of Long Pond and near Upper Saranac Lake [in what would become the St. Regis Canoe Area in 1972]. We spelled each other, sweating under the yoke and the upside-down boat, making our way over the roots and rocks of the trail. Clarence did the better part of the mile-long portage from Long Pond into Nellie Pond, probably worrying (and rightly so) that from the looks of me, I had a pretty good chance of stumbling and splitting his guide boat open like an egg.

For Clarence it was simply all in a day's work. But he was always aware of the intense public scrutiny that their investigations aroused:

There was terrific controversy about these wilderness areas when they were proposed years later by the Study Commission. One of the things I thought we should do was find out how far these places were from a public road or waterway. A lot of the people who were against wilderness and its restrictions on motorized access were saying, "These areas are so remote that nobody but the most physically fit can get in there." So I said, "Let's find out just how hard it would be to get into these places."

We would spend a good deal of time on that our last winter at the Study Commission, going all over with a map and finding out where the margins of these wilderness areas were—how hard it was to reach them. We found that 38 percent of them were less than a mile from a highway or public waterway and 82 percent were within three miles. It was amazing, really, and it didn't go over too well with those people who were saying that the wilderness areas were so remote. Because most of them were right along some public access point, and you could walk a mile or two or get in a boat and be there in a few minutes.

The Joint Legislative Committee drew up a plan that would have set aside twelve wilderness areas in the Adirondacks and four in the Catskills, of at least ten thousand acres each, in which motorized use would be banned. But the plan was much less clear with regard to what would happen in the rest of the Forest Preserve. By 1966 some committee members had come up with proposals to allow the development of recreational facilities on the preserve, including some so liberal that they would have allowed the building of restaurants at the end of wilderness trails.

Clarence and Neil finished their studies in 1962. "The reason we ended at that particular time was [because of] a situation which was really sad," says Clarence.

Commissioner Harold Wilson, unbeknownst to Watson Pomeroy, decided that he was going to require a bill along with the study bill that would allow cutting of timber around deer yards on state land in the Adirondacks. Of course, that would be a violation of article 14 and

R. Watson Pomeroy resting on the trail during wilderness studies, 1962. Courtesy of Neil Stout.

Watson would never go along with it. So the commissioner essentially killed our proposals right there. If he couldn't have his cutting bill, he wouldn't sanction our wilderness bill.

Neil and I were at a meeting with Watson, and Watson said to me, "We've been used." He was really disgusted. The commissioner should have told him, to begin with, that he wasn't going to support him unless he turned in a bill that cut timber off Forest Preserve land. Instead he waited and spent all that time, three years, and Watson was just devastated by it.

Eventually Watson Pomeroy turned in a minority report that identified the main uses of the Forest Preserve as watershed protection and those recreational pursuits that were in line with the mandates of the constitution. He stood by his belief that the cutting of timber would violate the constitution and threaten the wilderness environment in the preserve.

Despite Pomeroy's obvious disappointment with the outcome of the wilderness studies, the work was the most personally satisfying of his career. In a letter to Neil Stout in 1984, Pomeroy wrote: "Those were indeed fun days—as were all our trips studying wilderness, and I always enjoy thinking about them. There are snapshots of them in my 'Rogues gallery' in my office, which I always inspect whenever I go upstairs to it. Indeed, they were among the happiest and most gratifying days of my life."

No action was taken with regard to the Joint Legislative Committee's zoning recommendations. However, the research done by the committee's staff, that is, by Neil and Clarence, to determine which parts of the preserve were most suitable for special wilderness designation—with a capital W—would greatly influence the work of the Temporary Study Commission a few years later.

CHAPTER 16

Warming Up to Controversy

Through the 1950s the Pettys lived in Parishville, and Clarence commuted to his office in Canton. But in 1961 the new home he had been building three miles outside of Canton was finally finished. Its construction, primarily on weekends and other moments stolen from Clarence's extremely busy career, was one more example of his do-it-yourself nature. Though he clearly could have afforded to have the home built, he preferred that it be a family affair. His son Ed was a bit less enthusiastic: "I poured every inch of cement in that foundation myself," he remembers ruefully. Ferne began teaching sixth grade at the Canton Elementary School, and the two younger boys, Richard and Ed, attended Canton High School. Donald, half a dozen years older than his brothers, attended Canton Agricultural and Technical Institute (later College). Richard and Ed would eventually go on to the State University College at Potsdam.

Clarence's mother, Catherine, had died in 1959. "She'd been having some problems with blocked arteries," remembers Clarence, "and there was no such thing as a bypass at that time. She was eighty-two years old. We were still living in Parishville, and I got a call from the neighbors at Coreys who said someone was trying to get hold of me. It was Bill's wife. She'd gone over to pick up my mother who was going to get her hair done, and there she was, sitting right in the chair in the living room. I guess she was lucky to go like that. My father, mother, and brother Bill all died sudden like that."

Catherine had been the guiding light for Clarence and his brothers. If not for her, all three boys would likely have spent a lifetime guiding in the Adirondacks like their father. Instead, her constant prodding and obvious pride in her sons' educational achievements led them in other directions. Bill's working life paralleled Clarence's in many ways. He had been a district ranger at Middletown and later was stationed at Saranac Inn. Eventually, he became a regional director for the DEC for much of the Adirondacks. Their younger brother, Archie, was employed by the Fish and Game Department as a fisheries biologist, but was located outside the Adirondack Park.

Clarence and Ferne's new home on the Canton-Potsdam road was suitably situated on one of the highest points between the two villages and had a distant view of the Adirondack foothills. There was a fenced-in field for Ferne's beloved Morgan horses and several acres of land that would soon become the talk of area gardeners as Ferne put her indelible mark on the landscape. Somehow, Clarence also found time to operate a sugar bush and maple syrup-making operation behind the house.

Throughout their lives, Clarence and Ferne maintained very different interests. Ferne could not have cared less about flying. Clarence would have nothing to do with her horses. Even in gardening they went their separate ways, Ferne concentrating on flowers, Clarence on vegetables. Mary Jo Whalen, a close friend and riding partner of Ferne's, recalls preparing to go out on the horses one day when Clarence came in and announced that the tomatoes were ready for canning. "So we had to bring in the tomatoes and can them right then and there," says Mary Jo, "before we could go riding. It was *time* to do the tomatoes."

One area where husband and wife could usually agree was the environment. But not always. Again, Mary Jo Whalen:

> There was a horse barn with stalls up on the mountain at Coreys where we went riding and sometimes stayed overnight in a lean-to [probably near Calkins Creek]. Clarence was determined that lean-to was going to be taken down because it was in the wilderness. Forever wild—no buildings. Ferne was equally determined it would stay. So

she wrote many letters and talked to many people about the horse barn staying. And Clarence wrote many letters and talked to many people about having it taken down.

Ferne said, "You want to save the Adirondacks? People will tie their horses to the trees. The horses will eat the bark off the trees. The trees will die. People don't like to leave their horses out at night and let them be rained on if they're used to being inside." But Clarence prevailed and the barn was burned down by the DEC.

Ferne was probably the first person to ride the horse trails that were opened up into the wilderness areas around Coreys. She was the only person given permission by the Rockefellers to ride the trails in to Ampersand Pond. Avery Rockefeller had bought Ampersand Pond from the Santa Clara Lumber Company in the 1930s. Ed recalls riding with her on some of those early trips: "Mother would always tell me to ride along the side of the road so the caretaker wouldn't see tracks from more than one horse, because she was really the only one allowed to go in there."

Clarence was not fond of horses or of their impact on the trails. But while Ferne sometimes fussed over her husband's stubbornness, others admired the quality. For Clarence was now well known in Adirondack circles as a man of straight talk, strong principles, and inexhaustible energy. Those characteristics, in combination with his vast knowledge about the region, made him an authority on the Adirondacks. Occasionally, they also got him into hot water.

"There was one longtime commissioner at the Adirondack Park Agency," says Clarence,

who made a lot of enemies among the antienvironmentalists. When they burned her barn down, I began to suspect some of those people might try to burn my place too, because I'm a target. Have been for a long time. But I try not to antagonize anybody. I like to speak to issues rather than personalities.

One of the things I admired about Paul Schaefer was that he could stand up at a meeting, be the only one there on the side of the conservationists, and yet he would never get personal about it. He stuck to the issue. It's a great skill. You have to be really brave to be able to do that in some situations. I remember him getting up one time among a group of engineers who were promoting flood dams in the Adirondacks. He said, "We're not about to allow engineers to make mill ponds out of the Adirondack streams."

Another fellow who was a real antienvironmentalist once told me, "I attended a meeting over in Malone where they were talking about flooding land on the Salmon River. They were going to build a dam on it. Paul was the only man there that was against it. He stood up in that meeting and do you know, by the end of it, they all voted not to dam the thing." He said, "That guy has got power. He was the only guy there that stood up." Well, I have to give Paul credit for having the ability to do that. He was really devoted to the Adirondacks.

Clarence wrote letters constantly to nudge, to prod, and often to lambaste those whose ideas he felt would be harmful to the region. There were few who held positions of influence in the Adirondacks who did not hear from him sooner or later. Commissioners, governors, rangers, recreationists, and bureaucrats were all the same in the face of a perceived threat to his beloved wilderness.

This letter writing was an act of lifelong devotion for both Clarence and Ferne. "You've got to have input," says Clarence. "It's the only way you're ever going to change anything." Dick Beamish recalls seeing the couple, sitting side by side at the dinner table, writing letters. It was a Petty tradition that stretched all the way back to Ellsworth, who had written the governor in 1901, protesting what Bernhard Fernow was doing to the forests around Upper Saranac Lake. To this day Clarence uses a 1934 Remington typewriter to compose his letters. A few years ago he had to search out someone who could specially cut ribbons to fit the machine.

One fairly recent issue that Clarence blasted the DEC on repeatedly was the department's Adopt-a-Natural-Resource stewardship program:

> They had an application for snowmobilers to adopt snowmobile trails. Snowmobile trails! A snowmobile trail is *not* a natural resource. This is the sort of nibble-away process where they try to make people

believe that snowmobile owners are interested in natural resources. Maybe some of them are, but they're damn sure making a mess of things in a lot of places with these big machines. Some of them want to be able to go everywhere.

There's been a big fight over the disabled wanting access to everything by road. It's been tied up in a lawsuit for some time now. People were going in with bulldozers to improve the trails and so forth. The reason snowmobiles were allowed in in the first place was because they would be on the snow and they wouldn't be doing anything to the land, because it was covered. Now they want to use bulldozers. The DEC is not paying enough attention to their employees. Some of them have been issuing permits that have directly violated article 14. If I go out snowshoeing or skiing, I don't want to get run over by a damn snowmobile. The racket alone destroys the silence of the woods. New York State is thirty-two million acres and there's only three million acres total of Forest Preserve. Why in hell can't we keep that from being overrun by these things?

You have to keep putting pressure on if you're going to save anything. When I was with the DEC, a lot of my colleagues were foresters, and they were wood butchers. We used to argue endlessly over this. They felt that the maximum production of saw timber and pulp wood was the way a forester should go. I belonged to the Society of American Foresters for thirty-eight years, and I finally dropped out because all they would talk about in their meetings was the production of timber. I used to say, "Look, standing trees are a hell of a lot more valuable financially just standing there than they are once you chew them up into wall board."

Some of the people in Albany used to look at me as sort of an outcast. It was because a lot of stuff would come down to me, passed down the line when it was a sticky question that the governor or the commissioner didn't want to answer directly. One time my brother Bill took Governor Rockefeller on a horse trip up into Cold River. They got as far as Shattuck Clearing and something came up and the governor had to leave, so they went in there with a helicopter and picked him up and took him out.

Later, Rockefeller made a statement that he thought the area ought to be made more accessible to the public. Well, the statement appeared in the papers, and one member of the press wrote and said, "What did the governor mean by more accessible to the public?" It should have been answered by the governor's people, because they knew what he meant. But it went to the commissioner, and he bucked it to the Division of Lands and Forests, and it ended up on my desk to answer for the governor.

But rather than stick my neck out along with the governor's, I figured out a weasel way of saying that it would be preferable if we had better maintenance of the trails. And damned if he didn't sign it. The Conservation Department was even commended for replying to the press inquiry. I knew perfectly well what Rockefeller meant. But he didn't dare say it, because what he meant was there should be more people going up there, and to do that, he'd have to change those horse trails into vehicle trails.

One of those Clarence argued with on occasion was his brother Bill:

A lot of the businesspeople in the Adirondacks were anti-DEC. One of the first things I remember people jumping on the DEC for was a regulation that the fish and game people put through that required someone who killed a deer to bring it out whole or at least in pieces that showed the sex. Before, you butchered the deer right there and put it in a pack basket and carried it out. But a lot of people, what they were doing was they'd kill a doe and then they'd have the head of a buck they had killed earlier or an old hide that had the sex on it, and they'd put that on the pack basket and they'd walk out. Of course, nobody could catch them. This was the kind of thing that Bill was trying to ease off on, because he knew they were all against the DEC. Once the Adirondack Park Agency (APA) came in, then they were all against that.

One time we had a pretty good argument over a road. The state allowed a certain amount of Forest Preserve land to be taken for the purpose of straightening roads. For safety reasons, Bill wanted to straighten this road that would have meant cutting down a good stand of big pine. Well I went up there when it was slippery and there was slush on the road, and I drove forty-five miles an hour right around that curve. It didn't bother me any. So I said, hell, this is no problem—it's a sharp curve all right—but there's no need of making a race track out of it and losing all those pines. But Bill said to cut right through there. We had those kinds of differences of opinion a lot.

Bill was the forest ranger in charge of Cold River country in the late 1960s. This was one of the Adirondacks' most remote and wild places, yet he was permitting some questionable uses. Administrators were driving vehicles on trails that were supposed to be strictly foot paths. Bridges, stables, and horse trails were being constructed. Clarence and Bill argued over many of them. Clarence's feelings about these sorts of intrusions had clearly changed since his CCC days, when he actually oversaw the construction of jeep trails, bridges, and other backcountry accoutrements. Now he could see the handwriting on the wall as the Adirondacks began to be overrun with tourists, developers, and recreationists, all demanding comforts and improvements.

In addition to responding to concerns that would be bucked down to his office from the commissioner or from Lands and Forests, Clarence spent much of the mid-1960s doing inspections for the department:

> There were all sorts of things. I had to check for illegal advertising signs put up in violation of the Sign Law of 1924. Or they might have a problem internally or with people working for the department out in the field. They'd have to send someone to inspect the work. I did a lot of inspections in the western part of the state.
>
> I was still connected with the Division of Lands and Forests in the fire control unit, because of my work as representative for the Interstate Forest Fire Control Compact. The Forest Service wanted surveys made of the results of fires that had burned in New York State. So I would go out and take a map of where the fire occurred, and I'd run grid lines across it and check every tree along the line to find out whether they died or were still living. I was just stretched out with all these sorts of things.

Clarence would fly back to the office in Albany, first at the old campus site and later at the new office at 50 Wolf Road, where he would prepare his reports. Then he'd go home to the North Country.

Busy as always, Clarence was about to get even busier as a new job loomed on the horizon. The impetus that would propel him into the new position and resurrect his work at the Joint Legislative Committee earlier in the decade would come from an unexpected source: Laurance Rockefeller.

CHAPTER 17

Laurance's Modest Proposal

In the 1950s the five sons of John D. Rockefeller Jr. were the closest thing America had to a royal family. Overseeing a vast web of interconnecting family interests, the brothers were among the most powerful men in America. In addition to wealth, they inherited from their father a sense of duty to serve the nation that had given them so much. John D. Rockefeller Jr. had been the world's greatest philanthropist, giving away an astonishing half-billion dollars during his lifetime.

Rockefeller's sons were raised in a manner designed to teach them that philanthropy was the family calling. They were each given an allowance but were obligated to turn a percentage of it over to charity. Another facet of their education involved traveling the country, visiting wilderness areas and developing a strong attachment to places such as Grand Teton National Park in Jackson Hole, Wyoming, to which John D. Rockefeller Jr. had donated thirty-five thousand acres.

Laurance and Nelson were the closest of the five Rockefeller brothers. Just two years apart, they were inseparable as children and throughout their lives. As youngsters, they had jointly decided that their rather effete sounding names were not manly enough, so they adopted the practice of calling each other "Bill."

During one college summer, the two "Bills" talked themselves aboard as crew on Sir Wilfred T. Grenfell's sailing ship as the famous missionary headed for the Arctic. On the return trip, fogbound off the Maine coast, Laurance was suddenly stricken with appendicitis. The captain refused to sail through the fog to get Laurance to a hospital. But

Nelson told him, "Bounce your foghorn off the cliffs out there. That way we can judge the safe distance by the echo and make the harbor." Still dubious, the captain at last gave in to the forceful Nelson, bringing Laurance safely into port and probably saving his life.

Like Clarence, Laurance Rockefeller had been hooked on aviation since boyhood. While still in his twenties, he had given a crucial infusion of funds to a struggling, young Eastern Airlines. During World War II he spent four years in the navy, crisscrossing the country as an aircraft production troubleshooter. After the war he invested heavily in McDonnell Aircraft Corporation, which merged with Douglas, becoming one of the country's top three defense contractors. He was also an early investor in ITEK, the company that made cameras for the famous U-2 spy plane. It almost seemed, in some uncanny way, that extremely wealthy men, such as Laurance Rockefeller and Averell Harriman, with an interest in aviation were destined to have major influences on the course of Clarence's life.

Laurance had a long history of interest, too, in conservation projects. Some years earlier, he had given five thousand acres on St. John Island in the Caribbean to the federal government for the Virgin Islands National Park. And his "Rock-resorts," one of the world's most elegant resort chains, was a stunning example of his attempt to combine his conservationist heart with his businessman's savvy.

Like most New Yorkers, Clarence was dumbstruck to wake up on the morning of July 30, 1967, to the news that Laurance Rockefeller, then chairman of the State Council of Parks, had proposed the creation of an Adirondack Mountains National Park. It was to be made up of one million one hundred twenty thousand acres of state land and six hundred thousand acres of adjoining private land to be purchased over the next fifteen years by the federal government. It would become the third largest national park in the nation and would include the High Peaks area and a good deal of the lands and waters that Clarence called home. The settlements of Saranac Lake, Lake Placid, Indian Lake, Fourth Lake-Inlet, and Blue Mountain Lake would become inholdings within the national park.

The major hurdle was how the scheme would get around the New

York State Constitution. Article 14 had become a firewall of protection for the Adirondacks against politicians, lumbermen, developers, and others over the years who had their own, largely economic reasons for wishing to get rid of Forever Wild. National park administrators, on the other hand, were famously subject to the whims of political pressure. Adirondack preservationists, who had been pleased with the example set by Howard Zahniser's Wilderness Act of 1964, were nevertheless cognizant that a wilderness designation made by Congress could just as easily be taken away by Congress. They preferred to rely on the security of wilderness protected by constitutional amendment rather than by legislators.

The preservationists were hardly alone in their resistance to Laurance's proposal. In fact, the idea served to unite virtually all Adirondack interest groups against the scheme. Residents of the Adirondacks, who had for years been at loggerheads over the proper direction the state park should take, suddenly found common ground.

It is almost in the Adirondack character to resist any suggested extension of federal power. While the possibility of increased tourism was dangled as an enticement, the truth was that the park was already attracting millions of visitors a year. One of the factors that led Laurance to make his proposal in the first place was the completion of I-87 (the Northway) in 1967. The new highway placed the park within a few hours drive of millions of people, and developers of second-home communities were poised to cash in on the Adirondacks.

But while Laurance Rockefeller worried about too much development, others feared that a federal prohibition on building in a National Park would make the region's economy too dependent upon a single industry: tourism. For their part, sportsmen clearly understood that hunters were generally banned from national parks. Also threatened were the owners of large estates and hunting preserves, for Rockefeller had included a provision that would limit individual private inholdings to three acres. Lumbermen, too, were against the idea because it recommended condemning densely forested private land for inclusion in the park.

The grand plan was publicly eviscerated. By Christmas Laurance was backpedaling furiously, and the idea of an Adirondack Mountains National Park was as extinct as the giant Adirondack beaver of eons past.

But the entire episode was to serve an important function in the annals of Adirondack Park protection. Nelson recognized that his brother's proposal had aroused the state and forced its citizens to confront the park's problems. In response, he announced that he would appoint a "distinguished group of New Yorkers" to determine what the future course of the Adirondacks should be.

In this effort, Nelson Rockefeller was to show both persistence and patience. He would take a step-by-step approach to achieve state-supervised land-use planning for the region, despite fierce opposition from Adirondack legislators, local officials, and developers. The first step was the creation in 1968 of the Temporary Study Commission on the Future of the Adirondacks, whose principle recommendation was the creation of an APA, which the state legislature and governor did in 1971. The APA's first task was to draw up a master plan for the state-owned portion of the Forest Preserve. This was completed in 1972 and was approved by the governor as state policy. The APA's next task was to establish a zoning map and development controls for the park's private lands—a plan approved by the legislature and enacted into law in 1973.

Clarence approved of the governor's approach: "He did a very good job, but I think his emphasis on the environment came from his brother Laurance. Laurance was the one who tried to get a national park here. That was what really stimulated Nelson to establish the Temporary Study Commission. I don't think he would ever have done that unless his brother had pushed him."

Among the "distinguished group of New Yorkers" that the governor selected to serve on the commission was the man who would eventually become its chairman in 1970, Harold K. Hochschild.

Hochschild was a fascinating character. His family had a long association with the Adirondacks, dating back to his first visit in 1904. He spent many subsequent summer vacations at the family's estate at Eagle Nest, site of the mid-1800s home of the swashbuckling adventurer and writer Ned Buntline.

The Hochschild family business centered around a huge mining corporation, American Metal Company (later Amax, Inc.). This was the basis for their incredible wealth. But Harold never liked to talk about business with his Eagle Nest crowd. The Adirondacks were special in their own right and the center of his personal passions.

Harold's brother-in-law, Boris Vasilievich Sergievsky, had been a captain in the Imperial Russian Air Force and a World War I fighter ace awarded the St. George's Cross. He had even flown with Lindbergh. Boris came to Eagle Nest in 1930 as a chief pilot for the Sikorsky Aircraft Company. Arriving in a Sikorsky S-38 seaplane that the family was thinking about buying, Boris swept Harold's fortyish sister, Gertrude, off her feet and married into the family.

From then on, the gatherings at Eagle Nest took on an international flavor. Boris's Russian friends included a ballerina, an Arctic explorer, a princess related to the imperial family, and Alexandra Tolstoy, the famous writer's youngest daughter. Mingling with this odd and constantly changing assortment was Harold's own circle of business and political associates. Among them were American diplomats such as George Kennan and Adlai Stevenson; perennial socialist candidate for president, Norman Thomas; various African prime ministers; a chaplain of the South African prison system; and other figures whom Harold met as part of his duties running the family's interests around the world. Dinner table conversations raged in English and Russian.

A vigorous man, Harold rode for miles through the woods around Eagle Nest on horseback every day and swam across the lake and back every evening. Once a summer, he swam seven miles through the chain of lakes from the Blue Mountain Steamboat office to the Marion River Carry Landing. The swim usually took five and one-half to six hours.

As a youngster in 1906, Harold accompanied two college-age acquaintances as they drove the first motorcar ever to arrive in the central Adirondacks (a 1905 Winton that suffered five flat tires on the trip). He was a close friend of the entrepreneur and builder of the first Great Camp, William West Durant. Harold's father, Berthold, had purchased the Eagle Nest property from Durant, who had built a golf course and country club and subdivided it into many lots. Fortunately, the development never occurred, thanks probably to the Hochschilds. Harold went on to write a classic history of the Adirondacks, *Township 34*, and to establish a collection of Adirondackana that, under his guidance, grew into the Adirondack Museum in Blue Mountain Lake.

Clarence developed a close relationship with this extraordinary man. "Harold asked me to arrange to get the Temporary Study Commission members into West Canada Lake, which was one of the potential wilderness areas," remembers Clarence.

> He wanted us to go in there and see what it was like, because none of them had seen it. So I got Herb Helms, who was flying out of Long Lake at the time. He'd flown Hochschild before, even though he was on an entirely different side of the fence. Herb and I were also on different sides of the fence, but we worked together all right. [Herb Helms seems to have spent a great deal of time undermining his own occupation by flying around those who were working, among other things, to forbid planes from landing on wilderness lakes.]
>
> Watson Pomeroy was in the group, and Dick Lawrence and Peter Paine, and the whole bunch who were on the Temporary Study Commission. My job was to see that they got in and out okay and had a place to stay for several days during their meetings up at Old Forge. Herb came over, and we flew all this gang into West Canada Lake and back, back and forth.
>
> One of the interesting things was that Harold was never personally attacked or singled out as a target that I remember. I think it was a matter of people being almost afraid to attack him because he had all this money and a lot of folks were dependent on him. Many of the people around Blue Mountain Lake and the museum and so forth were funded by Hochschild. He used to invite all sorts to his home at Eagle Nest, politicians and artists and celebrities. He had a nice wine cellar there and a boathouse on the shore that was built to accommodate a DC-3 on floats. He used that to bring people in and out.
>
> He was a nice fellow—one of the best friends I had. He was really knowledgeable about the Adirondacks and did everything in his power to protect the park, yet he was in a corporation, a mining business that certainly did a lot of things that were antienvironmental when you got right down to it. He was the head of one of the biggest mining outfits in

Clarence and Harold Jerry at Henderson Monument on trip to Cliff Mountain, 1977. Courtesy of Gary Randorf.

the world. A number of times, I had to go down to New York City for meetings at the headquarters of his mining company.

He told me once how when he was younger, he spent two years in China for the company. And one time he had to walk into this place that his guide didn't really know, but the fellow kept saying, "Over the next hill, over the next hill." Harold said they walked over forty miles. It was the only time in his life he walked forty miles in a day.

In 1970, the year Hochschild took over as chairman of the commission, the legislature created a bureaucratic behemoth called the Department of Environmental Conservation. The move was in response to various environmental problems that were becoming of increasing concern to the state. The new DEC, as it was called, absorbed several state agencies, including the old Conservation Department. Some saw the governor's new creation as a way for him to favor Laurence Rockefeller's promotion of mass recreational opportunities in the park by transferring facilities such as ski areas and public campsites to the Office of Parks and Recreation. But Hochschild made a direct plea to the governor that he not make any policy decisions until the commission's work was completed. Rockefeller agreed.

The commission's staff, under its executive secretary, Harold A.

Jerry Jr., compiled extensive field reports and studies that would ultimately provide the commission with the basis for its hundreds of recommendations. One staff member of the new commission had once been given a little birch bark canoe by Governor Rockefeller on Upper Saranac Lake more than fifty years earlier. His name was Clarence Petty.

CHAPTER 18

A Walk in the Woods

The staff of the Temporary Study Commission included professional ecologists, economic planners, and wildlife experts. Two of the earliest employees, operating under the oversight of the executive secretary, Harold Jerry, were George Davis and Clarence Petty.

"Our office was downtown," Clarence remembers,

> almost in the same place where the old Conservation Department used to be, across from the railroad station. We were on the second, or maybe it was the third floor. George and I used to run up the stairs, because we would spend so much time on maps and stuff that we really needed the exercise.
>
> About two weeks before Laurance Rockefeller came out with his national park proposal, I had received a call from one of the fellows down in the Senate office, wanting to know if he could borrow the maps we'd prepared during our wilderness studies for the Joint Legislative Committee. He said, "I think we can help you on that." I didn't know what he meant at the time. But when Rockefeller's proposal appeared in the newspaper, I knew then he had used our study as a guide. It was nothing like what we'd prepared. He cut right through areas of the Forest Preserve, and it was a mess. Nobody thought much of it, least of all the people in conservation.
>
> Harold Jerry, who had been a state senator and lost his job, was hired by the Conservation Department to write a rebuttal of Laurance Rockefeller's plan. I was asked to work with him in preparing a treatise on why we should or shouldn't go for the national park. That's where I

first met Harold Jerry. As a result of that, when the governor decided to appoint a Temporary Study Commission, Harold asked me to work with them at least one day a week. The next week I went to two days a week, and by the third week I was on full time, because Harold kept asking the commissioner if I could be borrowed. So I worked

Harold Jerry and Clarence on Skylight, 1979. Courtesy of Gary Randorf.

with them on almost the same damn stuff that I'd been doing for the Joint Legislative Committee, and I worked right through until the commission released its report in January 1971.

Thirty years later, Harold Jerry recalled working with the commission's first two employees, Clarence and George Davis:

During the winter of 1968–1969 we decided to take a field trip, which was the first field trip of the study committee. On a Sunday, George, Clarence, and I went to Saranac Lake and checked into a hotel. In those days it was possible to call the FAA in Albany on a telephone and get a weather forecast. You can't do that now, but you could back then. From the hotel on Sunday night, we called the FAA and told them we were state employees and we had to go over to the top of Mount Marcy on the next day. We asked what the weather report was for the top of the mountain. I will never forget the reply of the FAA employee. He said, "If the cold bothers you, your luck has run out." I said, "What in the world do you mean?" He says, "It's going to start raining anytime. It's going to rain for the next forty-eight to seventy-two hours."

Well, I said to Clarence and George, "We've got to make up our minds now. We're going to cancel this trip or we're going to go." I said this was the first trip of the Study Commission, and it seems to me we ought to set a pattern for all state trips that are scheduled, regardless of the weather. So we got up the next morning and started for the top of Marcy. It was pouring, and it rained all day Monday, and it rained until the late afternoon on Tuesday.

We went into Marcy by way of Adirondak Loj. The snow was still on the ground, and as we approached the top several hours later, it was getting deeper and deeper. Finally, as we climbed up the peak of Marcy from the north side, the snow was probably four feet deep, and it was wet and it was raining. George had snowshoes made by his great aunt and Clarence had an old pair, and I had a brand-new pair that had never been used before. We stopped when Clarence's snowshoes broke, and he took a branch off a tree nearby and used it to try to wire them together. This was the first of thirteen breaks suffered by the party as a whole.

We went right over the top of Marcy and down the south side. We were soaking wet and the snow was coming down. We were breaking through with every step. We decided to make camp in a lean-to. I wasn't really too smart about building fires in the pouring rain, so I sort of watched Clarence and George try to do this.

The whole thing was a disaster from beginning to end. No matter where we put the fire, it went out, or the smoke got so bad that we had to move it. We tried to put it under the overhang, but if we got it out too far, the rain would put it out. If we pushed it further back, the smoke got so bad we couldn't stay inside. So we compromised and put it halfway in and halfway out. But it didn't work, so we let the fire go out, and the next morning, we were all very, very cold.

This was 1969, and we had on clothes from that period. The backpacks were canvas, which we covered with plastic as best we could. I had a cotton hat, as did Clarence, and we had on jackets and wool pants. The jackets were not much help after the first few hours. We got pretty wet.

On the second day, on the way out, along the Opalescent River, my snowshoe broke and everyone was very excited and pleased, because it established me as one of the party. Clarence and George had each had several breaks, but my snowshoes, being brand-new, had not yet broken.

This was the first trip of the Study Commission, and I think by the end of the work, we had had thirty-two field trips without a single cancellation. The policy had been established by that first trip, and we never deviated from it. Though the conditions were miserable, our morale was very high. We thought we were in a great job, which we were, and we never got disgusted or discouraged, although we did get very, very wet. Clarence always moved along as if we were out for a stroll in the sun.

Jerry also related what was to become a quite famous story among people who knew Clarence well—the boot story. It took place in the Mount Marcy region a number of years later:

The story begins at Panther Gorge lean-to. Clarence, Gary Randorf, and I spent the night there, Gary climbing Haystack after our arrival in the late afternoon. The next day, Gary and I climbed Skylight and Mount Marcy. Clarence climbed Skylight with us. We had a busy day and we worked hard. Clarence was having trouble with cramps in his legs, which was why he only did one peak.

Clarence had to leave early the next morning because he had a meeting someplace that he had to attend. So when Gary and I woke up at about five or six o'clock, he had already left and was on the trail. This trail was from Panther Gorge, out across Marcy Swamp, to Elk Lake. As Gary and I moved along, we suddenly came upon an old boot in the middle of the trail. It was an above-the-ankle boot with a hobnail sole, obviously a lumberman's boot, belonging to someone who had abandoned it in the woods.

Clarence, who was ahead of us, had taken the boot and placed it in the middle of the trail. In it there was a pencil sticking up and on the pencil he had affixed a piece of paper in the form of a pennant. And on the pennant he had written, "The last hike."

This was our first warning that maybe Clarence was through climbing high peaks. He spent an awful long time in the woods after that on brooks and rivers and trails, low slopes, and so forth, but I'm not sure that he ever climbed another high peak again. I'll never forget the fascination we had with that boot when we found it on the trail.

Hobnail boot with note from Clarence, "The last hike," on trail between Panther Gorge and Elk Lake, 1979. Courtesy of Gary Randorf.

Jerry was unable to put a precise date on this trip, and hesitated to tell the story without one, since it possibly signified the end of Clarence's High Peaks climbing. But Gary Randorf remembers clearly that the trip took place in 1979, after he had become executive director of the Adirondack Council two years earlier. Clarence was seventy-four at the time. For several years running, the three men maintained the tradition of an annual hiking trip. Clarence's recall of the outing generally coincided with Harold's, except that Clarence said he did in fact climb in the High Peaks a few more times after the incident. But the story of that boot and its cryptic message in the middle of the trail is vintage Clarence Petty.

George Davis has his own memories of working with Clarence in the state's remotest backcountry during those heady days. He first met Clarence in early 1969, when George was assigned to the Temporary Study Commission as staff ecologist:

> Clarence, of course, was a delight. We hit it off right away, despite our age difference of approximately forty years. Clarence's basic assignment was to teach me about the geography of the Adirondacks, so that I could draw my ecological conclusions. Harold Jerry had instructed us to spend a minimum of two and preferably three days each week on the ground in the Adirondacks. This was certainly one of the greatest assignments anyone with an interest in fieldwork could ever draw.
>
> I had already gone over all of the past studies of the Adirondacks and had a pretty good theoretical knowledge of the lay of the land. Clarence had studied the Adirondacks on the ground and from the air for decades and knew practically the whole park intimately. Our first field trip together was to a little-known area northwest of Stillwater Reservoir, which later became classified as the Pepperbox Wilderness.

This was an area that my map studies had indicated could qualify for wilderness, but which had never been recommended for wilderness designation in the past. I wanted to see why not.

I soon learned that Clarence liked to start his days early. He wanted us to be in a motel Sunday night in March 1969, and then on the road headed to the Pepperbox by 5 A.M. at the latest. I was certainly too young to argue with Clarence, who was, as far as I was concerned, the guru of the Adirondacks.

Thus we left Old Forge at 5 A.M. and headed up through Big Moose to the outlet of Stillwater Reservoir, where we donned our snowshoes and headed into the remote backcountry. It turned out to be a beautiful day, with the sun shining and not a cloud in sight. The snowshoeing was wonderful. It was an area of lowland with many stringer meadows that enabled us to avoid the dense swamp vegetation.

We came out of the woods and back to our car at approximately 4 P.M., an eleven-hour workday. I started driving down the road to head back to our motel, and when I got to Big Moose, perhaps fifteen minutes later, I pulled into the bar, for I wanted a beer. Clarence immediately became very nervous and asked me what I was doing. I said, "Well, I feel like having a beer. It seemed like a good idea." And he just kind of shook his head and couldn't believe it. He said, "You can't do that. It's not quitting time yet." I pointed out that we had put in an eleven-hour day and that even though it wasn't five o'clock, it seemed like that might be enough for one day. And he said, "But it's not quitting time yet and also, we've got a state car. We can't park a state car at a bar."

Well, I decided I really wanted a beer, regardless of that, and I had no qualms that we were doing anything wrong. Clarence muttered, as I was to learn Clarence often does when hit with a situation that he thinks is totally absurd. And I got out of the car and headed toward the bar, kinda looking at Clarence, hoping he would get out. When he saw that I was serious about this whole matter, he did indeed get out of the car. But instead of coming toward the bar, he went to the trunk of the car and opened it. He pulled out his bright orange, unmarked raincoat.

I said, "What in the world are you doing?" and he muttered again. But I realized that he had his conservation department uniform on and did not want to be seen wearing it in a bar. At any rate, in we went, and

George Davis, Clarence, and Greenleaf Chase on Wright Mountain, 1972. Courtesy of Gary Randorf.

I had my beer while Clarence had a glass of branch water, as he called it, still muttering most of the time we were there. We left about five o'clock on good terms, but both of us understanding the other a little bit better.

Clarence was soon to learn that this was going to be standard operating procedure for commission field trips from that point on. I don't think, however, he ever fully accepted this procedure.

George Davis is almost certainly one of the few who can honestly say he ever had a drink with Clarence in a bar, even though Clarence was only drinking water. Despite George's bad habits, Clarence speaks warmly of their association.

The trips that George and Harold took with Clarence during this period only increased their awe at their guide's knowledge of the Adirondack backcountry. There seemed to be, literally, no place that Clarence was not familiar with. It became something of an ongoing contest with the two men to see if they could come up with some spot where Clarence had never been.

During their studies of the proposed wilderness area northwest of Stillwater Reservoir, George and Harold asked Clarence one day if he had ever been to Pepperbox Pond itself, an impossibly remote spot. Clarence thought for a moment, then said: "That's a terrible mosquito hole. I wouldn't be caught dead going in there."

So George and Harold crossed the dam at Stillwater and hiked northwest into the mosquito hole that was Pepperbox Pond. When they got there, they made up a sign and mounted it on a tree. The sign read: "This is the only spot in the Adirondacks where Clarence Petty has never been."

Clarence kneeling, photographing, with George Davis and Greenleaf Chase on APA outing at Scott's Clearing, 1972. Courtesy of Gary Randorf.

Davis had one more Clarence story to tell:

> We had Clarence at a series of New York City board meetings of the commission, and some of the staff would go out every night to a local bar. Of course, Clarence would never join us. But one night he did. We tricked him a little bit actually, and we got him between several of us in a rounded booth where he couldn't get out. We sat around drinking beer, and Clarence drinking his water for a couple of hours. And, of course, we were feeling pretty good at that point. And I have to admit that although Clarence grumbled during the whole thing, there was no doubt in my mind that in his own way he really enjoyed that type of very non-Clarence behavior. I don't think we could get him to ever do it again, but he did enjoy that night, being out with the boys.

Clarence on Giant Mountain, 1975.
Photograph by Nancy Morton Trautmann,
courtesy of Richard Beamish.

In December of 1970 Chairman Hochschild submitted the Temporary Study Commission's report to the governor. It consisted of a summary report and a separate volume of technical reports. Among the main recommendations were that article 14, section 1, of the constitution (Forever Wild) remain unchanged, that a wild, scenic, and recreational rivers system be established in the park, and that "An independent, bipartisan Adirondack Park Agency should be created by statute with general power over the use of private and public land in the Park."

The commission report presented a bleak forecast on the future of the park if action was not taken at once:

> After two years of study, it is clear to the Commission that a crisis faces the Adirondacks. Failure to take prompt action will mean the certain destruction of the Adirondack Park as it is known to the millions of people who visit the Park each year. . . . With the present ownership pattern, the prospects for maintaining the Adirondacks as we know them are bleak. More than 50 per cent of the privately owned land is held by 626 individuals and corporations, each of whom owns 500 acres or more. In short, the future of the Park is to a large measure in the hands of a small group of private landowners. . . . If immediate action is not taken, many critical tracts will be broken up within five years and almost all of the large blocks of private forest land will be de-

veloped with second homes within less than a generation. There will be no Adirondack Park as we know it today.

A fierce struggle over passage of the governor's legislation was to ensue. After the APA land-use plan was passed in 1973, the Adirondack heartland would erupt as the battle was joined to find a middle ground between a constitutionally protected wilderness and the busy world of humanity that surrounded it. The ferocity of the emotions involved would ignite the state.

"Home rule," shouted local citizens. "No taxation without representation," replied Assemblyman Peter A. A. Berle. He reminded New Yorkers outside the park that it was their money the state paid in taxes to local governments on the state-owned Forest Preserve. George Davis received anonymous phone calls threatening to burn his house down. The town of Clare voted to secede from the park. Truckloads of manure were dumped on APA property, and one man, caught in the act, actually did attempt to burn down the new agency headquarters.

Clarence was sixty-five years old in 1970 when the Study Commission submitted its report. He had been thinking about retirement and a long-postponed vacation to Alaska. In June 1971 he left the Conservation Department and headed north. His respite from the building Adirondack controversy would be short-lived.

CHAPTER 19

Alaska

Clarence's interest in Alaska predated his meeting with Bob Marshall in 1931. As young boys running their traplines and snowshoeing to school, Clarence and Bill had often talked about Alaska. The Adirondack wilderness was a remote place to grow up, yet they wondered what it must have been like two hundred years earlier.

"We wanted even more wilderness than we had," says Clarence. "They had animals up in Alaska that we didn't, caribou and grizzlies and huge salmon. I read a lot about it, and I always wanted to go, but the place is so huge and it takes so long to get there that I had to wait until I had a whole summer free to do it."

That wait turned out to be nearly a lifetime, or at least in Clarence's case, two-thirds of a lifetime. A free summer was something he had never experienced. His life had been one long succession of jobs, with almost no time in between. Not until he retired in 1971 did he finally have the time to travel. Even then, that first retirement would last only a few months. He had barely begun receiving Social Security when he would be called back to work at the APA and would have to scramble to go off the government program until his second retirement in 1974. Brimming with excitement, Clarence and Ferne headed north:

> My son Ed agreed to take care of Ferne's horses, and we bought a little Trotwood trailer and headed out. Our rig didn't have a shower or refrigerator or much of anything else in it. While we were up at Haines, Alaska, where the inland ferry comes in, we got to talking with some

people who had an Airstream trailer, and they invited us in to look at it. Well we thought, boy, this is the thing to have. It had a refrigerator, shower, gas stove, and heater, everything compact. Soon as we got back home, Ferne started looking in all the magazines, and she found one for sale down in New Jersey. We drove down and bought it. It wasn't very big, but it had everything we needed.

That first trip, we learned that you never go over the Alcan Highway without busting your windshield. All the trucks flying over that road kick up big stones, and you always had a broken windshield. They didn't even require you to replace them—you simply drove with them broken.

Our first trip we spent a lot of time just looking around. We went to Fairbanks and up to Circle City. There were only eleven people there and about four buildings. We wanted to get up to Fort Yukon but couldn't make the connection with the pilot, so we came on back. I used to wonder where all the Piper Cubs and Aeroncas went. Well, boy, they're up there. You'd drive along the road and there'd be a propeller sticking out. They used the road to land on. There's more people have planes up there—Hood Lake had a greater concentration of float planes than anyplace in the world. When you realize New York State has thirty-two million acres and Alaska has three hundred and sixty-eight million with very few roads, well . . . airplanes are the only way to go.

That first trip, I was supposed to take a flight physical in the summer. I got a list of examiners from the FAA at Anchorage and got a physical from a Dr. Jones at Haines. He said, "If you want a job, I've got one for you flying passengers." I guess if I'd been alone, I would have just stayed there forever. Alaska has that effect on people. It's a tough country to make a living in, yet we found people up there, kids that went up for the summer, and they'd work in the canning factories and go home with five, ten thousand dollars in their pocket.

Clarence made a half-dozen trips to Alaska through the 1970s and 1980s. The great northern wilderness pulled him in like a salmon on a line. He felt instantly at home. Gary Randorf, who would work with Clarence at the APA shortly after Clarence's first visit to Alaska, vividly recalls the effect the state had upon the Adirondack native: "Clarence fell in love with Alaska. Next to his great love for the

Adirondacks, all the letters he's written, all the money he's poured into protecting it, he's spent probably the next amount of time, as far as trying to protect another place, focusing on Alaska. They always tried to do the trip on the cheap, taking food with them and camping out. I think they did trips up there and back spending something like five or six hundred dollars maximum."

On one of their early trips, Ferne could not go along, so Clarence packed everything into the back of a pickup truck and lived out of it the entire time. Instead of taking nine days to drive up, he "willed it right through," driving seven and eight hundred miles a day, making it in five days. With the extra time saved, he left his car at the airport in Anchorage and flew to Katmai National Monument (Land of Ten Thousand Smokes), because someone had told him that it was true "wild country." Another bush plane then flew him to the inlet of remote Naknek Lake. As he had once felt upon returning to the Adirondacks after living in New York City so many years earlier, Clarence again felt completely content and in his element:

> I was alone. I took my camping equipment and enough food to last eight or nine days. Where the rapids dump into Naknek Lake is where all the grizzly bears are. You've probably seen pictures of grizzlies catching salmon there on TV. It was on this trip, about 1980, that one of Dr. Craighead's sons, John, and his wife camped right next to me. John and his brother spent a lot of time studying the grizzlies in Yellowstone, made some documentaries, and so forth. Harold Jerry told me how he went down there with them one time. They were out shooting grizzlies at the dump with tranquilizing darts so they could put a tracking collar on them. They were doing it at night and they didn't have any lights or anything. So they'd shoot a bear and of course they wouldn't know where the thing would run. I guess there were bears going every which way, and Harold said it was pretty nerve-racking.
>
> There were grizzlies all over the place up on the Naknek. I set my tent up about fifty feet from the shore of the lake and put my stuff, toothpaste and everything, in a cache about thirty feet in the air. I

didn't take anything into the tent. In the morning, just as soon as it was light, I'd look out, and here's grizzlies walking along the shore within fifty feet of me. But I knew as long as they were after food, they probably wouldn't bother me.

You're really out in the backcountry there. We were near one of the places on the DEW [Distant Early Warning] line. They flew us in in a Grumman Widgeon. Coming out, there was a bunch of Germans with us who had been camping not far from where I was. They overloaded the plane. I mentioned it to the guy. I said, "You're gonna have a time. We're loaded too far forward." He says, "Oh, I think we can make it. We'll try it anyway." So it's overcast and we take off, and we must have gone more than a mile before we could get off because he was so heavy. This was a huge lake. By the time we were three hundred feet up, we were miles and miles from shore. There's not a damn device in the plane that you could float with. They're supposed to have flotation devices, but because it was a float plane, they could get away with it legally. But if that thing ever went down and you damaged the hull and it sank, no way you could survive. I said to the guy, "I can see why Alaska has the highest accident rate."

It's a huge place compared with the Adirondacks, and different, with all the animals. You are on your own, and that's what I liked about it; one of the real values of wilderness, that you have to recognize that it's your fault if you get into trouble. Like Rondeau used to say, "You got no business cutting yourself with an ax."

On several of their trips, Clarence and Ferne took along fishing gear. They caught ten- and twelve-pound salmon but quickly realized that they could not begin to eat what they caught. They began to take a pressure cooker along to process the fish. They had quantities of pint jars, and they would stick a chunk of salmon in each jar, load it into the pressure cooker, and in a few minutes the salmon would be cooked, bones and all. They brought back well over a hundred jars each time. Friends remembered the Pettys eating that jarred salmon all year long. As a collector of bear stories, Clarence can not resist telling one set in Alaska.

We met a lady who had been up there most of her life. She married a guide and they lived at Talkeetna. She said they had a cabin, and one day she and her husband and another man decided to go cut some poles for the cabin. They drove out about three or four miles down a dirt road. There were a lot of blueberries, so she went picking while the two men cut poles. After a few minutes she looked up, and a grizzly was standing on its hind legs looking down at her. She called to her husband and said, "There's a grizzly." He yells at her to get back to the jeep. They all jumped in the jeep just as the bear started coming down the mountain. They drove the three miles back to the cabin and had been there a few minutes when sure enough that grizzly comes right along. He'd followed them all the way back to the cabin.

So the man takes his thirty-ought-six and goes out and shoots the bear, and then they all ducked inside. There was a pile of wood on the porch, and the bear went right up there onto that pile and died right there on the porch. She said, "That's the only time I ever knew a bear that would chase you like that." Why it did, there's no way of telling. She'd never seen the like before in all her years. But all it takes is one time.

Clarence returned from his first Alaska trip in September of 1971. He was up on the hill behind his house at the spring when someone began yelling down below. He went down and found George Davis waiting for him. Davis said, "The Temporary Study Commission's recommendation for an Adirondack Park Agency has been approved. They want to put some staff members on, and you and I are the first ones they want."

Clarence had plans to return to Alaska the next year, but he decided to work for the new APA over the winter. That decision would delay his next Alaskan trip for three years and place him directly in the forefront of the growing Adirondack controversy.

CHAPTER 20

Wilderness Battle Lines

$g$overnor Rockefeller selected Richard Lawrence, a member of the Study Commission, to be the Adirondack Park Agency's first chairman. Lawrence was independent-minded and worked diligently to get the young agency on its feet. "He told us not to stir the pot," Clarence recalls, "so we all tried to avoid getting in a conflict with anybody. But invariably these would occur."

One conservationist who worked with the new chairman told historian Frank Graham Jr. that Lawrence lacked the common touch and was unpopular with park residents. But others felt it was the state's plans that were unpopular rather than Lawrence himself. Peter Van de Water was the leader of Citizens to Save the Adirondack Park (CSAP), formed in 1972 to resist the development plans of the Horizon Corporation. "Lawrence was the guy who was charged with interpreting the private land use plan at public meetings around the state," Van de Water recalls. "You wouldn't believe the fervor of the opposition inside the park. People were threatened and shots were fired. Dick would stand up at those meetings, very cool, very much in command and control, very civil. He dealt with some pretty rough comments."

Peter Paine, a lawyer and member of the Study Commission, drafted the State Land Master Plan. He joined Lawrence in presenting the private land use plan in public meetings across the state. Paine told Van de Water that "Dick Lawrence was one of the real heroes in this scenario. The agency would not have survived without him."

Nevertheless, the importance of good public relations did not seem to register in the early APA approach. The agency took too long to process applications and then chose its fights poorly. The first criminal summons issued for a zoning violation was served on a forest ranger. The second went to a land developer about to set off at the head of a Boy Scout troop. The result of such missteps was predictable. Those opposed to the creation of a private land use development plan had plenty of ammunition for their argument that the APA wanted to take over the entire park, or that it threatened to destroy the local economy with its onerous restrictions.

There were two plans that had to be developed, one for state land and another for private land. In the case of the state-owned Forest Preserve, the classification system that had been designed a decade earlier for the Joint Legislative Committee became the basis for the new agency's plan for state lands. It relied upon the maps and studies done by Clarence and Neil Stout. The preserve was divided into seven categories: wilderness, primitive, canoe, wild forest, intensive use, travel corridors, and wild, scenic, and recreational rivers. Following a series of public meetings on the plan, the final version of the State Land Master Plan, developed in coordination with the DEC, was submitted to the governor on June 1, 1972. Just seven weeks later, it was declared state policy by the governor.

But developing a land use plan for the private lands inside the park would not be so easy. It would encounter resistance from developers and legislators, several major legal challenges, and a great deal of horse trading between the governor and his two major opponents, Assembly Minority Whip Glenn Harris and Senator Ronald Stafford. The precedent-setting nature of the private land use plan, destined to become one of the most visionary in the country, was a big pill for residents to swallow. Only a handful of towns in the Adirondack Park had any zoning at all, and the antipathy toward regulation from outsiders in Albany was palpable.

The land use plan was submitted to the legislature for action in 1973. But Harris and Stafford, strong advocates for home rule, sponsored a bill to delay a vote on the plan for a year. To the surprise of the conservationists, the "delay bill" passed both houses of the legislature.

But Rockefeller vetoed the bill, and the backroom dealing began in earnest.

Fortunately for those in favor of the APA and its private land use plan, a major subdivider, the Horizon Corporation of Tucson, Arizona, came along at exactly the right time to force the issue. Early in 1972 Horizon purchased twenty-four thousand acres in the northwestern Adirondacks and announced plans to build ten thousand new homes along with access roads, golf courses, skiing facilities, and a number of dams on the Grass River. Other schemes were also in the works, including the so-called Ton-Da-Lay vacation home development north of Tupper Lake in the town of Altamont, to include four thousand units on nearly 18,500 acres of forest land. The newly proposed APA would be the only thing standing in the way of these and several other grandiose development schemes.

One of the largely untold stories of this period centers around Citizens to Save the Adirondack Park (CSAP), founded by Peter Van de Water in 1972, though he is quick to rattle off a long list of others who were heavily involved—Jane Eaton Gage, Richard Grover, Max Coots, Rod O'Connor, Alan Schwartz, Jonathan Fairbanks, Bob Plumb, Scott McRobbie, Ruth Blankman, and, notably, Ferne Petty.

"Paul Jamieson and Ed Blankman helped out on the fringes," Van de Water remembers,

> writing letters and being supportive, because they were influential people, but they weren't regular members. Ruth Blankman cut her teeth in CSAP and then went on to become mayor of Canton. Bob Plumb let us use one of his paintings for a poster that said "Save the Adirondack Park. Stop Horizon."
>
> I went down to New York City and met with David Sive,[1] one of the country's foremost environmental lawyers. We hired him to be our attorney and paid him about ten thousand dollars. He was one of those hired guns that you paid whatever you could afford because he made the opposition quake. Very well known and very powerful.

1. David Sive was the first Chairman of the Environmental Planning Lobby.

As a staff member of the APA throughout this period, Clarence was in an exposed position, especially with regard to his involvement with CSAP through Ferne. He had long believed that as a state employee he needed to be circumspect in his public comments. He took his representation of state government seriously, as George Davis, who had once watched Clarence put on an orange slicker over his conservation department uniform before venturing into a tavern, could testify.

Yet there was no question where Clarence's sympathies lay. If he felt the need to stay in the background, his wife had no such compunctions.

"People used to run in fear when they saw Ferne coming," Van de Water remembers. "She would call me at home and launch into these long spiels. She was a hard-core environmentalist, and she helped funnel information from Clarence and George Davis to the organization that was helpful to us."

The ad-hoc citizens group played a critical role in bringing the plans of the Horizon Corporation before the people of the state and in building public and legislative support for the newly formed APA and its private land use plan.

When Horizon made its initial foray into St. Lawrence County in the spring of 1972, a consensus seemed to be forming that the proposed project would bring jobs, rising land values, and "progress" in a general sense to the depressed economy of the region.

But gradually letters began to appear in county newspapers raising new questions. What of the impact on water quality of impoundments on the Grass River? What of rising taxes, sewage disposal, and the obligations of local government to provide roads, schools, and police and fire protection? Horizon was talking about creating a city of thirty thousand people in the Adirondack forests of St. Lawrence County.

The County Environmental Management Council denounced the project, as did St. Lawrence County Planner Richard Grover. Grover sent two rolls of color film to a public interest group in Albuquerque, New Mexico, that had been raising questions about Horizon's developments and asked it to send someone out to take pictures. He took the

resulting photographs of sagebrush prairies under development and produced a slide show, interspersing the Western photos with others showing the pristine forests of the Adirondack Park.

In an eloquent appeal at a conference on the Adirondack Park at St.
Lawrence University in 1972, Grover said,

> People are scared; people are threatened, threatened because a
> band of speculators, a band of subdividers, of developers, are threaten-
> ing to take over the entire Adirondack Park and the North
> Country. . . .
>
> Somewhere along the line, when we took the land from the Indi-
> ans and started chopping it up and giving it away, giving deeds to peo-
> ple, a concept got out of control. When you had a deed to something,
> you had the right to do anything with it that you wanted to. Land be-
> came regarded as a commodity, like a ball-point pen or a sport coat,
> something that you could sell or exchange, alter, or tear up and throw
> away. I don't think we have that right. The land must be regarded just
> like water or air. Everyone owns it, and everyone has a certain interest
> in it, and the right to alter for any purpose must be rejected.

Clearly, some voices against the massive development were beginning to be heard. But Horizon was gambling that it could push its project through while the new APA was still in its formative stages and
before the private land use regulations, due in early 1973, could be
enacted.

"There was a lot of opposition to what we were doing," says Van de
Water. "I was accosted by Congressman Bob McEwen, and Senator Ron
Stafford called me one night and tried to get me to back off. This was big
stuff, because we were halting economic development in the North
Country."

In an October 1978 article in the *Quarterly*, the official publication
of the St. Lawrence County Historical Association, Van de Water outlined CSAP's role: "Citizens to Save the Adirondack park, which eventually gained a membership of 2,600, was particularly effective in
bringing the issue to the attention of New York State Legislators and to

national media. Environmental groups, and especially the Environmental Planning Lobby (EPL), gave their full support. Legislators were flooded with mail asking them to preserve the Adirondack Park."

The efforts of CSAP proved to be a crucial factor, not only in defeating Horizon's development scheme but in swaying public opinion in favor of the APA private land use plan. Soon after the plan was approved in May 1973, Horizon backed out of its ambitious project for the Adirondacks.

Horizon's stock value plunged and the company sued the state of New York. In 1976 the Court of Claims ruled that the private land use plan of the APA did not constitute an illegal "taking" of private property, and Horizon's suit for thirty-six million dollars was dismissed. The following year Horizon sold its twenty-four thousand acres to Lyme Timber Company of Lyme, New Hampshire, for just over two million dollars.

Conservationists had been forced to accept concessions in the drive to pass the private land use plan. Shoreline setback restrictions along lakefronts for septic systems and new building were relaxed. As a result, most shoreline development was exempted from APA jurisdiction. Consequently, most private lakeshores have been overdeveloped in the past thirty years. The governor also agreed to authorize a twelve-member Local Government Review Board to advise and monitor the agency. In addition, the state promised not to phase out the payment of taxes to towns on the state land within its boundaries.

The concessions on shorelines, Peter Paine told Van de Water, were a "tragic compromise." Existing shoreline restrictions were already inadequate in his view, and now they would be further weakened to subject lakes and their water quality to gradual degradation. "The deal was done at 4:45 A.M.," he said. "I wouldn't agree to it, and they threw me out of the room."[2]

The absence of clear and strong development standards would

---

2. For this and additional material and quotes concerning the APA, I am indebted to Peter Van de Water for permission to quote from his unpublished paper on the Adirondack Park Agency.

make the work of APA commissioners much more difficult. "For the twenty-four years I was there," Paine said, "we always had an environmental edge, although sometimes it was thin." He believed that local governments had no interest in restricting development because they were always desperate to increase their tax base. "Never once," said Paine, "in twenty-four years on the APA have I seen local governments oppose in public any kind of development." In later years, he and four other proenvironment commissioners—Arthur Savage, Elizabeth Thorndike, Anne LaBastille, and John Collins—called themselves the "Gang of Five." When Governor Pataki was elected, he replaced them with some commissioners less friendly to the environment. "We came goddam close to losing the agency then," said Paine.

Today, some observers maintain that the big developers such as Horizon and Ton-Da-Lay were not the main threat, though they were the big threat before the APA plan was enacted. John Collins, a fifth-generation Adirondacker and a former park agency chairman, told Van de Water that "The APA has been moderately successful in limiting larger developments in the Park. But people thought the APA would preserve the Park forever. What's happening is death by a thousand cuts. It's not the big developments that are a problem, it's a lot here and a lot there. They add up, especially along sensitive areas like lakeshores."

But the heart of the private land use plan remained intact. The park's 3.8 million acres of private land were divided into six categories, with the APA given the authority to regulate new land uses of potential "regional impact" in each area. Governor Rockefeller signed the legislation on May 22, 1973, declaring, as he did: "The Adirondack Park is preserved forever."

With the successful defeat of Horizon and the new, private land use plan in effect, Van de Water felt it was time for Citizens to Save the Adirondack Park to disband:

> We had done what I thought we could do, and I never did believe in ad-hoc citizens' groups going on and on, because I don't think they have any future. As soon as the APA was set up there was no longer any need for us in my opinion.

We'd raised quite a lot of money. I can't remember exactly what the figure was, but it all came in nickels and dimes really. We didn't have any major contributors. Eventually it went to environmental organizations. Courtney Jones, one of the founders of the Adirondack Council, got a good deal of it. And I think some went to the Adirondack Mountain Club. But we did have a little parting of the ways at the end, because there were a few, including Clarence and Ferne, who wanted to keep the thing going.

After his second retirement, this time from the APA in 1974, Clarence felt free to emerge from his background role of advising CSAP. "Helen Brouwer," Clarence recalls, "who later became a member of the Potsdam Town Board, came to a meeting and urged CSAP to continue. It was voted to continue the organization and I was elected chairman. I think I served for about two years and then Helen became chairman."

Brouwer recalls attending the meeting where she urged CSAP to continue:

There were a number of people who wanted the group to go on. Clarence was a strong and unique individual, but he didn't have an abrasive character. He was sort of the opposite of Ferne in that regard. She could be difficult to get along with. I can't remember how long Clarence was chairman. Then I followed him as chair for maybe two more years.

It was sort of ironic, because I was the one who had urged the group to continue, but then the APA and other groups began to do the job we had done, and I ended up urging our membership to dissolve at the end. We weren't doing much besides our newsletter, but even so it was actually hard to get people to stop sending us money. People want a cause sometimes. They were pleading with us not to disband.

It is interesting to note how closely Clarence and Ferne worked on CSAP. It may well be one of the few times they ever collaborated so intensely, for their personal interests usually diverged greatly. But the prospect of a city nestled in their beloved forests, virtually within sight of their Canton home, was too much for either of them to stomach.

One of the reasons the crucial role played by CSAP in these years has been largely forgotten is because most of the organization's papers were lost. Van de Water explains what happened:

> Paul Schaefer said to me several years after we ceased operations that he would like to have all the papers of CSAP for the Adirondack Library at Union College. I agreed and said I would bring three boxes of papers down to him that had been in my attic.
>
> I drove down to his home in Schenectady, but he was gone, so I left the boxes with a neighbor. I tried unsuccessfully to contact Paul about them several times, and then he died and I never found out what happened to those boxes.
>
> I spoke recently to Barbara McMartin and David Gibson, who are working on the project to start an Adirondack library in Paul's home. They were going to see if they could locate the papers. But there's a huge gap there, more than twenty years. It's a sad tale, but it's why nobody knows about CSAP when they write the history of the Adirondacks.

CHAPTER 21

Back on the Job

In the fall of 1971 the new staff of the APA moved into the old log building that had housed the DEC in Ray Brook. Joining Richard Lawrence, George Davis, and Clarence were Park Naturalist Gary Randorf, Executive Director Harry Daniels, Assistant Director of Planning Resources Richard Estes, counsel William Kissel, and biologist Greenleaf Chase. "We started out on a shoestring. We didn't even have a place to sit," remembers Clarence.

This was soon rectified, as Harry Daniels explained a few months after the agency became official: "One of the most prudent purchases that was made was ten cases of toilet paper. It was delivered promptly, and those magnificent large cardboard boxes became desk, conference table, and chair. . . . Our total staff [was] sixteen people, including myself, the three clerical staff, and the janitor. [That boiled] down to a rather minimum staff to do a rather major job in a spectacularly short period of time."

"We were sitting on those boxes," says Clarence, "until my brother Bill came over and offered some furniture left by the DEC after its move into new Region 5 headquarters next door. So George went over and got a bunch of that stuff, and we set up our tables and started into business."

Bill Petty, who was DEC regional director for much of the Adirondack Park, was also headquartered in Ray Brook. Thus, the two brothers were now working in different environmental organizations next-door to each other. Their views, as we have already explored, often clashed, but the conflicts did not interfere, apparently, with the sharing of office furniture.

"The APA took all the maps that Neil Stout and I had done back in 1962," says Clarence,

> and that was the base for what the organization did in establishing the wilderness areas. And the APA added to it a couple of areas that we didn't have, [such as] the St. Regis Canoe Area and another over in the Blue Mountain area near Hochschild's place that became the Blue Ridge Wilderness Area.
>
> One of the first things I had to do was go over every public road in the Adirondacks from the point where it entered the park in order to determine sight distances. They used this to identify scenic vistas, which were supposed to get extra protection, but they never did. I picked out about fifty or sixty altogether. I had to do this when the leaves were off the trees, so it was mostly in the winter. Then when it warmed up, I went to the river studies.
>
> Most of my three years were spent on the river studies. We had time limits on all this stuff. The legislature wanted certain things in on certain dates, so we were pushing a lot of the time. We'd often be working till two o'clock in the morning getting the written stuff out. One of the things I've noticed with every organization I've been with, when you start out, there's a lot of enthusiasm, a lot of drive. But after it goes for a while and you get more people in, that enthusiasm sort of fades. You begin to get in a kind of a rut. It happened with our work at the APA. I noticed the same thing in the CCC, and I saw it in the Temporary Study Commission. We'd go in full bore and then it sort of fades a little bit.

Part of the problem, perhaps, lay in Clarence's extreme work ethic, which few of his colleagues could come close to emulating. Dick Beamish recalls how he and others working at the APA would get ready to leave for the day at five o'clock and Clarence would just shake his head. "It happens all the time," he would say. "You've become a bunch of bureaucrats. Five o'clock and the factory whistle blows and you all leave and go home."

Clarence and Anne LaBastille cutting wood, 2001. Courtesy of Anne LaBastille.

"Clarence, of course, had been there since seven in the morning," says Beamish, "working through lunch at his desk, and continuing on after everyone else left in the evening. He had a real Puritan work ethic."

Anne LaBastille, a longtime friend of Clarence's, has also experienced this work ethic firsthand. After the blowdown of July 1995 devastated her land, Clarence offered to come out and help her clear the debris. He arrived on a mid-September day, writes LaBastille in *Woodswoman III*, "with his neatly woven packbasket, scarred timber-cruising axe, large Stihl chain saw, gas, oil, and a sackful of groceries and garden produce." He proceeded to spend most of the day clearing, cutting, or resetting and saving trees where possible. He also cut and stacked a considerable pile for firewood. Spending a full day in such labor at the age of ninety-one was once again simply the way of things for Clarence. His work twenty-five years earlier for the APA had been similarly intense.

"One of the first things we had to decide with regard to the river studies," says Clarence, was whether we should follow the lead of the Forest Service out West, where they had already started to separate the rivers into wild, scenic, or recreational. So a couple of us went to Washington and talked with the forest service people to find out how they went about deciding which river would be wild, which scenic, and so forth. We felt they were going about the same direction we wanted to, so we pretty much patterned our approach on theirs.

We were particularly interested in the sight distance from the river. If a person is going to canoe a river, you want to know how far it is to the nearest road and those sorts of noises that will intrude. The wild rivers were pretty restricted when you realize they had to be at least a mile from any road, and if a bridge

Clarence filling out data sheets on APA river studies, West Branch, Sacandaga River, 1974. Courtesy of Gary Randorf.

went across, well, that killed it as a wild river. And of course motorboats were prohibited. They were also prohibited on most scenic rivers that would not only be scenic but would have limits as to the stuff that could be near it, like highways and buildings and so on. Then the recreational rivers would pretty much take all those that didn't fit into the other categories.

Most of the work was done by canoe or by walking along the shore, if rivers were not navigable. Pushing through trailless backcountry was hot, hard, bug-ridden work, probably not unlike the sort of conditions that Verplanck Colvin and his crews experienced one hundred years earlier.

Dick Beamish relates the story of one river studies trip in about 1973 when he accompanied Clarence, Greenie Chase, and a writer for the Associated Press named Dave Schaefer:

We spent the day not only canoeing but walking beside the river, bushwhacking areas where it was impassable. Clarence carried the canoe through some pretty rough conditions. At the end of the day, I asked Dave if he'd enjoyed the experience, and I figured he'd say "Yeah, it was a great time." But instead he said, "This has been the most humiliating day of my life." I said, "What do you mean?" And he said, "Here I am, carrying nothing but a notebook and a pencil, not able to keep up with this elderly man who is carrying a sixty-five-pound canoe, bushwhacking through the woods on a riverbank."

Clarence, who was then sixty-eight, may have initially seemed elderly to his youthful companions, but to Dave Schaefer at least, who was then in his twenties, it was a mistaken impression.

Most of the river studies were carried out in this exhaustive fashion. "There was only one river that I had to do by air," recalls Clarence.

It was on the Whitney property. They didn't want anyone in there. I knew the caretakers for all the others that went through private property. But I didn't know the caretaker at the Whitney property because he was new. He said he would refer my request to the Whitneys, and they said they didn't want any surveys made on their rivers. So I flew that one, checking still water and the rapid areas and so forth. The Whitney property was the only one out of the whole Adirondacks that I had to use aerial reconnaissance for. Even the Adirondack League Club gave us no problem. We told them what we were doing, and they invited us right in.

I don't know who was responsible for the Whitney's decision on this. But I got to know all the other caretakers when I was with the department, and they all gave me keys to the places that were locked up. It was very important to have those keys while we were doing the stream surveys so we could get close to the source. I would start at the source, and I had a sheet made out for each mile of each river. There was the width of the river and the depth of it and the speed. I would put a piece of wood in one place and time it in seconds to give me some idea about the flow. And then it was important to note any special things along the side of the river, like a deer yard, or any unusual vegetation, and so on. Each mile of river had a sheet, and there were thirteen hundred miles.

It was a lot of work. Gary Randorf and Greenie Chase would help me some of the time. But when they were assigned to do something else, then I had to go out alone. There was a lot of opposition to the whole thing. People were very hostile to anything that looked like more regulations. This could be expected, and I think one of the big mistakes that was made was in setting the thing up without first going to the local people and telling them and actually involving them in the process. Even though a lot of them still would have been opposed, at least they might have felt they had a voice in the matter, and it would have made them more agreeable.

I think every organization that's trying to do something has found that the first thing to do is contact the local people. Because they immediately get suspicious that you're trying to force something down their throats. And I can understand that. Too many of these things are decided by too few people, by some state organization without fully informing the public. You need to get all the voices out there, whether it's for or against. That's very important, because there is so much misinformation. You have a lot better success if you get all that stuff out at the start.

Gary Randorf is a photographer who became the Adirondack Park Agency's first park naturalist. He spent ten years as executive director of the Adirondack Council and then returned to the APA to help with the opening of the Adirondack Park Visitor Interpretive Centers. Randorf worked closely with Clarence during his time at the APA and offers a vivid look at the man who guided him all over the region in the early 1970s:

> I first came into contact with Clarence when I started to work for the Adirondack Park Agency staff in the spring of 1972. I realized early on how wonderful it was going to be to work with such a great group of people, particularly the old-timers, Clarence Petty and Greenleaf Chase. It didn't take long to realize that as far as the geography of the Adirondacks was concerned, Clarence was the most knowledgeable

person around and, I suspect, that's ever been around. There's nobody that knows the park better than Clarence or loves it more than Clarence. Greenie was a plant biologist, but he didn't have quite the grasp that Clarence did of the land of the park, the geography of the park, from one corner to the other.

Shortly after I started, the APA was getting ready to submit the Adirondack Park State Land Master Plan to Governor Rockefeller for his review and, hopefully, his stamp of approval. And he did approve it fairly quickly, and by doing so, it became state policy. But we needed to get out and take some photographs to accompany the text of the report to Rocky on the park's state lands. And so we were asked by our boss, George Davis, to run around the park and get quintessential photos of the various state land classifications—wilderness, wild forest, primitive, and intensive use. Clarence being the fellow who knew where they were and me, the guy with the camera.

I remember it was May, because we had eight days in a row that were beautiful, crystal-clear weather without a cloud in the sky, and Clarence said that he never recalled eight days in a row of cloudless, beautiful days in May or in any other month or any other year, since he had been alive. So it was a grand time. I soon realized that Clarence's knowledge was just an astounding thing, and he took me to wonderful representative locations to get the photos that we needed.

Randorf went on to work with Clarence for two and one-half years on the river studies. When the Wild and Scenic Rivers Act was passed, the APA was mandated to investigate thirteen hundred miles of "study rivers" to see if they rose to the level of being outstanding rivers that the state should preserve in their free-flowing form.

"We started at the headwaters and followed the rivers right to the boundaries of the park," says Randorf.

And any place that we went, no matter how far in the back country it was, I realized that Clarence had been to those places before. There wasn't any place that we headed for that Clarence wasn't familiar with.

Even though the rest of the staff thought we had the best deal going, a lot of times it was arduous, difficult work. Sometimes streams that we had hoped would be canoeable weren't, so we were carrying a canoe for miles, sometimes along the river banks, thick with vegetation, thick as hair on a dog, swatting black flies and mosquitos and putting up with some pretty rough conditions. We ended up recommending most of the "study rivers" for inclusion in the system, and virtually all, in the final analysis, were included.

When we first started talking about doing the rivers, Clarence had the idea that we should build a raft. He got a four-by-eight sheet of plywood, and we tied it to a bunch of truck tire inner tubes. He thought we could go down a river and just let the thing kind of find its own course. We took two canoe paddles along to try to steer it a little bit, but it pretty much guided itself.

Well, we got to the point where we were going to give it a first try. Clarence thought the section of Saranac River below Bloomingdale heading for Franklin Falls was a good, frisky little section that would have all the conditions—rapids, big rocks, and the various obstacles—that would test the raft quite handily. So we started down the river on this stretch. It was April. Ice had recently left. There was probably still some ice around the edges when we jumped on the raft and started down the river.

We'd hit a rock and rotate around it and off she'd go, and we'd struggle to get the front end and the back end back to where it made some kind of sense, and on we'd go again. All of a sudden, I looked up and we were heading straight for a rock that was about ten feet across and six to eight feet high. We hit it straight on, and instead of the raft rotating around it, it went straight up in the air and came down over our heads, upside down, with us under it.

Needless to say, I was very nervous about what our future was to be, and all I could think of was diving down low enough to have the raft clear me and then head for shore as fast as I could. I looked downstream and there was Clarence, hanging onto the raft and trying to guide it in to the shore, so we wouldn't lose our equipment. I couldn't wait to get to the bank, because of that damn cold water. Once I got there, I ran down and helped Clarence pull the raft up onto the side of the river bank. But he stayed in the water longer than I did, far longer than I would have cared to.

I don't believe we ever took the raft for another trip. I think the truck inner tubes were pulled off of it, and the plywood was absconded with by one of our staff, who cut it up and made a doghouse out of it. Clarence was subsequently convinced that the way to go down the rivers was in a canoe if they were "paddlable," and those that were not, because they were too narrow or too rough or whatever, we would walk along in winter time.

Despite the upsets, the cold water, and the clouds of insects, Clarence and his colleagues thoroughly enjoyed their work. They recognized its importance and understood clearly the impact their studies would have. The APA act regulations have been called the most comprehensive, ambitious, and enlightened regional land use controls ever put in place in the United States. Clarence's contribution, through his work with the Joint Legislative Committee, the Temporary Study Commission, and the APA, was at the heart of the entire system.

As residents started to feel the effects of the new regulations and the need to get permits for new construction, resentment grew, eventually permeating every facet of life within the park itself.

But the vision that the framers of the APA had in mind was one of a unified park, protected from the worst ravages of development by a series of controls that were predictable and parkwide. They followed in a long tradition of stewardship of the Adirondacks that stretched back to the 1800s, and they would eventually outlast the loudest voices of opposition.

By 1978 Historian Frank Graham, Jr. wrote: "Forever wild and the APA survive in the Adirondacks now because they are in tune with sentiments that are in the ascendancy . . . crowding and blight are hastening an acceptance of land use planning far beyond what its proponents might have hoped for even a few years ago."

Gary Randorf, by this time executive director of the Adirondack Council, agreed. In July of 1978, in a letter to the *Watertown Daily Times*, he wrote: "In recent months it has become clear that more people are learning to accept the land use restrictions administered by the Adirondack Park Agency. As people become more knowledgeable of park agency law, it becomes evident that many are little affected by this forward-looking legislation."

Clarence's primary role was now completed, but the home-grown woodsman-become-bureaucrat was about to begin a whole new career as senior statesman and outspoken defender of the Adirondack wilderness.

CHAPTER 22

Taking It Easy

as Clarence began his second retirement in 1974, the Adirondack Park was entering one of its most turbulent periods. He was now almost seventy years old and at a point in life when most people begin to cut back and think about tropical vacations and playing with grandchildren. As it happened, Ferne retired the same year from teaching the sixth grade in the Canton school system.

But the word retirement was never really in the Petty family lexicon. Ellsworth had worked until he collapsed at the age of ninety-three in his guide boat in the middle of Upper Saranac Lake. In fact, few of the old-time Adirondack guides ever entertained the notion of retirement. How could they? There was no such thing as social security. Who could imagine asking some vague government to take care of them? Such a notion was contrary to the self-reliant code of the wilderness.

Clarence's life had been one of strict discipline. The values instilled by Catherine ran deep: hard work, independence, responsibility, self-reliance. He had not touched a drop of alcohol in his life nor smoked a cigarette.[1] One can scarcely imagine another navy man being able to claim such a thing.

Discipline had seen him through hard times as a boy living off the

---

1. At his 95th birthday party in August 2000, thrown for him by *Adirondack Explorer* publisher, Dick Beamish, Clarence broke his lifelong taboo. He knowingly sipped two glasses of spiked lemonade punch. Beamish reports that he thought it was "pretty good."

land. It had seen him through the Depression while leading hundreds of war-hardened Bonus Marchers in the CCC. It had got him through the war in the Pacific. It had saved his life when he fell through the frozen ice of a snow-covered lake. It had given him the fortitude of character necessary to serve on government commissions with men often much more highly educated. And it had given him the foresight to nurture a second career as a pilot.

Clarence's so-called retirement was hardly worthy of the name. In addition to his burgeoning responsibilities as Adirondack spokesman, for the next twenty-five years he would continue to operate his own business, a flight training school for pilots based in Potsdam, New York. In fact, the school had been an ongoing proposition for many years prior to his retirement. Now, with more time to devote to it, the business could expand.

Beginning with the instruction he had first given in the 1930s, Clarence trained pilots for an astonishing sixty-five years. Though he never kept count, he believes he has trained thousands of pilots. Given the numbers of other jobs he has held, without interruption, over the course of his life, this is a remarkable achievement.

Clarence has seen innumerable changes in aviation over the years: "When I got my license in 1930, my ticket number was 19,059. That's how many pilots there were in the entire country of all types, private and commercial. In the 1980s there were almost a million pilots. That's dropped off now to something over six hundred thousand, and there's a real shortage of pilots for the airlines. After the war, there was a surge and everybody wanted to fly, but people seem to be dropping out of it now."

Speaking about the Alaska Airlines crash of January 2000, Clarence says, "Some parts of that plane were only inspected every eighteen months. Even though they had a record that there was a need for repair, they let it slide. I'm afraid to fly the airlines today because of the lack of maintenance. Most people that own airplanes have to have them checked every year, no matter how many hours are on them. And if you operate commercially you have to have them checked every hundred hours. Here's a major airline allowed to go eighteen months when they knew there was something needed to be fixed. Is there any wonder they're having accidents?"

The Potsdam flight school quickly became a fixture of the North Country aviation scene:

> I had a pretty good variety of clients. There were a lot of students from the area colleges and about half were local people, including some older retirees who decided they wanted to fly. Most of them had to take lessons on weekends, so I got in the habit of taking a day or two off in the middle of the week.
>
> A lot of the fellows I trained went on to fly for the airlines. There are two guys flying for Delta now who got their licenses with me. I hear from them every once in a while. And there are others in the military that trained here. There was one fellow from Canton who was a politician. He came over one day and said, "I'd like to learn to be able to take off and land a plane." Well, I said "okay" and figured by the time he got so he could land it he'd probably want to go ahead and continue. So I got him to the point where he could solo, he took his flight physical, went up and flew around, came down and landed, shook my hand and said, "That's just great. That's all I want to do." That was the end of it right there.
>
> I had a woman who said she was afraid of flying. She said, "I have relatives on the West Coast and I'd like to fly out there. Do you think if I had some flight instruction, that would help me any?" I asked her what she did for a living and she said, "I'm a psychologist over at the Psychiatric Center in Ogdensburg." I said, "Well, you ought to know better than me if it'll help." So she came over and had some lessons, soloed maybe seven or eight hours by herself. Then she says, "That's all I want to do. I haven't got the money to go on."

One of Clarence's students, Ken Alger, took lessons from him in 1985 when Clarence was eighty years old. They trained in Clarence's Cessna 150. At first, Alger had some concerns about flying with someone of such an advanced age. He wondered about his teacher's competence and about the possibility of Clarence being stricken one day while they were up in the air. But this soon dissipated as he came to realize just how competent Clarence really was. The experience actually changed Alger's perception of old people, causing him to realize that they could be very competent indeed.

"The physicals Clarence had to take to get certified as an instructor were much more demanding than just for a regular pilot," Alger recalls.

The doctors who certified him took a certain risk.

Our lessons took place during the winter in February and March and it was very cold. The engines would be preheated by a Salamander kerosene heater that sat on the floor and had its hot air ducted into the engines to warm them up. One day some of the heat got onto the brakes of one wheel and heated it up. When we taxied out onto the runway, the hot wheel hit the snow and melted it into water, which apparently sat in the wheel well.

I got out and did my exterior visual check prior to takeoff. Then I began my final turn to line up for takeoff, and one of the brakes wouldn't work and the plane wouldn't turn. I didn't know what had happened. But Clarence did. The brake had frozen up. Clarence reached over and turned off the key, and the plane rolled across into a snowbank, burying the engine.

Clarence said, "Well, just sit still." He got out of the plane, went around, and pushed the tail down, lifting the front of the plane where I was sitting back up to level position. Then he tugged the plane back onto the runway, turned it around, climbed back in, and said, "Let's go." This was an eighty-year-old man running around in the cold doing this stuff.

Clarence didn't like to use car fuel in his planes. He also didn't like the aviation fuel they had available at the Potsdam airport. So he used to drive to Ogdensburg or Massena in a pickup truck and fill fifty-five gallon drums with eighty octane aviation fuel. This was the fuel his plane was designed for, and Clarence insisted on having what he was supposed to have. He would hand pump the fuel out of the drums into the plane.

I remember looking down once as I was taking off years after I'd gotten my license, and there was Clarence down below on top of a

Clarence refueling the Cessna at Potsdam's Damon Field, 1985. Courtesy of Stephanie Coyne DeGhett.

stepladder, holding up a five-gallon tank and pouring fuel through a filter to fill his plane with the best fuel he possibly could. He was in his nineties by then.

Clarence taught his students to fly the plane rather than the instrument panel. He would often tape a piece of paper across the various instruments on the panel so students couldn't rely on them. This sort of thing is not too common today, and there are some instructors who did not believe Clarence always taught students in the best way possible.

Alger felt that Clarence mellowed as he got older: "There were a lot of people back in the forties and fifties who thought he was pretty hard on his early students."

If true, this probably grew out of Clarence's military background. He had endured many strict trainers himself, going all the way back to Weems in the 1930s who had once asked him, "Are you still alive?"

If there is any place where strict attention to discipline ought to be required, it is in piloting an aircraft. Clarence has little tolerance for sloppy attention to checklists, inebriated pilots, or pilots who do not keep up on their flight ratings and training.

Nevertheless Richard, the only Petty son to develop an interest in flying, remembers one instance when his father allowed his honed discipline to slip: "The only time that Dad did anything flying that could in any way be considered showing off came when he flew over Uncle Bill's house at Saranac Inn. Spotting Aunt Ruth's wash hanging out on the line, he proceeded to dump a load of water on the wash."

Richard frequently accompanied his father on flights in the 1950s to spot forest fires. He also flew with Clarence in the department's De Havilland Otter when the aircraft was used to take pictures of the newly completed St. Lawrence Seaway. The first flight Richard ever made was in 1954 aboard his dad's Aeronca. He was just eight years old: "It was the same day that I was thrown from Lucky, my mother's horse. I loved the flying, but I never got onto another horse until I went on an elk hunting trip when I was forty-six. And I was scared to death."

Richard took to flying with much of the same enthusiasm that his father had so many years before:

> I spent a lot of weekends in Ogdensburg, Massena, and at the grass strip outside Canton, passing the entire day by myself just so I could get a ride at the end of the day when Dad was finished giving lessons. One experience, however, stayed with me and made me fearful. One evening in the Aeronca, we went out of Potsdam just before dark. I was in the front seat and Dad announced we would do some stalls. Without any other warning (or me knowing what a stall was), the next thing the nose of the plane was pointing skyward and I was looking at the moon. I recall attempting to push the stick forward to get the nose down and Dad in the back pulled back on the stick until the plane stalled. The next moment I was looking straight down on the outdoor theater in Potsdam with my stomach in my throat.
>
> I don't think Dad knew how much this scared me. When I started flight training in 1983, I told the instructor about this experience, and it took me quite a while to practice stalls to get over that fear. I'm sure, though, that I would not have started flying had it not been for my childhood experiences. Hopefully, Dad is proud that I did.

Many pilots were willing to share memories of learning to fly with Clarence. Virtually all had glowing reports of their teacher's skill.

Stanley C. Bingham and his college roommate learned to fly aboard Clarence's Aeronca Champ in the 1960s:

> In no time it became very apparent that we'd made the correct decision. Clarence's vast experience in the world of flight in the military as well as civilian aircraft made him a superb instructor.

I was a college student, married, and with a child. Clarence realized the difficult financial aspects of my situation. It was not until sometime later that I realized what he had done. He asked me to be manager of his airplane during the week while he was at work with the DEC in Albany. There were many students who had soloed and were building flight time. I was given the keys to the hangar and was to keep track of flight hours, fuel used, plus other incidentals related to the aircraft. I also "groomed" the grass runway by picking up any rocks or stones that might cause problems with landings or takeoffs. In return I received a dollar for each hour the plane flew. In addition, I was given the task of tutoring math to his son. All of the money I earned went back into purchasing flight time.

As a result of Clarence's understanding and financial help, Bingham was able to go on to a lifetime of flying. Years after he left Potsdam, whenever he and his family made trips north, they were invariably greeted by Clarence and Ferne with open arms, home-cooked meals, and a place to stay.

Another Potsdam man had a somewhat different experience. Gus Thomaris wanted to learn to fly and decided to take lessons with Clarence. The only problem was that the night before his first lesson, Gus went out drinking with some friends. When he got aloft the next morning, he began to get sick. He started looking around for a bag or something to throw up in.

Clarence, seeing him in some sort of distress, said, "What's the matter?"

Gus replied, "I think I'm going to be sick. I was out drinking with some of the guys last night, and I don't feel so good. You know how it is."

Teetotaler Clarence stared at him for a long moment and then said, "No. I don't."

That was the end of Thomaris's flying lessons.

In the summer of 2000, after seventy years as a pilot, Clarence put his Cessna 150, the last plane he owned, up for sale. It was the end of an era. "The time comes for everyone," says Clarence. "You have to have twenty-twenty in each eye to pass a commercial flight physical, and I know my right eye is not so good. I don't think I could pass the flight physical, so I said to hell with it. I'm not going to push it anymore. It wasn't too long ago that I heard about a flight instructor in his forties who had a stroke. That makes you think . . . maybe the blood vessels aren't as good as they used to be. I wouldn't mind if I was alone, but I don't want to take somebody with me. You get to be ninety-four years of age, you damn well know something like that can happen."

Richard believes that his father was the oldest active flight instructor in the United States when he finally quit: "The FAA has that information but in all my attempts to verify it, they refused to confirm my belief. I attempted to get confirmation through the Aircraft Owners and Pilots Association (AOPA), but they said only the FAA would know for sure. I had wanted to get him a plaque confirming it before he quit, but I couldn't verify it. In 1998 I was told by AOPA that the oldest one they knew of was an eighty-nine-year-old woman in the Midwest, at which time Dad was ninety-three."

But plaque or no, Clarence knew it was time to stop and that he had had as long a run as anyone:

> It's been good to me. It's given me a good income. You can do better in a ground school, having forty students all at once. There's more money in that than instructing. But I enjoy it . . . to see someone come out, start from scratch, and get his license. You have to be realistic, though, about this business as a career. It can be risky, because whether or not you're going to keep a job depends on your physical condition. And I'm telling you, if you want to see someone that's disgruntled, it's a guy who has given up a higher education to become a pilot and then he loses his flight physical. Where is he?
>
> I had one woman, young girl, come in and she says, "I want to be an airline pilot." Just like that. Well it didn't take her long after going up a few times to decide that flying wasn't for her. She would get sick. So flying isn't for everybody. I just happened to like it. I always liked it.

CHAPTER 23

"A Good Soul"

Stephanie Coyne DeGhett teaches literature and creative writing at the State University of New York at Potsdam. In 1983 she became one of Clarence's many flight students. The two quickly developed a rapport based partly on her own deep Adirondack connections.

"My father was an artillery spotter in World War II," says DeGhett, "and he had lots of stories about flying. He went down a couple of times, not shot down, but engine trouble, hopping over the hedgerows of France behind enemy lines. He always made it sound like great, exciting stuff. So when I decided I had to try it, I looked in the phone book and called someone up who gave me Clarence's name. I went out to the Potsdam airport and found this very interesting man whom I liked immediately."

DeGhett's roots in the Adirondacks go back five generations. Her grandfather was a guide. He was born the same year as Clarence in a slab-sided cabin on the Forest Home Road, between Saranac Lake and Lake Clear. The two young guides knew each other, although DeGhett's grandfather was closer to Bill Petty than to Clarence. "My mother had the same teacher as Clarence in high school," says DeGhett. "So when he spoke about where he stayed on Lake Street, I knew the place he was talking about. I'm an only child of an only child whose father was one of fifteen kids. So I have a lot of very old Adirondack relatives. Clarence and I just connected right away."

DeGhett became fascinated by engines at an early age and used to work on Volkswagens. It surprised her to discover that airplanes involved so much engine work.

> The first plane I flew was 73 Juliette, one of Clarence's Cessnas, and I quickly realized that these planes were like VWs with wings. Clarence started talking about aerodynamics instantly. There were no preliminaries. We were in the middle of flying as if I'd always been flying. There was no initiation period. It was immersion from the beginning and a lot of expectation that I'd keep up.
>
> He had this tiny little airplane, a broken piece off some sort of flying trophy. I remember him holding it up and explaining Bernoulli's principle of lift using this little airplane, and then explaining to me about what crabbing into the wings would be and showing me the different postures of the airplane. That's my first image of him, of Clarence standing in a much-mended shirt with a broken airplane off an old trophy, showing me about aerodynamics and telling me stories. I realized then that he was this great storyteller, and also a wonderful teacher.

It was immediately obvious that whatever kind of flying her father had done, she was not going to do a bit of it because the emphasis was so much on safety: "My father would say to me, 'So, you're learning to fly,' and I'd say, 'Yeah,' and he'd say, 'Do you ever just jazz it up?' And I was appalled. 'Jazz it up? No, not a bit. Not with Clarence.' "

Under Clarence's guidance, DeGhett learned the rigors of the preflight check. She ran her hand over every surface and got to know the plane by touch and by feel. She checked the fuel, the gauges, and the pressure in the tires. She checked everything, and she learned the cardinal rule, which was not to simply try to remember if the checks had been done.

> You always did it by the list, which was this thing that Clarence had typed up and that had taught so many students that the masking tape around the plastic was yellow and grimy like a menu holder. You didn't stay clean with airplanes. Clarence never skipped a thing, and it

was never from memory because it was too important. I felt a deep confidence in him from the beginning.

He put students in charge from the first. There's so much to do all at once that if you had a nervous person beside you it would make it very hard. But Clarence was always just deep down relaxed. I mean, no matter how nervous the student was. I would say on a scale from one to ten, I was about a five, but I saw him take eights and nines up. I saw him take a ten up. And he was always just very routine. It would take a hundred times of reminding you to do something because everything is new. Yes, you have to look at your gauges, but you have to look outside. And then you're looking outside too long, it's time to go back to your gauges. There was never any grabbing or sudden moves. He would just reach out with that big hand and this very calm presence, explaining everything.

I'm not sure what he used as a gauge to determine when I was ready to solo. He certainly wasn't using precisely my confidence level. But I watched him with other students, and he didn't take chances. He wasn't going to send anyone up who couldn't do it with his airplane, and that's what he'd say, "I won't let you wreck my airplane." And when your time came, you'd just go up. He'd stay on the runway and look for four-leaf clovers—so you'd look down and there he'd be, searching for four-leaf clovers.

He'd have us do short field landings over an obstacle. He called them carrier landings because they were short and there was no fudging. The field was short in an imaginary way and it was an imaginary obstacle, but that was how he taught students to land in the first third of the field. When I went down later for my flight check and the trainer hollered, "Your engine's on fire, you're over forty foot pines and you've got to get down." And I would just be, "Hmm. That's cool." And the trainer would look at me and say, "One of Clarence's students, right? Carrier landings."

Clarence was never in love with flying over mountains in his single-engine plane. He always said that almost everything was survivable, but you don't go into hardwoods, you go into softwoods. I always wondered how much nerve it would take to know that you were going down in the trees but yet have the presence of mind to pick softwoods, because it made a difference. He was very cautious, but I mean in an intelligent way that loved adventure, because he clearly loved the airplanes that we flew. The only time he would ever fly the mountains was when someone asked him to go up so they could take pictures or do surveys, that sort of thing. But he didn't do pleasure cruises over the tops of the High Peaks, because as scenic as they are, he saw them as dangerous places, and rightly so.

DeGhett never saw Clarence get mad at a student, not even when one young man apparently lost his temper while up in the aircraft. But Clarence would never take him up again, no matter how hat-in-hand he came. DeGhett relates, "He had tremendous tolerance for mistakes, for insecurity. He never, never raised his voice, never was impatient, and he didn't let you fool around with the airplane. There were never any jokes with the plane. He appreciates machinery, likes machines that accomplish work, but he had this thing about noisy machines not necessarily having a place where they could disrupt animals—I don't think he was so worried about disrupting people."

Among the many stories Clarence told her was the one about almost losing his leather flight jacket in a tree while clearing trails after the hurricane of 1950. "Back then, when the wind was in your ears, a leather jacket must really have meant something," says DeGhett. "Later, it was stolen out of the back of his car along with his whole flight bag. He told me that he'd gotten over it, but there was something

Clarence, wearing his freshman beanie from Syracuse College of Forestry, with his Cessna at Damon Field, Potsdam, 1985–86. Courtesy of Stephanie Coyne DeGhett.

about how he said it—I think it pinched still, that it was lost. Those sorts of things were very important to him, part of his history, and he hung onto them. He would still wear his freshman beanie from Syracuse when he was in his eighties and working around the hangar."

DeGhett has her own theory regarding why Clarence came to feel so strongly about alcohol:

> Clarence doesn't like anything he has to depend on. The only thing he's never been able to shake as far as I know is chocolate. I'm sorry, Clarence, if I give something away with this. But oh, he struggles with chocolate. When he was a kid living on Lake Street, the people he stayed with had coffee every morning and so Clarence had it too. And one time they were out of it and he got a headache, and he realized the headache was from not having the coffee. I'm amazed that he knew instantly something that a lot of people don't figure out right away. He had a headache from not being able to have the coffee, and it made him mad. He didn't actually tell me it made him mad, but the look on his face said it all. He wasn't going to be ruled by anything, and he quit coffee then and there. He wasn't going to fool around with something that clearly had snared people.

DeGhett views Clarence as someone who has an uncanny ability to see right to the core of things. And she believes he values that ability highly, which is why he absolutely refuses to diminish it through any kind of altered state. "When he told me about their trips into town," she says, "into Saranac Lake, it only slowly dawned on me that he was making these very long treks when he was a little kid, just three and four years old. It occurred to me that his parents needed to ask the boys to come up to a household standard of safety so that everybody could manage. And I think he responded with his whole being to that. I don't know how the other boys reacted, but it seems like it was a calling to him, like it mattered. It was a duty. It was almost like he intuitively understood the whole system."

DeGhett thinks Clarence grew much more social as he grew older. When she was appointed to serve with him on the St. Lawrence County

Environmental Management Council, she had the opportunity to watch him closely in his dealings with others:

> He always knew what to say and seemed so socially capable. I could see it register on his face that it was time to be social, and he would ask the questions and then as soon as he was warm, he would tell the story. And I think he had confidence in his stories, because his stories are worth telling. He has a good sense of timing. Maybe that's something to be honed with airplanes.
>
> I don't know why he's so different from his brothers, except that his brothers, I think, were more ordinary. They took a more ordinary route, and I think they wanted more ordinary things, more comfortable things. Clarence has evolved over time. He doesn't think now what he thought fifty years ago. He always seems to be part of his times and has this kind of acquired wisdom about things that didn't stop when he was forty-two. He stays open to new views, stays fluid, absorbing, passionate in a contemporary sense about the things he cares about. It is really amazing to think that they wanted him in the APA as much for what he thought currently as for what he remembered. My family was all anti-APA, except me, and so Clarence and I used to talk as resident renegades. It's something different for a native Adirondacker to think these things.

She often listened to Clarence talk about "Mother." His mother's vision affected him greatly, but it was his own personality that made him receptive to her certain set of values. Clarence only told good stories about his mother:

> He was very close to her and always wanted her admiration. She was a big influence—a sort of power to be dealt with. But he was close to his father too. He adopted a lot of his father's attitudes, and I think he feels a completeness now in being back home where he wants to be, at Coreys.
>
> He admired both of them, respected them. I think it would be wonderful if all parents were such a good influence. Look at all the things they gave him, along with that incredible self-reliance. Can you

imagine what was in Catherine Petty's head when she sent her kids off from the woods to go to college. To college? I mean, that's unreal. It's unreal that she had that as an aspiration and what it must have taken for the family to float those experiences.

Clarence's personality is so—I hate to use the word—but it's so authentic. It so clearly proceeds from spirit and experience. He's just a good soul.

CHAPTER 24

Senior Statesman

at the same time that Clarence's primary retirement career as a flight instructor was progressing, a second career developed, flowing seamlessly out of his lifetime of work in the out-of-doors. Now a senior statesman on all things Adirondack, he maintained a disciplined and highly focused interest in wilderness protection.

Freed from the restraints of government service, he could now speak out more forthrightly on the issues that mattered to him most. He did so with an eloquence that made him a highly sought ally among conservationists and legislators trying to protect the Adirondack Park.

"When I was with the federal and state government," relates Clarence, "I never joined anything except the Society of American Foresters. I felt it would be a conflict of interest. The only one I ever joined while I was with the government was the Wilderness Society. I did that when I was on the staff of the Temporary Study Commission."

Many organizations wanted to claim the Pettys as members. It sometimes seemed as though Clarence and Ferne had an ongoing competition to see which of them could belong to more groups. Ferne listed the Adirondack Council, the Sierra Club, the Save the Redwood League, the National Wildlife Federation, and the Adirondack Nature Conservancy, among a host of others.

Clarence belonged to many of the same groups but would also generally be asked to come on as a board member or trustee. At one time or another he has served on the board of directors of the Adirondack Council, the Adirondack Nature Conservancy, the Adirondack Land Trust, and the Environmental Planning Lobby. He was an honorary trustee of the Association for the Protection of the Adirondacks and a member of the St. Lawrence County Environmental Management Council. He has been a member of the advisory committees for the Wildlife Research Programs of the New York State Environmental Science and Forestry College and for the DEC Region 6 Land Acquisition Program. In his mid-90s he was a member of the Region 6 Open Space Planning Committee and the Citizens Committee on Feasibility Study of Wolf Reintroduction to the Adirondacks.

During one of the twenty-two years that Clarence served on the St. Lawrence County Environmental Management Council, his fellow members sent his name in to the county legislature to act as chairman. But the legislature refused, saying that he was "too much of an environmentalist." Clarence believes, in his typically blunt manner, that the legislature's members only wanted the public to *think* that they were actually interested in the environment.

Clarence and Dean Cook at Adirondack Council Awards dinner, 1995. Courtesy of Gary Randorf.

As he entered his tenth decade, many organizations took to honoring Clarence with banquets, certificates of appreciation, laudatory speeches, editorials, and honorary degrees. The modest home at Coreys began to run out of wall space for the plaques, medals, and commemorations. He was named a fellow of the Forest Preserve by Governor Cuomo and received the Adirondack Stewardship Award from the DEC, the Howard Zahniser Adirondack Award from the Association for the Protection of the Adirondacks, and the Adiron-

Clarence with Arthur Crocker along South Branch of Moose River, 1984. Courtesy of Gary Randorf.

dack Museum's Founders Award. He was named Environmentalist of the Year by the Environmental Planning Lobby. St. Lawrence University presented him with a North Country Citation and Potsdam College, its Distinguished Service Award. Most prestigious of all was the Robert Marshall Award, presented to him by the Wilderness Society in 1999.

In 1994 Clarence received the Lifelong Achievement Award from the Association for the Protection of the Adirondacks. Executive Director David Gibson describes what Clarence has meant to the organization:

> He and Paul Schaefer thought highly of each other and communicated closely. And he did that with Arthur Crocker and other leaders of the association during that tempestuous time that led to the creation of the APA.
>
> Clarence has a great sense of timing, and he chooses his words carefully so that when he makes a statement, it's forceful and memorable. He's very sympathetic with the plight of organizations that are always looking out for the next dollar and the next member. He has managed his meager resources extraordinarily to be able to support at the level he does the organizations he chooses to support. It's just amazing.
>
> He recognizes what organizations need to survive and speaks forcefully for the welfare of the institutions he cares about. He'll make statements about what is *realistic,* but also about what is needed to make organizations effective. And then he will make sure that the Forest Preserve and state land issues are uppermost in the minds of the groups he serves.

Clarence feels strongly about issues like the reintroduction of the wolves. Wildlife in the Adirondacks is of the utmost importance to him. He's observed so many changes over his long life. I wouldn't be surprised if the first wolves to be released are in the Cold River region, and that he does it himself.

The extraordinary thing is that he has gone through so many different careers, and he has tried to manage and shepherd so many organizations to enable them to reach their potential, and yet he has never burnt out. He provides a constant infusion of enthusiasm, sage advice, and cajoling to make sure that we are reminded of our mission and what we should be caring about and paying attention to.

He also wants us to be aware of our historical mistakes, both as institutions and in our mission to protect the Forest Preserve. He is remarkably rejuvenating every time I have contact with him. His letters are in a file and they are referred to frequently. And that is the touchstone—the archetype of a member who is obviously a leader but who also leads by example.

One of the most interesting elements of Clarence's long connection with the Adirondacks has been this ability to grow and to change his thinking. As we have seen, his early use of leghold traps as a boy was something he deeply regretted. He came to view the backcountry construction of truck trails and tent platforms and the haphazard cutting of trees during his time with the CCC as mistakes, ones that he worked to correct when he became a ranger, though it often put him at odds with his coworkers and even his brother Bill.

Perhaps the greatest mistake he ever made, which Clarence freely admits, was his work spraying DDT. The insecticide was subsequently shown to have devastating effects on many forms of life, but especially on the bald eagle and the osprey.

This ability to recognize past mistakes, to admit them, and to move on is one reason he has proven so valuable to the groups he belongs to. His core principles are bedrock solid, forged from a lifetime of experience. But he is constantly growing, even well into his tenth decade of life. It is not only remarkable that he has never burned out, but also that he has maintained his ability to consider new thinking.

*Clarence leading kids at
Camp Sagamore, 1992.
Courtesy of Gary Randorf.*

"It's crazy really to belong to sixty-four organizations the way I do," Clarence declares. "And I get more every day wanting me to join. I write and ask why don't they consolidate. Because they're all spending money on solicitation and office space and all that stuff. There's just too many organizations that could be combined. They're all competing with each other. The same thing's going on up in Alaska. I belong to ten or twelve groups up there. No one wants to give up his own thing. They write back and say, 'Well, our group sees things a little differently from so and so's group.' So it never ends."

The issues never seem to end either. While he has been a central figure during some of the most contentious times in Adirondack history, his years in "retirement" have witnessed a host of important new concerns rise to the fore.

Clarence keeps up a steady drumbeat in support of the work of the APA and against efforts to develop more of the park. In a letter to the editor of the *Albany Times-Union* on May 30, 1991, he wrote, "As an Adirondacker who was born here and lived here for more than half a century, I never found it easy to obtain the kind of income that people 'outside' were able to acquire, but I always considered it worth the sacrifice because of the quality of the relatively unexploited wildlands. . . . The Adirondack Park is a special treasure of this state; dependent upon its wild lands, not upon 'growth and development.' That is best carried on outside of all parks."

Clarence strongly supported the state's 1.2 billion dollar Environ-

Clarence holding forth at Sagamore Lodge, 1992. Courtesy of Gary Randorf.

mental Quality Bond Act of 1986, which appropriated 250 million dollars to acquire land. He supported the "Bottle Bill," which would help keep litter out of the park. He opposed low-level training flights of FB-111 air force fighters and B-52 bombers over the Adirondacks because of noise pollution. He supported the failed Twenty-First Century Environmental Quality Bond Act of 1990. He fiercely derided the antienvironmentalism of the Reagan administration, calling Interior Secretary James Watt "a throw-back to the robber baron era of the past whose priority is turning our public lands over to private industry."

The 1990s were shaping up to be nearly as contentious as the 1970s had been. In addition to the never-ending bickering over the APA, environmentalists were growing more concerned over the "death by a thousand cuts" forecast by John Collins. Many also believed that the 1990s would be the last decade during which the Forest Preserve could be significantly increased. A number of large, privately owned parcels, such as the Follensby Pond tract and the Whitney Park lands, were tantalizingly close, if only the state could come up with the money. The faltering wood products industry also offered the prospect of adding large portions of timber lands to the Forest Preserve.

In 1989 Governor Cuomo called for a new study to look into the park's future. The Commission on the Adirondacks in the Twenty-First

Century, chaired by Peter A. A. Berle, president of the National Audubon Society, issued its report the following year. George Davis was the commission's executive director. "I was really proud of that report," he told Peter Van de Water. "We had excellent recommendations to protect open space and to help the forest products industry, and we dealt with Adirondack people's concerns—health, education, the economy. But the recommendations for a moratorium on development and on aesthetic considerations, such as telling people what color to paint their houses, shouldn't have been included," Davis admitted. "They caused all hell to break loose."

A minority report issued by commission member Bob Flacke stirred the ire of Adirondackers. Flacke's report was "full of misconceptions and outright lies," said Davis. In trying to explain the Cuomo Commission report to Adirondack audiences, Davis found himself needing an escort of state troopers in order to escape with his skin intact.

Though environmentalists believed the Cuomo Commission had made many worthwhile recommendations, some of them felt its uncompromising tone played into the hands of those who called it "extremist." Even Dick Lawrence thought the report was "not a bit helpful." [1]

Van de Water describes the final outcome of the commission's report: "Opposition groups sprang up like weeds after a summer rain: the Adirondack Fairness Coalition; the Adirondack Citizen's Council; the Blue Line Council; the Adirondack Solidarity Alliance. A protest caravan of over 1,000 cars plugged the Northway. According to Dale French [founder of the Adirondack Solidarity Alliance], 'the politicians scrambled to get in the lead cars.' "

But despite the dismissal of the report, many important goals would be achieved during the 1990s. An environmental protection fund provided money to the state to purchase new lands. A large chunk of Whitney Park and twenty-nine thousand acres of timber lands owned by Champion International in the northern part of the park were added

1. Quotes from George Davis and Dick Lawrence from Van de Water's unpublished manuscript.

Clarence in guide boat, Stony Creek Ponds, 1987. Courtesy of Gary Randorf.

to the preserve. Another one hundred thousand acres were protected by conservation easement. Governor Pataki, an avid outdoorsman, proved to be more of a friend to the park than many had anticipated. He supported additions to the Forest Preserve and added funds for stewardship.

However, as the 1990s drew to a close, Van de Water wrote, "The APA remains in limbo; repeatedly excoriated and wary of conflict; understaffed and underfunded; short two Commissioners; awash in paper and slow to act; suspect by environmentalists, developers, and local government officials alike; just getting by."

Nonetheless, important strides in protecting the future integrity of the Adirondack Park have been made. Many of the most strident resistance groups have come to accept that the APA is not going away. An uneasy truce seems to have descended across the park. Local residents and developers are not content. Neither are environmentalists. But both sides seem to have wearied after decades of intense conflict.

Clarence still sees challenges on the horizon. The fight for the protection of his homeland will never end, and he shows no signs of tiring as an active participant in the battle, even as he nears his own century mark.

Faced with the defeat of Al Gore in the 2000 presidential election, perhaps the best chance ever for an environmental leader to achieve the presidency, many environmentalists bordered on despair. Dick Beamish was among them, wondering aloud to Clarence one evening if there could possibly be any hope left.

"You can't think that way," Clarence replied. "You've got to fight. You can never give up. I will write twice as many letters."

As uncompromising as ever when it comes to wilderness, Clarence, at ninety-three, told Van de Water: "I'd just as soon stand on the capital steps in Albany and look toward Montreal and not see a damn thing except wilderness."

CHAPTER 25

Family Ties

The work ethic that Catherine instilled in her boys came from her own "iron will." Clarence's son Ed was able to recognize this hard core in his grandmother when he was just a boy in the 1950s: "She was very strong-willed. She felt she had a role to play in her children's lives. She expected them to be doing things for her. Even when Dad was very busy working through the forties and fifties and we were living in Parishville, he'd go up there and be doing things. He did an awful lot for them. It was just expected."

Richard, Clarence's middle son, also remembers how Ferne and Clarence deferred to Catherine:

> "As a child I suffered from various allergies and hay fever. For some reason, whenever we drove to Tupper Lake from Parishville, the motion of the car made me sick every single time, but it only happened on the trip up there, never on the return. After several of these episodes, Grandma insisted that before I left I had to take her concoction which contained honey so I would not get sick. I protested that I never got sick on the trip home and I did not want the concoction, but my parents would stay on the sidelines and Grandma would force me to drink the stuff. To this day, I cannot even stand the smell of honey, much less the taste. So I would certainly characterize her as extremely strong-willed."

From a diary Catherine kept that has since disappeared, Ed recalled a few interesting tidbits, in particular, Catherine's thoughts upon

Ellsworth's sudden death on Upper Saranac: "She said that he never wanted to die, that he really enjoyed his time on the Upper Saranac, which he thought was one of the most beautiful places. He just enjoyed being there. He lived on Deer Island where his employer's camp was located in the summer, because that was expected of a caretaker. You had no time off. And they were just dirt poor. They were paid little or nothing."

Catherine had a temper to go along with her iron will. And she never lost her strong spirit. After Ellsworth died, Bill's wife, Ruth, would drive Catherine around. On one occasion, when Catherine was about eighty years old, Ruth was driving them up a steep incline over a slippery road surface, and Catherine became fearful that they would not make it. She jumped out while the car was still moving and began to push the vehicle up the hill. Ruth was petrified that the car might slip backward and kill her.

It would seem obvious that Clarence must have gotten his teetotalism from Catherine. But this was probably not the case, according to Ed: "She had card meetings with friends up at Coreys, and she served drinks to them and drank herself. There were always bottles up there in the cabinet. Aunt Ruth said that she'd be up there sometimes playing cards when Clarence was staying there. He'd make derogatory statements about card players, you know, what a waste of time it was and how they ought to be doing something worthwhile."

It remains unclear precisely how Clarence came to have such strong feelings against alcohol, though Stephanie Coyne DeGhett's theory about his sense of family duty and his distaste for ever losing control are probably pretty close to the mark. Both his brothers drank socially. Bill often had parties at his home at Saranac Inn, parties that Clarence studiously avoided. And Archie once drove his station wagon into the driveway at Coreys, opened up the back where he had a bar set up, and began to serve people drinks. Richard felt that both Uncle Bill and Uncle Archie were much more social than Clarence: "Dad is very reserved and, in my view, happy as a hermit."

Ed never could get over how different Clarence was from his brothers: "He's just completely different. Uncle Bill was very political. He had good connections and was close to Nelson Rockefeller. I've been told there was no one else in the Adirondacks had as close a connection to Governor Rockefeller as Bill Petty did. I don't think Uncle Bill had an enemy. He played the field in a way that kept everyone satisfied. Dad could get along with people okay, but he was much more willing to speak his mind. You can't do that and be a DEC regional director like Uncle Bill. You tick too many people off and you're in trouble. Bill had an art for knowing how far he could go."

Yet on at least one occasion, Bill showed he was capable of turning his radar off. Ed had gone up for a visit at Saranac Inn in the early 1970s: "Bill was there with some other people, and they were really damning the APA, and I just thought, 'you know, you don't have to do that in front of me.' They all knew how I felt and that my dad was on the staff at the APA. Dad and Bill just built up a lot of animosity during that time over the agency."

The APA was setting policy for managing state lands, and DEC people had to carry out those policies. This naturally caused antagonisms, especially in the area of wilderness management, as ranger cabins were removed and the right to drive vehicles into wilderness areas was restricted.

"But even through all of that," says Ed, "they still came together to work on the place at Coreys. They did a huge amount of work there together and got along fine. Their way of handling it was simply not to talk about the areas where they disagreed."

Despite Catherine's dominance in the family, Clarence patterned much of his personal behavior after Ellsworth. He adopted his father's attitudes toward drink and religion. He loved the woods with the same passion and would likely have lived the same life as a guide and caretaker if not for his mother's intervention. He also developed Ellsworth's laissez-faire attitude toward child-rearing.

Clarence worked hard to support his family, for that was what a man did. That was his role. Beyond that, however, Ed felt he did not have much to do with day-to-day family life: "He had little connection with us, really, for church or school when we were growing up in Parishville. He was never involved in community affairs or connected with neighbors. I don't ever remember him going to a school event for any of us. All that stuff was on my mother. Dad was in his own world of his work."

But Richard took a different view: "My dad provided well for us and supported me financially through college. I don't think that it would be fair to say that Dad was primarily a working father who spent little time at home. He was at home as much as possible and, in my view, did take an active role in our upbringing."

Perhaps the extra time that Richard spent flying with Clarence and the bond they must have formed from this gave him his different perspective. In point of fact, Clarence's parental approach was completely in synch with the philosophy of the period. In those seemingly quaint days of the 1950s, most families really did consist of a working father and a stay-at-home mother. Of course, Ferne always worked too, but taking care of the children and the home life remained the woman's domain.

Though Ferne joined many groups and had a variety of interests, from gardening and showing her horses to environmental causes, none of this translated to socializing. The family rarely entertained at home during the years when the boys were growing up. "Dad was too preoccupied," recalls Ed, "with a combination of work and all the stuff he had to do up at Coreys."

One thing Clarence did do with the boys was take them camping and fishing. Still, the occasions were rare, and Ed did not care for the outings: "I didn't like all the hauling and canoe carries. We went on some long trips, but Dad just didn't have the time to do a lot of it. Being a ranger was a twenty-four-hour-a-day job. You just couldn't expect it to be a nine-to-five thing."

Richard, on the other hand, has better memories of the camping trips and of hunting and fishing with his father: "In hindsight, my lifestyle was probably more closely patterned after my father's. I recall him letting me carry the rifle on deer hunts and us getting up at ungodly hours at Coreys to take the guide boat to the end of the lake. Of course, he never had any luck when I was around, and he would keep turning around to look at me with a glare every time (which was often) that I would break a twig or make a noise. He could go through the woods like the Indians must have."

Richard and Ed's memories of how preoccupied their father was with work may explain another characteristic, his distaste for hospitals, which were simply one more distraction. In the late 1950s and early 1960s, when Ferne's mother was dying, the family made regular trips to visit her, first in Montreal and then in the sanitarium at Gabriels. Ed could only remember Clarence going on one or two of those trips. When Noah Rondeau was dying of cancer in the Lake Placid hospital, Ed and Ferne visited him several times. But Clarence would never go to see him.

The trips meant a great deal, however, to Ed: "Jay O'Hern, who's writing the books on Rondeau, told me that he found my name and mother's name in Rondeau's diary. Noah remarked that we had made a visit in the spring and brought him a geranium. When he died, I was working up at Lake Placid for my aunt and uncle, and they had a red Lincoln Continental, and that's what I drove to Rondeau's funeral."

Clarence's avoidance of hospitals is in keeping with his feelings about the end of life. He accepts death as an utterly natural occurrence and appears to have no fear about it whatsoever, joking about going to "the Happy Hunting Grounds." This does not reflect any belief in an afterlife, however. Rather, he takes deep content in the idea of returning to the earth and becoming a part of the natural world once again. His "aversion" to hospitals reflects simple disinterest. He feels people should enjoy their time, do their work, and when the end comes, accept and even welcome it.

Ferne's passing in June of 1994 followed an accident in which she fell off some steps and broke her knee the previous year. Shortly after, she was diagnosed with colon cancer and given six months to live.

Clarence, and later Ed, helped to care for Ferne, who remained independent as long as she could. Clarence continued to teach flying and to attend meetings on the Adirondacks around the state. It was the habit of a lifetime. This was the role he felt it was his duty to play. He had worked voraciously all of his life in support of his family. He honored his parents above all. This must have stemmed from his beginnings in the isolation of Adirondack wilderness. Here, the family was the center of everything. It alone could be relied upon. Yet when it came to his own family in later life, that same closeness seems to have been at least partially undermined by the demands of his all-consuming career.

The key to Clarence's personality lies in Catherine, that strong-willed, in some sense almost abandoned child from New York City, who forged a new life on the outskirts of civilization. If she was the controlling figure in the family, it was because her world needed control. If she tended to take the lead, it was in response to Ellsworth's retiring ways that left the family essentially in her hands. In truth, Catherine was a woman ahead of her times. Despite just a fifth-grade education, she had strong beliefs, a clear-eyed view of the world, and an understanding of the tremendous importance of the schooling she never got.

It is hardly surprising that the woman Clarence eventually married was also strong-willed and, in many ways, not unlike Catherine. In the end, the roles that Clarence and Ferne established for themselves were remarkably similar to the ones that Catherine and Ellsworth had also fashioned.

Throughout Clarence's long life, the central, overarching principles have been the importance of work, of contributing to society, and of providing for family. Catherine's vibrant spirit and her determination to educate her boys guided the family. But it was Ellsworth's belief in self-reliance that affected his sons' characters as much as any other factor.

That self-reliance has guided all of Clarence's days. It has been the rock upon which he built his amazing career. The key to success and happiness in any life lies in discovering the work one loves. Clarence found that key early on in his near-century of work in the Adirondack wilderness. For there has never been anyone who loved his work more than Clarence Petty.

Postscript

On a cool and breezy but sunny May day in the year 2000 (Clarence's ninety-fifth year on this earth), my wife, Kathy, my friend Joe, and I drive down Coreys Road and pull into the short, steep driveway of the Petty home.

Clarence is expecting us and is already out the door as we stop. I never quite knew what Clarence might be doing on my many visits over the past few years. One time, he had an electrician rewiring the entire house. The man's assistant had failed to show up, so Clarence was spending the day helping him run wires through walls and ceilings. He still allowed me to conduct my interview, though, jumping up every few minutes as needed to stretch a hand through lathe and insulation in search of an electrical wire.

On another occasion, in January, I became very nervous when I pulled in to see him atop a twenty-five-foot ladder, busily chopping away at an ice dam on the roof with a hatchet. Once he was out back digging a two-hundred-foot trench to run a new waterline to the house. I learned not to worry about waking Clarence with early-morning calls. Usually I got no answer, since by five or six A.M. he would already be outside, stacking wood or shoveling snow off his steep driveway.

Clarence shovels all winter, seemingly continuously, often shaving just an inch or two from the surface as the snow comes down at nearly an equal rate. It is necessary, he maintains, in order to keep ahead of the snowplow, which inconsiderately fills his driveway entrance. He would never consider hiring someone to do the work.

236

He lives frugally, rarely spending money on himself. But he can not resist any environmental organization that asks for help. He has always done this, giving money at a rate that would seem beyond his means. But then, he has worked nonstop at two careers, pilot and forester, all of his life. At the age of ninety-six he has begun to will money to organizations after he dies. The Natural Resources Defense Council, the National Audubon Society, and the Defenders of Wildlife will all receive substantial bequests. In addition, he plans to leave his Canton and Coreys homes to the Nature Conservancy after his son Ed's lifetime tenancy.

Clarence looks forward to returning to the earth upon his death. It also appears that he plans for much of the wealth he has accumulated to go to the tending of the earth as well.

He takes his seat in the front passenger side of my car. On past outings, he has sometimes offered to drive us himself. Once I asked him to accompany me to the opening reception for the new Adirondack Center for Writing in Saranac Lake. I think he really wanted to drive that night, because he appeared just a little nervous that I might partake of a glass of wine at the gathering. Drinking and driving or, worse yet, flying were nothing short of taboo. I drove, and we drank branch water. We were undoubtedly the two soberest members of that happy crowd.

Our first stop this windy morning is a mile down Route 3. Just short of the turnoff to Bartlett's Carry, we pull over as Clarence points out the site of Putnam's, his home in the Adirondacks from the ages of about three to six. There is little left to see. A low stone foundation marks the site of the large icehouse, once used to store meat and other essentials for the ill-fated grocery a century ago. Back in the woods behind it, Clarence gestures, was where the house once stood. We do not stay long. The black flies are fierce.

Our next stop is the Indian Carry, a mile back again toward Tupper Lake. This is what I had long been waiting for, a chance to visit with Clarence the place where he spent his first three years of life, in his father's tent and later shanty on the shore of Upper Saranac Lake. There are a couple of cars in the lot and a few walkers about, none of whom have any idea that this sprightly, ruddy-faced man with the picturesque

Clarence crossing boardwalk leading to former site of Ellsworth's shanty on Upper Saranac Lake, 2000. Courtesy of Kathleen Straka.

walking stick was, with his family, the original homesteader on this verdant peninsula thrusting into the lake.

We follow Clarence out onto the hundred-foot-long boardwalk that leads across the small outlet of Church Brook. He moves carefully, for the walkway is slightly tilted. Only a week before, he tells me, the entire thing had been underwater, and part of it was tipped nearly on its side. But today the boards have settled back into place and are dry, just a few inches above the waterline. Fiddleheads and painted trillium line the entrance to the woods. Clarence notes that his father built the first crossing here more than a hundred years ago, pounding stakes into the water and mounting a number of precarious planks to walk across.

We enter the woods, and Clarence leads the way to the highest point of the headland, where his father had built the family's first home. The path contains numerous exposed roots, providing perfect stumbling traps. Clarence steps cautiously. "I walk with the speed of a tranquilized snail," he says. Mercifully, there is a brisk breeze to keep the black flies in check.

Standing near the highest outcrop, Clarence points with his stick across several large downed pines to the relatively level spot where the shanty had stood. I recall a picture I had seen of this early home, nestled in deep winter snows.

"We were never cold," Clarence says, seeming to guess what I am thinking. I doubt, somehow, that this still-imposing figure who once snowshoed thirty-six miles in a single day, and who on more than one occasion fell through river and lake ice in minus thirty degree temperatures, could possibly have any concept of cold that I might identify with.

We stand on the shore beside several huge boulders. Clarence points across one bay to where the Rustic Lodge once stood with its cabins and golf course, and where his father had worked as a guide. Across another bay was the camp to which Clarence delivered mail at the age of six because the mail boat carried too much draft to enter the shallow water.

He stares out across the white-capped lake. I wonder what thoughts of a young boyhood and of a family of whom only one other brother still survives might be passing before his mind's eye. "Mother used to sit on this rock and catch fifteen-pound trout," he says suddenly. I try to imagine the pretty young mother from New York City raising three boys here in such splendid isolation.

We have one more stop on this beautiful morning, back down Route 3 to Bartlett's Carry. I have never ventured down this road, for it is heavily posted. But Clarence, sitting in my front seat, gives me courage. Who has more right to be here?

We stop just short of the bridge over the Saranac River and get out of the car. It is a magnificent, wild Adirondack place, despite the road and a nearby home. On one side of the bridge, the high spring water surges through the river channel, flanked by large trees. On the other side, the forest pulls back as the river meets the lake. The fresh breeze kicks up the water's surface. Here, Burdette Parks and Fran Yardley, who live nearby, once told me they had stared for nearly half an hour at a bald eagle perched in a tree not twenty feet from them.

This is the fabled river along which old-time guides such as Clarence's father, Ellsworth, carried their guide boats. The trail beside this stream has felt the padded feet of Indians, the fancy shoes of a queen's lady-in-waiting, and the store-bought boots of Ralph Waldo Emerson. It has witnessed the passing of presidents, writers, artists, surveyors, historians, and explorers. Here, beside Bartlett's two-story, unpainted frame tavern, Alfred B. Street landed in the 1850s to confront "A huge, savage-looking bull-dog, with porcupine quills clinging to his coat, and his black lips curled over his white fangs . . . looking powerful enough to bring down even a moose."

"Mother and I saw an elk coming down this road about 1909," says Clarence. "He was one of those western elk captured and released by the Elks Club in Tupper Lake. Will Dukett shot one. The others didn't last more than a year or two."

We pile back into the car and Clarence tells me to turn into the posted entrance to the Bartlett Club. A red pickup turns in just before us, and I have a suspicion the driver might be a caretaker, but Clarence just waves me on. We follow the truck in past several elegant cabins. It is an unexpected treat to see the club buildings. The pickup turns off and, after half a mile or so, we decide to head back rather than follow the road to its natural end at a point on the lake. As I maneuver into a space to turn around, the pickup suddenly reappears, cruising past slowly, the driver staring at us hard. Clarence simply raises a slightly annoyed hand and ushers the man past.

Caretaker or no, the man in the red pickup's father, or maybe even his grandfather, were not yet born when Clarence Petty first ambled through these woods.

Bibliography

Books

Abbott, Henry. 1980. *The Birch Bark Books of Henry Abbott.* Harrison, N.Y.: Harbor Hill Books.

Abramson, Rudy. 1992. *Spanning the Century: The Life of W. Averell Harriman, 1891–1986.* New York: William Morrow and Company.

Ambrose, Stephen E. 2001. *The Wild Blue—The Men and Boys Who Flew the B-24s Over Germany.* New York: Simon and Schuster.

Bilstein, Roger E. 1984. *Flight in America, 1900–1983: From the Wrights to the Astronauts.* Baltimore: Johns Hopkins Univ. Press.

Berg, A. Scott. 1998. *Lindbergh.* New York: G. P. Putnam's Sons.

Birmingham, Stephen. 1967. *Our Crowd: The Great Jewish Families of New York.* New York: Harper and Row.

———. 1968. *The Right People: A Portrait of the American Social Establishment.* Boston: Little, Brown and Company.

———. 1984. *The Rest of Us: The Rise of America's Eastern European Jews.* Boston: Little, Brown and Company.

Bond, Hallie E. 1995. *Boats and Boating in the Adirondacks.* Blue Mountain Lake, N.Y.: Adirondack Museum/Syracuse Univ. Press.

Brumley, Charles. 1994. *Guides of the Adirondacks: A History.* Utica, N.Y.: North Country Books.

Bryan, Charles W., Jr. 1964. *The Raquette: River of the Forest.* Blue Mountain Lake, N.Y.: Adirondack Museum.

Burdick, Neal S., ed. 1985. *A Century Wild: Essays Commemorating the Centennial of the Adirondack Forest Preserve.* Saranac Lake, N.Y.: Chauncy Press.

243

Burns, James MacGregor. 1970. *Roosevelt: The Soldier of Freedom*. New York: Harcourt Brace Jovanovich.

Carson, Rachel. 1962. *Silent Spring*. Boston: Houghton Mifflin.

Clostermann, Pierre. 1952. *Flames in the Sky*. London: Chatto and Windus.

Cohen, Stan. 1980. *The Tree Army: A Pictorial History of the Civilian Conservation Corps, 1933–1942*. Missoula, Mont.: Pictorial Histories Publishing Company.

Collier, Peter, and David Horowitz. 1977. *The Rockefellers: An American Dynasty*. New York: New American Library.

Colvin, Verplanck. 1873. *Report on a Topographical Survey of the Adirondack Wilderness of New York*. Albany, N.Y.: Argus Company.

Commission on the Adirondacks in the Twenty-first Century. 1990. *The Adirondacks in the Twenty-first Century*. Albany, N.Y.: State of New York.

Commission on the Adirondacks in the Twenty-first Century. 1990. *The Adirondack Park in the Twenty-first Century: Technical Reports*. 2 vols. Albany, N.Y.: State of New York.

Cross, David, and Joan Potter. 1992. *The Book of Adirondack Firsts*. Elizabethtown, N.Y.: Pinto Press.

Curth, Louis C. 1987. *The Forest Rangers: A History of the New York State Forest Ranger Force*. Albany, N.Y.: New York State Department of Environmental Conservation.

DeSormo, Maitland C. 1969. *Noah John Rondeau: Adirondack Hermit*. Utica, N.Y.: North Country Books.

———. 1974. *The Heydays of the Adirondacks*. Saranac Lake, N.Y.: Adirondack Yesteryears.

———. 1980. *Summers on the Saranacs*. Saranac Lake, N.Y.: Adirondack Yesteryears.

DiNunzio, Michael G. 1984. *Adirondack Wildguide: A Natural History of the Adirondack Park*. Elizabethtown, N.Y.: Adirondack Nature Conservancy Committee/Adirondack Council.

Donaldson, Alfred L. [1921] 1989. *A History of the Adirondacks*. 2 vols. Reprint, Mamaroneck, N.Y.: Harbor Hill Books.

Everett, Susanne. 1980. *World War I : An Illustrated History*. New York: Exeter Books.

Fowler, Albert Vann. 1959. *Cranberry Lake, 1845–1959: An Adirondack Miscellany*. Blue Mountain Lake, N.Y: Adirondack Museum.

————, ed. 1968. *Cranberry Lake from Wilderness to Adirondack Park.* Syracuse, N.Y.: Adirondack Museum/Syracuse Univ. Press.

Gilborn, Craig. 1981. *Durant: The Fortunes and Woodland Camps of a Family in the Adirondacks.* Blue Mountain Lake, N.Y.: Adirondack Museum.

————. 2000. *Adirondack Camps: Homes away from Home.* Blue Mountain Lake, N.Y.: Adirondack Museum/Syracuse Univ. Press.

Graham, Frank, Jr. 1984. *The Adirondack Park: A Political History.* Syracuse, N.Y.: Syracuse Univ. Press.

Hammond, S. H. 1857. *Wild Northern Scenes.* New York: Derby and Jackson.

Headley, Joel T. [1875] 1982. *The Adirondack, or Life in the Woods.* Reprint, Harrison, N.Y.: Harbor Hill Books.

Hochschild, Adam. 1986. *Half the Way Home: A Memoir of Father and Son.* New York: Viking.

Hochschild, Harold K. 1952. *Township 34: A History, with Digressions, of an Adirondack Township in Hamilton County in the State of New York.* Privately printed.

Holland, Kenneth, and Frank Ernest Hill. 1942. *Youth in the CCC.* Washington, D.C.: American Council on Education.

Jamieson, Paul, ed. 1982. *The Adirondack Reader.* Glens Falls, N.Y.: Adirondack Mountain Club.

————. 1986. *Adirondack Pilgrimage.* Glens Falls, N.Y.: Adirondack Mountain Club.

————. 1992. *Uneven Ground.* Canton, N.Y.: St. Lawrence Univ./Friends of the Owen D. Young Library.

———— and Donald Morris. 1987. *Adirondack Canoe Waters: North Flow.* Glens Falls, N.Y.: Adirondack Mountain Club.

Jerome, Christine. 1994. *An Adirondack Passage: The Cruise of the Canoe "Sairy Gamp."* New York: Harper Collins Publishers.

Jerome, John. 1997. *Blue Rooms: Ripples, Rivers, Pools, and Other Waters.* New York: Henry Holt and Company.

Joint Legislative Committee on Natural Resources. 1963. *Report of the Joint Legislative Committee on Natural Resources.* Legislative document.

Kaiser, Harvey H. 1982. *Great Camps of the Adirondacks.* Boston: David R. Godine.

Kudish, Michael. 1996. *Railroads of the Adirondacks: A History.* Fleischmanns, N.Y.: Purple Mountain Press.

LaBastille, Anne. 1976. *Woodswoman.* New York: E. P. Dutton.

———. 1987. *Beyond Black Bear Lake.* New York: W. W. Norton and Company.

———. 1997. *Woodswoman III: Book Three of the Woodswoman's Adventures.* Westport, N.Y.: West of the Wind Publications.

Lindbergh, Charles A. 1970. *The Wartime Journals of Charles A. Lindbergh.* New York: Harcourt Brace Jovanovich.

Longstreth, T. Morris. 1917. *The Adirondacks.* New York: Century Company.

MacArthur, Douglas. 1964. *Reminiscences: General of the Army.* New York: McGraw Hill.

Manley, Atwood. 1968. *Rushton and His Times in American Canoeing.* Syracuse, N.Y.: Adirondack Museum/Syracuse Univ. Press.

Marsh, George Perkins. 1864. *Man and Nature, or Physical Geography as Modified by Human Action.* New York: Charles Scribner.

McMartin, Barbara. 1994. *The Great Forest of the Adirondacks.* Utica, N.Y.: North Country Books.

New York State Forest, Fish and Game Commission. 1901. *Sixth Report.* Albany, N.Y.: James B. Lyon, state printer.

O'Hern, William Jay. *Life with Noah: Stories and Adventures of Richard Smith with Noah John Rondeau.* Utica, N.Y.: North Country Books.

Oppel, Frank, comp. 1988. *New York: Tales of the Empire State.* Secaucus, N.J.: Castle, Book Sales.

Payne, Daniel G. 1996. *Voices in the Wilderness: American Nature Writing and Environmental Politics.* Hanover, N.H.: University Press of New England.

Persico, Joseph E. 1982. *The Imperial Rockefeller: A Biography of Nelson A. Rockefeller.* New York: Simon and Schuster.

Schneider, Paul. 1997. *The Adirondacks: A History of America's First Wilderness.* New York: Henry Holt and Company.

Sears, George Washington [Nessmuk]. [1920] 1963. *Woodcraft.* Reprint, New York: Dover Publications.

Seaver, Frederick J. 1918. *Historical Sketches of Franklin County.* Albany, N.Y.: J. B. Lyon.

Simonson, G. R., ed. 1968. *The History of the American Aircraft Industry: An Anthology.* Cambridge, Mass.: MIT Press.

Splete, Allen P., Judith DeGraaff, and Robert A. Clark, eds. 1973. *Third Conference on the Adirondack Park.* Canton, N.Y.: St. Lawrence Univ.

———, Paul F. Jamieson, and William K. Verner, eds. 1971. *First Conference on the Adirondack Park.* Canton, N.Y.: St. Lawrence Univ.

———— and William K. Verner, eds. 1972. *Second Conference on the Adirondack Park.* Canton, N.Y.: St. Lawrence Univ.

Stillman, William J. 1901. *The Autobiography of a Journalist.* 2 vols. Boston: Houghton Mifflin Company.

Stoddard, S. R. [1874] 1983. *The Adirondacks: Illustrated.* Reprint, Glens Falls, N.Y.: Glens Falls-Queensbury Historical Association.

Street, Alfred B. 1865. *Woods and Waters, or Summer in the Saranacs.* New York: Hurd and Houghton.

Taylor, Robert. 1986. *Saranac: America's Magic Mountain.* Boston: Houghton Mifflin Company.

Terrie, Philip G. 1985. *Forever Wild: Environmental Aesthetics and the Adirondack Forest Preserve.* Philadelphia: Temple Univ. Press.

————. 1994. *Forever Wild: A Cultural History of Wilderness in the Adirondacks.* Syracuse, N.Y.: Syracuse Univ. Press.

————. 1997. *Contested Terrain: A New History of Nature and People in the Adirondacks.* Adirondack Museum/Syracuse Univ. Press.

VanValkenburgh, Norman J. 1979. *The Adirondack Forest Preserve: A Narrative of the Evolution of the Adirondack Forest Preserve of New York State.* Blue Mountain Lake, N.Y.: Adirondack Museum.

Wallace, E. R. 1887. *Descriptive Guide to the Adirondacks.* 12th ed. Syracuse, N.Y.: Watson Gill.

Wallhauser, Henry T. 1969. *Pioneers of Flight.* Hammond, Inc.

Welsh, Peter C. 1995. *Jacks, Jobbers and Kings: Logging the Adirondacks, 1850–1950.* Utica, N.Y.: North Country Books.

White, Willam Chapman. 1954. *Adirondack Country.* New York: Duell, Sloan and Pearce.

Van Dyke, Henry. 1897. *Little Rivers.* New York: Charles Scribner Sons.

Zahniser, Ed, ed. 1992. *Where Wilderness Preservation Began: Adirondack Writings of Howard Zahniser.* Utica, N.Y.: North Country Books.

Periodicals

Bauer, Peter. 1989. "Watersheds." *Adirondack Life* 20, no. 2: 88–101.

Beamish, Richard. 1987. "Clarence Petty: A Lifelong Fight for Forever Wild." *Adirondack Life* 18, no. 6: 52–55.

Cartledge, Jerry. 1958. "Trout 'Bombed' into Mountain Ponds." *Albany Times-Union,* October 26.

Decker, Janet P. 1991. "Early Settlers on the Indian Carry." *Franklin Historical Review* 28: 45–49.

Duquette, John J. 1991. "Tracing the History of One of the Area's Grand Hotels." *Adirondack Daily Enterprise*, August 17.

Glover, Jim. 1985. "The First Forty-sixers." *Adirondack Life* 16, no. 1: 17–23.

Hale, Ed. 1986. "Boat 'Scrapbook' of Guide's Life." *Watertown Daily Times*, December 14.

Jamieson, Paul. 1992. "The Embowering Woods." *Adirondac* 56, no. 3: 12–13.

Jones, Robert Courtney. 1972. "The Agency: A Review." *Adirondack Life* 3, no. 4: 44–47.

Ketchledge, Edwin H. 1992. "Born-Again Forest." *Natural History*, May, 34–38.

Marshall, Bob. 1933. "Great Adirondack Guides: No. Four, Herbert Clark." *High Spots* 10, no. 4: 8–11.

McKibben, Bill. 1991. "Adirondack Reprise." *Outside* 16, no. 11: 124–31, 172–75.

Smith, Mason. 1981. "The Adirondack Council." *Adirondack Life* 12, no.1: 25–27.

Van de Water, Peter. 1978. "The Voice That Cried Out in the Wilderness: The Story of Citizens to Save the Adirondack Park." *The Quarterly* 33, no. 4.

———. 1999. "The APA: Tyrant or Savior?" *Adirondack Explorer* 1, no.7.

Vickery, Jim Dale. 1985. "A Hunger for Wilderness: Bob Marshall." *Sierra*, November-December.

Wuerthner, George. 1999. "The Healing Woods." *Adirondack Life* 30, no. 8, 58–63.

Interviews

Interviews were conducted by the author in person or by telephone, letter, e-mail, or audio recorder with the following people: Ken Alger, Richard Beamish, Stanley C. Bingham, Helen Brouwer, Charles Brumley, George Davis, Janet Decker, Stephanie Coyne DeGhett, Jean Freeman, David Gibson, Richard Grover, Jay Hutchinson, Paul Jamieson, Harold Jerry, Anne LaBastille, Archibald Petty, Clarence Petty, Ed Petty, Richard Petty, Gary Randorf, Neil Stout, Gus Thomaris, Peter Van de Water, Mary Jo Whalen, and Pat Whalen.

Video Recording

Hutchinson, Jay. 1997. "Clarence Petty Interview." Canton, N.Y.

Index